HEINEMANN SCHOOL MANAGEMENT

Working with Parents

by
Monica Shah

Series editor: Michael Marland

Heinemann Educational Publishers
Halley Court, Jordan hill, Oxford OX2 8EJ
a division of Reed Educational and Professional Publishing Ltd

OXFORD   MELBOURNE   AUCKLAND
JOHANNESBURG   BLANTYRE   GABORONE
IBADAN   PORTSMOUTH (NH) USA   CHICAGO

Heinemann is a registered trademark of Reed Educational and Professional
Publishing Ltd

Text © Monica Shah, 2001

First published in 2001

05 04 03 02 01
10 9 8 7 6 5 4 3 2 1

British Library Cataloguing in Publication Data
A catalogue record for this book is available from the British Library

ISBN 0 435 80057 4

Typeset by J&L Composition Ltd, Filey, North Yorkshire
Printed and bound in Great Britain by Biddles Ltd, Guildford

Acknowledgements

The author would like to thank all those who contributed to the research for
this book:
Roger Hancock, Lecturer in Education, The Open University; Bob Sproson,
Head of Cambridgeshire Secondary Support Service; Lin Taylor and Patricia
Alexander at the University of North London; Ms Vanessa Wiseman, Ms Anne
Macaulay and staff at Langdon School, East Ham, London; Mr David Jordan
and staff at Llanedeyrn High School, Roundwood, Cardiff; Mrs Melanie
Saunders and staff at The Philip Morant School, Colchester; Mr Des Malone
and staff at Deptford Green School, London Borough of Lewisham; Emma
Beresford, Sue Botcherby (M-SIS) and staff at St Matthews High School,
Manchester; Rosie Parker, parent, author and psychotherapist; Luke Norton
and his father, Kingsley; Mrs Gill Williams and staff at Cantonian High
School, Cardiff; Mrs Ann Springford-Stahler and staff at New Heys
Community Comprehensive School; Mrs Lesley Andrews, Mr Gareth Roberts
and staff at Llanrumney High School; Brenda McHugh at the Marlborough
Family Service Unit, London; Mr Angus Hardie and staff at Instep, Castlebrae

Community High School, Edinburgh; Mr Keith Allen and staff at Willows High School, Tremorfa, Cardiff; Dame Tamsyn Imison, Mr Phil Taylor and staff at Hampstead School, London; North Westminster Community School; Wafa Hussein; Mrs Gill Bal and staff at Wembley High School; Mr Marland and staff at NWCS; Deborah Jackson and staff at Camden School for Girls; Oaklands School, London.

For the transcripts included in Chapter 6, thanks to: Barbara M. Walker and Maggie MacLure at the University of East Anglia; Dr John Bastiani on behalf of the Community Education Working Party, Nottingham.

Pioneers such as Dr John Bastiani and practitioners in the home-school movement have uncovered the problems and pitfalls, and have substantially improved practice in primary schools nationwide. I would like to thank all those who have gone before me in writing and thinking about parent-teacher relations, and to pay a special tribute to the schools who have participated in the making of this book. In the schools that feature and some that do not, despite enormous workloads, the staff interviewed have been interested and willing to help other schools to learn from their experience.

Thanks also to: my husband, Sam, who accepted this extra project and supported me throughout; my parents from whom I inherited the energy and optimism to believe in it; family, friends and colleagues at work who gave me the space to write; the publisher and editor; co-thinkers with whom conversations have been invaluable – Michael Marland, Roger Hancock, John Bastiani, Gill Bal, staff at INCLUDE especially Martin Stephenson, Marianne Anglaret, Jacqui Stevenson and Andrew Pasterfield, and the school staff involved in the Cardiff GEST project 1994–1996; tutors from the Lincoln Centre and the Tavistock Institute who fostered analytic skills and emotional honesty; and last but not least, library staff at the University of East Anglia in Norwich and the Institute of Education in London who have been very helpful and provided access to essential resources.

The publishers would like to thank the following for permission to reproduce copyright material: The Plain English Campaign, p. 108; St Matthew's RC High School, p. 106; The Times Educational Supplement, p. 38.

The publishers have made every effort to contact the copyright holders. However, if any material has been incorrectly acknowledged, the publishers would be pleased to correct this at the earliest opportunity.

Tel: 01865 888058 www.heinemann.co.uk

Contents

Introduction

School and home traditionally leave each other alone. Although it is widely acknowledged that an overly self-sufficient culture works against the interests of a school, we have become accustomed to a division of labour between teaching children and raising them. The home–school divide is not in fact a neat one, as is proven in teachers' everyday pastoral care of children, as well as in the classroom, where understanding home lives is crucial. Within the family, too, parents and carers often adopt an educational role, even if they leave formal teaching to the teachers. But when teachers and parents meet, they encounter obstacles that prevent good communication about individual pupils. These obstacles often appear to be purely practical, but on closer examination they prove to be underpinned by powerful attitudes that prevent change. The intensity of a parent's feelings about their child and a teacher's ownership of education makes the task of changing the status quo particularly challenging. Yet change is imperative. The communication gap between home and school restricts the amount of information that parents feel they can give to teachers. It also prevents teachers and school managers from contacting parents until there is a serious problem.

Parental involvement has been shown to have real outcomes for pupils. Better communication between parents and school staff will improve teachers' understanding of the people they are trying to teach. It sets individual pupils' personalities and behaviour into context. It will improve parents' understanding of their child's development at school and its place within their life as a whole. Parental support for a child's education can transform pupils' experience of school and their ability to develop realistic future ambitions. Working with parents will also allow children to make connections with the communities in which they live. There are other benefits, from the practical to the cultural, in good communication between the two worlds. It will provide a means for a school to support staff in their daily task of teaching, even if there are enormous differences between school culture and family culture. The school will also increase its support base in the local community. There are important differences between home and school but mutual understanding will strengthen pupils and the whole school.

Creating a dialogue about learning between the adults responsible for individual pupils is a particularly crucial step for schools that prioritise the issue of equity. Without action, the poorest children are likely to suffer the most, as difficulties in communication between parents and teachers are currently reinforcing socio-economic inequalities. Working-class parents and those who do not have experience of education in this country are the parents who tend not to make a claim to get involved with their child's learning at school (Martin, Ranson and Vincent, 2000). The least advantaged in society feel that they are outside the teacher's realm. Remaining outsiders prevents them from making vital connections between what a child learns at school and what they learn in their particular family and community outside school. Unless schools reach out to change parents' expectations, those with the least opportunities in life are effectively being encouraged by a lack of home–school communication to see themselves as powerless in relation to their child's learning. Working with parents is therefore crucially important in determining the level to which a school can call itself comprehensive.

There is another factor that calls for improved home–school relations, given the findings of research in which patterns of communication between teachers and parents have been studied and the socio-economic background of parents has been taken into account. Off-putting encounters with staff quickly discourage parents in all social classes from contacting the school and discourage a large proportion from supporting state schools at all. Studies have found that parents do not wish to complain; they hesitantly challenge teachers on occasions, and then simply try to limit the damage to their children as best they can, within their means (Walker, 1998; MacLure and Walker, 2000; Vincent and Martin, 2000). Those who value education either try to help the school and their children despite the inherent difficulties, or divert their energies and their private resources elsewhere. The resources and tradition of private education in the UK combined with under-funding in the state sector have created an image of impoverished comprehensive schools, dissuading some parents from even considering sending their child to the local state secondary school. Respecting the views of parents in this context can therefore tackle the two-tier education system that has evolved in British education.

This book aims to challenge a lack of communication between parents and teachers that has persisted in secondary education despite decades of work to improve home–school relations in the UK. How can we achieve a better dialogue and how have others found successful home-school strategies in keeping with their whole-school priorities? Options are needed as schools re-think their work with parents. Although primary schools have made great advances in the last 20 years, effective strategies in secondary schools tend to rely on determined leadership rather than well-researched lessons from other schools. It is vital to disseminate good practice in secondary schools further. In the chapters that follow, different approaches are recommended to help schools to focus parental support for learning. Not all require parents to become more visible in the daily life of a school, because they can give effective support quite appropriately out of school time. Parents can either reinforce school learning or add to it from home life. Whatever the requirements of the school, their own contribution should not be side-lined, and teachers need to respect home learning before directing parental support.

> *'Homes are increasingly regarded as outposts of school learning, progressively colonised through training parents ... , activity sheets and workbooks – some of the paraphernalia of informed parental support.'*
> (Wolfendale and Bastiani, 2000, p.25)

As Dr John Bastiani points out, a school-centric view of family involvement and support can narrow the educational benefits to children overall.

Unlike in primary school relations with parents, active parental involvement in the curriculum or on the school site is only recommended in secondary schools on a time-limited basis amidst a range of other initiatives to improve communication between parents and teachers. Term-planners, newsletters and home–school diaries that allow regular contact will ensure parents are kept in touch so that they can provide less tangible but equally powerful support from home. At secondary level, it is more important to attend to how to maintain genuinely open channels of communication, which will have implications for the use of non-teaching, pastoral and senior staff time.

Parents and carers

Family structure needs to be understood to be sure that a school is working with the relevant parties. It is also important to be clear as to whom the child thinks of as their parents, and what communication is appropriate with other carers. Adoptive parents, where the birth parents are known, may welcome an acknowledgement of their different situation and might need time to liaise with birth parents or social services on certain decisions. In many families, where other carers are responsible for the children, or the parents responsible have to liaise with partners outside the main home, communication problems can be complicated to resolve.

The use of the term 'parents' throughout the book is evidently not always accurate given the number of children whose carers are not their birth parents or their legal parents. The influence of the one or two adults with whom the child has the most important relationships at their main home must be identified and incorporated into discussions with the 'legal' parents. Step-parents and new partners are often thought of as parents by the children even if they do not carry legal parental responsibility. They will be a determining factor in the pupil's success. This book effectively recommends that a dialogue should develop between staff at a secondary school and parents who hold legal parental responsibilities as well as those who are parents in practice, whether foster parent, childminder or extended family member. The nature of the issue to be discussed will influence who should be included. It may be appropriate to include after-school carers in invitations to a meeting about helping with homework, for example. Parents could suggest who else could attend if they cannot be there in person.

▓▓▓ Children with particular needs

State-appointed carers and teachers have a special responsibility to communicate in some situations regardless of the capacity of the child's original family, especially at times of transition and crisis in a child's home life. It is now well known that children can suffer disproportionately at school from the stigma of being in the care system (Fletcher, 1993). As the stigma can be created by teachers as much as peers, the responsibility on schools is to monitor a child's well-being without making them feel awkward about their home situation. This can be done by maintaining high expectations of their attendance and achievement, not singling children out to talk to them unless there is good reason to do so, being vigilant to prevent teasing by their peers, and helping them to deal with ordinary situations such as where their friends can telephone them out of school. Teachers may lose communication with the birth parents during these times, but need to keep focused on the child's progress despite the turbulence and uncertainty of which they become aware. School can be a lifeline, as illustrated by this pupil's view:

> 'My schooling hasn't altered because I have lived in children's homes and at present I live with foster parents. It is quite strange really, because although I have been in many awkward predicaments I have not let my education slip. The staff and foster parents have helped me.'

(Fletcher, 1993, p.35)

Children with physical disabilities are also in a particularly difficult situation, but this need not translate into difficulties with their schoolwork. As bullying is common, their inclusion demands whole school policies that apply to them as much as to other children without physical disabilities. Behaviour problems also need to be addressed fairly, discussing with them and their parents appropriate responsibility for their age and abilities together with honest acknowledgement of the stress factors that may be induced by either pupils or staff in the school or weaknesses in the school's policies and procedures. Their needs confer a responsibility on teachers to handle relations with their parents with the sensitivity due to parents who are understandably nervous about their child's inclusion in a mainstream environment. One researcher comments:

> *'One of the main factors to emerge from this study was that teachers interviewed felt they had insufficient training to enable them to understand the needs of the children in their care ... Parents felt the lack of staff training meant that their children's needs were overlooked by teachers in mainstream classrooms ... it was simple things like the fact that [child 3] uses a laptop computer in school to write but the teachers often ask pupils to copy something off the board (e.g. a diagram) which her son cannot do.'*

(Llewellyn, 2000, p.112)

The study reveals an atmosphere of mutual blame and discontent:

> *'Dealing with staff in school was one of the most stressful aspects of caring for a child with disabilities.'*

(Llewellyn, 2000, p.113)

A health visitor or nurse might be able to act as an advocate to prevent a breakdown in home–school relations, but schools should also consider the needs of school staff for their own support when dealing with very difficult situations and families in distress. Teachers who work with children with a whole range of special needs may find themselves in need of peer support, and few schools have clear channels that they can use.

Some teachers, such as form tutors, heads of year and senior managers, occupy a role that already carries clear responsibility for working with parents, and in schools that are developing their communication with parents, responsibilities may begin to extend further in the staff team. Teachers at all levels feel their lack of training to undertake and improve in this work acutely.

▓▓▓▓ Teachers' views

The Association for Teachers and Lecturers (ATL) conducted a survey of teachers' views which demonstrated teachers' awareness, particularly in secondary schools, of the urgent need for increased parental support for learning (ATL, 2000a and b). In the survey, 62% of the teachers said they were aware that: *'The majority of parents want to help their child's learning but do not know how best to do so.'* (ATL, 2000a, p.4) Parents often express dismay that they do not know how to encourage their children. Teachers for their part feel at a loss as to how to advise parents. The survey revealed *'overwhelming support [75% of 936 respondents] for working with parents forming a greater part of both teacher training and professional development.'*(ATL, 2000a, p.26) New teachers are completely unequipped and unsupported, as teacher training gives no preparation for this aspect of the schoolteacher's role. If they are to hold more senior responsibility, they will need this experience and it is hard to obtain.

Teachers who responded also expressed their resentment of parents and described very bad experiences of trying to talk and work with them. Disappointment, fatalism and disrespect in the teachers' open comments echo the sentiments voiced in staffrooms, behind closed doors. Problems such as the inequality of home–school work to date have allowed resentment to fester against middle-class parents, while a lack of understanding of working-class and minority ethnic parents has created an unbridgeable divide in many cases.

The persistent lack of meaningful communication between teachers and parents indicates the nature of the territory of this book. We have become inured to difficult home–school relationships. Working with parents is not a task for the faint-hearted.

▓▓▓▓ The home–school movement

At a well-attended conference entitled 'Families and Schools: creative ideas for collaboration' in 1998, the National Home–School Development Group invited a secondary headteacher to speak, but there were only a few secondary school delegates, greatly outnumbered by the primary school representatives from across the UK. Only 65 delegates attended the national conference hosted by the Manchester School Improvement Service in 1999, although work with secondary schools in this authority has been exemplary. Primary schools have worked on their communication with parents and carers with increasing success since the 1980s. When children are very young, the division and differences between home and school are less stark. Parents and teachers see each other regularly and informally during the infant years, while classrooms still reflect the world of childhood that is familiar to parents at this stage. An infant teacher's role spans the emotional development crucial to learning and has not become as specialised as is the case later on. Many of the issues with parents do not therefore arise in the same way in primary schools. Large primary schools confirm that the issue of keeping up good relations with parents is more difficult at the junior end of the primary phase, when new communication problems start to appear. A practical handbook does exist describing the experience of six secondary schools (Beresford, Botcherby & McNamara, 2000). Good practice in working with parents of older children needs to be promoted even more widely.

Even when education could have been described as entering the progressive decade of the 1970s, Tim Brighouse's mission to remove the 'NO PARENTS BEYOND THIS POINT' signs at school entrances was daunting. He has since written about the challenge:

> 'In any consideration of the progress made towards parental partnership in education, one must not forget such inheritances and the reality of flawed practice on the road between good intentions and delivery. Not only were the off-putting notices the rule rather than the exception, even when they disappeared there remained a mental 'so far and no further' approach on the part of many practitioners. Schools and LEAs which boasted parental policies theoretically designed to welcome partnership continued practices which suggested otherwise.'

(Brighouse, 1993, p.176)

Policy-makers still widely espouse the notion of partnership, but as Dr Sheila Wolfendale writes,

> 'A number of schools have maintained a rather suspicious not to say distanced view of the benefits of closer working relationships and still regard too much parental presence within schools as an intrusion.'

(Wolfendale and Bastiani, 2000, p.3)

Central and local governmental policies and school practice have tended to adopt a traditionally narrow view that does not take families into account. Government departments like most professions have become specialised, based on their remit and the extent of their strict control. Teacher training and school developments have followed suit. Consideration of work with parents during initial teacher training courses is limited to the presence of new teachers at parents' evenings, where the brief delivery of a verbal report is all that is required by the inspectors (OfSTED, 1999). Schools provide a service for children first, and in many, parents are only approached as an afterthought or if absolutely necessary.

▚ The legislative context

The burgeoning of education legislation in Britain of supposed relevance to parents has inferred unpopular political values to home–school communication. Some of the regulations, such as those governing parental choice of a school, have proved more abstract than realistic and more political than parents really want. From a number of teachers' perspectives, making parents into customers was an ideological betrayal of the non-consumerist ideal of developing children's minds. Giving parents power as clients of the school was read as an attack on teachers. The public listing of assessment results was also threatening to teachers and it encouraged parents to be seen as academically ambitious and choosy. Subsequent research, such as the 1994 Keele surveys (Barbet, 1994), showed what parents actually think as opposed to what they are assumed to think. Parents tend to make balanced and practical judgements about choice of school, on criteria such as distance from home. Associating parents purely with initiatives to improve examination results places them in a judgemental role more openly than their opinions and views suggest they wish. Framing parents as parties in opposition to the teaching profession, who have a right to knock on the doors of schools or angrily claim more involvement, is equally unhelpful and unrealistic.

Some teachers see the promotion of parents' rights as offensive because their rights appear more important to the government than the pupils' or teachers' rights. Perhaps this is one of the reasons why the parents' rights movement commonly meets with resistance among teaching staff. Parent power raises the hackles of the most experienced pastoral staff. It promotes the idea that teachers are unfriendly or are too powerful and suggests that parents are a force to contend with, not ordinary people engaged in the difficult task of bringing up children. The progression within public services towards taking views of the general public seriously found early expression in the form of the Parents' Charter. It became obsolete at the end of the Tory administration, presumably with the hope that so too would the consumerist perspective with which it was associated. If parents are a 'force', they are made into a group, whereas in fact they do not tend to come together in any formal way, or use group events to express themselves. The depiction of parents as a group, and furthermore as a group of 'customers', was generally thought inappropriate amongst comprehensive school teachers, who provide a free service to society and directly to children rather than a private service to individual parents.

The psychological effect of 'parent power' on teachers can be to close ranks against parents instead of recognising the media image for what it is. Parents are less powerful than teachers within schools, so the promotion of their individual rights is only useful if it bolsters their personal confidence and thus indirectly benefits the pupils. Recognising parents' rights is useful when it depoliticises home–school policy that otherwise too easily gains political overtones. Thinking about parents as people with individual rights counterbalances the tendency to see them as a uniform group. Generalising about parents has become the norm in many schools and needs to be challenged.

It is interesting that, alongside attempts to boost self-determination and raise national standards, successive political administrations have not increased the headteacher's or governors' duties to involve communities of local parents effectively in crucial decisions. The increase in the number of parents on governing bodies shows the desire to accommodate parents' opinions but parent governors have not been given formal responsibility as representatives, so these governors cannot carry the power of the actual body of parents. Even if they were invested with this power, it is unlikely they would be in a position to lead the school by sharing governmental authority. State schools have more structural accountability to Local Education Authorities than to parents. David H. Reilly, an American educationalist, advocates leadership of schools by parents and teachers themselves rather than by politicians, bureaucrats or interested others (Reilly, 1995). Perhaps actual leadership and increased control would not solve problems between teachers and parents. Nevertheless, the opinions of parents need to be channelled fruitfully to benefit the majority of different children within the school. There is room for improvement here. In Israel, for example, parents have an explicit and legislated right to specify 25% of the curriculum, whereas influence by parents in the UK is extremely rare, indirect and a matter of negotiation from school to school (Katz, 1997).

Given the importance attributed politically to parental opinion, the lack of government guidance to schools on the day-to-day management of home–school relations is surprising. Reports are a legal requirement, and certain standards are required in the handling of admissions, exclusions and special educational needs. Parent Partnership schemes are now a requirement in each Local Education Authority, but can take a variety of forms. The White Paper *Schools achieving success* pledges that the DfEE will 'continue to help schools to find new ways to involve and respond to parents' (DfEE, 2001, p. 63). Although it does not specify how this will be achieved, it does refer to involving parents more at key moments in children's education such as the primary–secondary transition, and working with schools to share good practice.

The School Standards and Framework Act 1998 highlighted one practical and concrete tool for discussion with parents, the home–school agreement, which was accompanied by guidance on good practice in introducing it (DfEE, 1998c). Home–school agreements, like policies, should not be dictated, as their effectiveness is reliant on the consultative and engaging powers of the school staff and their communication about the shared responsibility represented in the mutuality of the agreement. The government guidance for schools introducing the agreements gives examples of how some schools have created partnerships with parents, rather than just sending out a list of school-led requirements, produced in a vacuum of consultation. In contrast with an era of prescription, the government is feeling its way towards offering effective options and setting standards, in keeping with their inevitably remote role. But the government has not drawn attention to vital ingredients for good relations, such as the need for teachers to educate themselves about the cultures and families in the particular communities served by their school. Presumably, in the production of guidance rather than more legislation, the approach of illustrating, not enforcing, good practice is weighed against the risk of schools doing nothing.

Change does appear to be on the horizon. Recommendations have started to appear from effective schools, parents' interest groups and researchers. The text of the government-produced booklet for parents in all schools introducing home–school agreements was subtitled 'What every parent should know', and it reads as if schools will respond to parents with more than the minimal statutory required information:

> 'There are many ways you can help your child in school. By law you are responsible for making sure he or she goes to school regularly, and on time. But you can also help by supporting the school's rules, and its arrangements for homework. Make sure your child knows that you support the school's policies.
>
> Ask your child's teachers how you can help your child at school. Tell them about anything which might affect your child's work at school and talk to them if you are worried about your child's progress. Make sure the school knows that you want to be told as soon as any problems arise which involve your child. Let them know about anything else you would like them to tell you.'

(DfEE, 1998d, p.1)

Unfortunately, few secondary schools claim success in responding to parents' queries and even fewer monitor their track record in such work. Most teachers concentrate their energies on parental involvement in meetings at school rather than taking into account home-based support for schoolwork (Johnson and Ransom, 1983). Most parents concentrate on caring for their children at home and rarely attend meetings at school. As parents have commented, even if they go to meetings, it may be with the feeling they will not achieve anything. They might just be going to show they care. Teachers are indeed heard to pass judgement on parents who do not turn up to events and meetings as uncaring. In other, more difficult situations, parents may be aware they could make things worse for their child by attending a meeting with teachers. Many teachers also fear the meetings, and avoid in-depth conversations about individual progress, as Barbara Walker and Maggie MacLure's analysis of secondary parents' evenings has conclusively shown (1998, 1999, 2000). One of the aims of this book is to encourage teachers to confront the facts of this problem more thoughtfully.

Forcing schools to do more with parents could lead to increased tension in the interactions between them. The more requests the government makes of schools, the less time teachers will have to respond to parents' concerns in a thoughtful way. The DfEE booklet can therefore be seen as a colourful, attractive and readable piece of information for parents that schools can use off the shelf rather than going to the trouble of having to devise and produce it themselves. Giving the advice directly to parents may communicate the powerlessness of the position of government administrations to change the role of a teacher in a creative and visionary way. It also seems to be an attempt to make direct communication with parents in a way that will carry political advantage. But it does nothing to influence the way teachers perceive parents and behave towards them. It also implies that civil servants are trying to do for parents nationally what schools should be doing for themselves, particularly as issues such as the amount of homework given can be school-specific. Although the government has started to advise parents directly about what they can do through leaflets, a magazine and a new website, parents are more likely to need advice at a particular moment of need and seek advice from local schools from staff they know and can confide in.

School staff who have managed to avoid looking to the government for guidance in home–school relations have had more success than others. All of those interviewed for this book happened to be parents themselves, and have a role within the school that allows them to use personal empathy, such as those with pastoral responsibilities. This points to the fact that the necessary experience of being a parent on the outside of a school will certainly already exist within your staff team. Non-teaching staff will be an invaluable resource.

Secondary schools that have addressed the lack of communication with parents have had to find new ways of informing and talking with parents, as at secondary stage they are bound to be somewhat at a distance. New approaches that encourage parents and carers to attend meetings at the school such as the Academic Review day (Chapter 7) are starting to achieve good results. I have aimed to describe opportunities to work both regularly and at key points in time with parents, following interviews with secondary school teachers, leaders and other contributors in the field. Information is also provided in the Table of Information on Case Study Schools (p.305) on socio-economic and practical facts of relevance so that others can take into account the culture and the context of the strategies described. The schools that feature have created an ethos of respect for parents and improved channels of communication to resolve problems. Most have refined their approach over a number of years.

It is important to resist the temptation of taking particular strategies or techniques as perfect remedies or whole solutions. The case studies in this book illustrate that substantial change is achievable but staff in each school will still need to adapt them to suit their local community. Regardless of the actual time parents have available to attend meetings or to help in concrete ways, if they can promote the value of learning, they will provide essential support to teachers behind the scenes. This aspect of parental support does not depend on their level of education or on the day-to-day problems of stressed parents.

At the beginning of the road, the journey is a long one. Poor relations created by the lack of communication require staff within a school to change their attitudes towards work with parents, not just their practice, which is not an easy task. Understanding the barriers between teachers and parents is the first step towards breaking them down.

1 BARRIERS TO EFFECTIVE COMMUNICATION

Home–school communication promotes a consistent engagement with education and the life of the school community and thus strengthens a child's progress. Close, understanding communication is also likely to moderate the disruption caused by crises. Children at infant school have regular support from teachers and parents who are in touch with each other on a daily or weekly basis. Junior schools report communication becoming more difficult because parents are more often working or busy with other children. At secondary school, the pupil's attitude towards work continues to be fundamental and they need joint encouragement from parents and teachers to persevere, but teachers' relations with parents of older children are often found to be weak or sporadic. Studies of communication between parents and school staff reveal unspoken and invisible barriers to constructive discussions about pupil progress or behaviour (Teacher–Parent Interviews, 1983; Walker, 1998; MacLure and Walker, 1999, 2000). These barriers lead teachers, even those who are themselves parents, to respond briskly or defensively to parents' queries about academic work. Parents often become diffident and do not volunteer relevant information unless an urgent situation demands their involvement. In the first decade of the twenty-first century, intangible but powerful obstacles still make it difficult for teachers and parents to communicate effectively, even when they most urgently need to do so.

A caring and wise parent has to place great trust in a school as an institution that will protect their child from danger through good supervision. Once the child has started to develop a sense of belonging in the new, larger secondary school community, questions will naturally occur to any thoughtful parent. Parents understand that the education service aims to develop their child's minds and their whole personality, and see it as part of their job as a parent to make the child's education their business. Many of the formative experiences in their child's development take place at school, so they rightly wonder at times if an aspect of the school experience has been designed in such a way that will contribute to their child's ability to learn rather than detracting from it. At intervals, and certainly within a five-year period, they may need to check that their child's needs are being met or that pupils are exercising their abilities fully. Some of their questions might be answered by the child's description of school life. Accessible staff at reception or in the front office respond to many general enquiries. When a parent's worry is of a nature clearly delineated as personal rather than work-related, pastoral staff often respond. Welfare issues such as bullying, for example, usually prompt concerned communication with a pastoral head of year or tutor quite quickly.

But when a parent needs, or wishes, to discuss a newly problematic aspect of either schoolwork or behaviour with a teacher, substantial difficulties arise. Effectively, parents have 'delegated' some of their parental responsibilities to the school and, like any responsible carer, should not allow this to become an abdication of responsibility. So why is it that many teachers find parents' questions difficult and intrusive? Interpersonal factors play a large part and can be complex. Although the people involved in home–school relations are adult authority figures in their roles with children, with each other their power and their different perspectives on pupils can present a challenge. They may feel shy of each other. A reticence to talk makes it unlikely that either party will engage in a full and informed discussion about a child.

▬ An example of brief communication

A parent, interviewed for this book about her conversations with secondary teachers, described a typically brief exchange on the telephone in which she had aired a concern about her son's inability to complete a school project:

> I managed to speak to the Biology teacher and said, 'I'm worried about Sanjiv, I think there might be a problem. He does not seem to get his homework done. In this project too, he says he does not know what to do, as if he does not know what is expected of him.' The Biology teacher sounded surprised, saying, 'Oh I don't think there is a serious problem Mrs Desai, ... there is really nothing to worry about.' ... She later talked to my son and told him that my worries were unfounded.

Parents are frequently invited in school materials to 'contact the school with any queries'. In this example, a parent had thought about the pupil's attitude towards schoolwork and felt a pattern was emerging which might indicate a deeper problem. But when the parent first tried to speak with a teacher, she felt silenced. The feeling that the teacher holds all the power, placing the parent in a vulnerable position, starts to set in when parents contact the school but feel instantly rebuffed by the staff member with whom they have shared their thoughts. Their acknowledgement that a pupil's attitude to learning is jointly managed from home as well as school has been rejected by their school counterpart, giving them no alternative channel to communicate their concern.

The subject teacher may have felt alarmed when called to the phone, as parents rarely telephone subject teachers and the call may have come out of the blue. She could probably hear the anxiety in his mother's voice, which may have made her react quickly rather than thinking about whether the parent had a point worth considering. It is hard to judge, in a brief moment on the telephone, how seriously to take a parent's concern. In an attempt to be reassuring, she made this parent feel that her worries were being dismissed, as if she was interfering unnecessarily or being neurotic.

In fact, Mrs Desai had been told at a parents' evening, and had observed herself, that her son was underachieving. She was in a better position than a subject teacher to notice his behaviour and achievements in homework and coursework across different subjects and thus to observe the range of subtle ways in which her son was showing deeper worries. From her perspective, his personal insecurities were interfering with his progress at school. She felt responsible for his development overall, and could see the school was a key site where his future life chances and attitude would be moulded. In the case of his problem with homework, Mrs Desai said in her interview that she could imagine straightforward methods that might help her to monitor his work more successfully, such as more information about how much work at home to expect.

Many parents are likely to be able to make suggestions as to how to improve a situation after talking briefly with a few teachers, but they can feel helpless because there is no standard route to discuss possible solutions except an often inadequate annual meeting in the other's domain. Very few schools have pastoral or curricular systems that can take a parent's insight into account. All the staff who answer parents' telephone calls and letters should first acknowledge that parents' concerns about a school issue will be recognised as valid and worthy of consideration, even if the first staff member to whom they speak cannot instantly understand the problem. It is a sign of being a good parent that they care enough about their child to ring in, and a good teacher will recognise this before going into the detail of the problem.

▓ The nature of parenting

A parent's role lends itself to understanding the psychological and emotional hue of behaviour in their children, but many do not try to share their understanding with teachers. To leave the parent to try to encourage pupils in their homework and their attitude towards school at a distance from the teachers who set the work is expecting them to play a part with their hands tied. Modern standards of teamwork between adults in other work environments rely on frequent communication, but most junior and secondary schools have not been part of this sort of revolution. Parents quickly become aware of the limits in the discussion about a child that a school feels is possible and they try to conform. Many parents work or are busy all day, so the lack of communication will suit them. However, if they sense a problem emerging, parents are then acutely aware of the fact that they may not even be able to recommend a solution. They become dependent on teachers to find one.

Parents, in contrast with professional teachers, are meant to work things out at a human pace. There is no training to be a parent and it is common to hear parents ask other parents for advice while defending their own approach, because the state of parenting is a naturally insecure one. Well-known authors on the subject of parenting have identified a common underlying fear of not being 'good enough' amongst parents (Bettelheim, 1987; Miller, 1987; Winnicott, 1986). Domineering parents are the ones who think they always know best, whose apparent confidence might veil deeper insecurity. Even experienced parents with humility need to think carefully about how to sort out problems affecting their child and may not be sure they have got it exactly right. Their uncertainty can be positive in a family setting; it helps to accommodate other views and children learn from seeing their parents learn. In a school setting, it can make them hesitant, and prevent them from making suggestions to teachers for what would help their child.

There is no such thing as a perfect parent, and even very good parents are going to have weaknesses and not always be up to all that is required. But parents feel extremely defensive talking to professionals about their relationships with their children and how they handle them. Faced with the confidence of a professional, a good parent will tend to defer to their judgement even if it has taken a lot to speak up. By implying too hastily that a parent is over-worried, as is so easy to do, teachers are likely to shatter the fragile voice of a deferential parent, playing into their fear of not being good enough and undermining their hard-won confidence. The majority of parents are aware of the power a teacher has over their child, so they will be easily put-off if they hear a lightly dismissive tone when they call. This is why, in the case of minority parents, schools can easily be experienced as discriminatory and even racist.

The Biology teacher may have taken the concern about Sanjiv 'not knowing what to do' as a possible criticism of her setting of the work in question. Perhaps she did not understand what the parent was observing because she did not have the whole picture presented to her. Perhaps she felt sorry for him that his mother was on the warpath. She may even momentarily have felt nervous because she was talking to a parent, the closest party to whom a teacher feels accountable outside the informed world of the school.

▨ Accountability

Difficulties arise when one or both parties feel accountable to the other instead of sharing responsibility for a child's development. Teachers have a sense of professional, managerial or contractually defined accountability, depending on the type of school at which they work but equally onerous throughout the education service. Central government's plethora of regulations and a question from one's manager can provoke an anxious response in the same way as a query from a parent. It is easy to confuse contractual responsibility with moral responsibility to parents. Both types can feel the same.

Teachers may be conscious of the real power that parents inevitably have – to make them feel guilty, to take up their time, or ultimately to take their child away from school. Parents carry a strong sense of moral, personal, and limitless responsibility for their child's life and future and they feel accountable to the world, including teachers, for their part in the formation of their child's character. This can make a parent feel afraid and shy of being honest if a child is behaving very badly. Feeling called to account is a disincentive to confronting the issues openly, so opportunities must be created for conversations that are not punitive or complaining. In the example above, the basis for the parent's worry needs to be clarified rather than trying to field the enquiry as if it were an attack. A sense of joint responsibility for child development can help a parent to feel less threatened and isolated. It may help if both teachers and parents can express their fears about the other's opinion. Simple questions like: 'Is it a problem with Biology in particular?' or 'How long have you felt worried?' could have opened up the conversation. There may indeed be nothing to worry about, but avoiding the issue will compound the parent's anxiety.

A school that accepts the notion of accountability to parents is reciprocating the level of trust placed in the school by parents who believe their child will be well cared for and well educated. David Jordan,

Deputy Head of Llanedeyrn High School, places this sort of accounta-bility in its context in a western democracy in his Report to Governors:

> 'The principle is generally accepted that those with a stake in the enterprise should have the opportunity to influence decisions affecting that enterprise. In Wales we have a highly decentralised school system, and important decisions are taken at school level which affect the teaching and learning of the children entrusted to our care.'

(Jordan, 1998)

Trust develops where there are few reasons for suspicion, so it is fortu-nate that, legally speaking, the accountability of teachers to parents is remote in the UK. It is extremely unlikely that parents will sue a school for breach of contract or that pupils will bring an action in negligence for compensation. The world of legal action is thankfully still less of a concern than the moral implications of our duty to pupils for their edu-cation. In cases where negligence is implied, the emotional and social impact of the accusation is far more likely to have damaging conse-quences for the whole school.

In any case, local education authorities have tended to protect schools from direct litigation, both dealing with legal issues on their behalf, and being deemed ultimately responsible for duties to parents. In the Phelps case in 1997, it was held that the education authority was liable vicari-ously for negligence by an educational psychologist who owed a duty of care towards a pupil with a learning difficulty and failed to diagnose dyslexia. This decision was reversed on appeal in 1998 and the damages previously awarded were ruled irrecoverable, which implied that even a local education authority is far from any real danger of being deemed responsible for professional negligence in the eyes of the law. However, the House of Lords subsequently overturned the Court of Appeal's decision in July 2000 and reinstated the original decision (EPLI – 280, 2000, p.56–7). In this case, the judge ruled that the school was entitled to rely on the advice of the educational psychologist. Teachers had acted reasonably. The case is nevertheless a landmark in deeming educational professionals legally accountable for specific decisions about children. It is also possible that the new Human Rights act will lead to a review of the obligations of schools as public authorities.

▓ Sanjiv's story continued ...

The instinctive response of the subject teacher in the example above, when she heard the parent's tone of alarm, was to attempt to reduce the anxiety level, even if later on in the staffroom she might find that several teachers had complaints about this boy and some would find it helpful to be able to join forces with the parents to address Sanjiv's developing educational problems. Without intentionally undermining his parent's authority, the teacher in this instance effectively allied with the pupil by minimising any difficulties. By the time this pupil's school problems had developed in the following year (Year 9), his mother said he had been given the ammunition by a friendly alliance with some of his teachers to turn round defensively and say, 'No-one at school is worried about me so why are you going on about it?'

▓▓▓▓ Expressing emotion

Sometimes the problems that arise in relations between home and school are a result of the difference between communication styles of professional teachers and parents. Parents will almost universally be concerned about the place where their children spend the majority of their waking hours. The job of a parent is to support and provide for their children, and the providers they choose to trust in general will try to show the care they take of their children. If these providers appear to be careless of the feelings or views of their child, it is their job to object. Being a parent demands extreme love for their child. It allows intense feelings which sometimes help and sometimes hinder the task of bringing them up as best they can. It is a sign of their love for their children when they feel strongly, given that their child's quality of life is at stake. The parent's investment is highly emotional, as it involves their children. It makes them feel dependent on the school. Their stake is not financial, but it is equally powerful.

Parents may justifiably feel angry when they feel they are not being heard. They do not belong to the school, however, in the same way as pupils and staff, so they are expressing concern as an outsider. This can make them nervous too and so their attempt at self-expression may easily backfire. When they appear off-putting to teachers, because they seem unnecessarily anxious, it can help to remember that this is their proper role as a parent. By projecting the possible consequences of the present into the future, they are trying to predict how a situation will develop and whether it could reduce their child's achievements in the future. As Bettelheim notes, the intensity of feeling that parents experience on behalf of their child can be an inhibiting factor as well as a spur to their courage. They may repress their worries until they become serious, or feel inhibited and reluctant to get involved. If they wait for too long before contacting a teacher, they are likely to unload these excessive feelings onto that teacher instead of just discussing the current concern.

'Parental reactions often extend beyond what the present conditions may warrant to worries about the future, and this kind of anxiety may provoke an undue severity or intensity of inhibition. This is doubly unfortunate because the child relates only to the present situation, and thinks his parents are doing the same. Also, when a parent's concern is limited to the present problem, and not aggravated by considerations of possible future trouble, it is much easier to think of alternative conduct to propose to the child.'

(Bettelheim, 1987, p.158)

Teachers justifiably feel anxious, guilty and even afraid when they cannot think of a way to respond to parents' requests but tend not to express their feelings as they are playing a role. A teacher's response may help a parent to break a problem down into its constituent and actual parts. This will reduce their level of distress through focusing on the small current problem instead of the imagined escalation of the problem. This sort of work with parents will have an impact on the pupil's motivation even if it does not involve working directly on school issues. A teacher can easily prevent the parent's anxiety or annoyance being communicated to the child, for example, by using their less emotional perspective to help to work out with the parent if their worry is justified.

A conversation between adults can also appropriately refer to much larger worries than a younger person might understand. As Bettelheim explains, a parent's worries may not be in proportion with their child's current particular situation and their child may not therefore understand why their parent is worried now. A teacher as another adult should be able to see the parent's point of view, whether it concerns the behaviour, academic work or general well-being of their child. They need not assume they should necessarily share that same point of view – listening does not mean agreeing – but it is unhelpful to tell them not to worry. Adults have to weigh up the possible positive and negative consequences of current behaviour or progress, thinking further ahead than a pupil can. To turn their joint thinking into a developmental influence, they need to decide on the best way to encourage the pupil to take a particular interest in their work rather than suggesting they need do nothing to change as mum is worrying needlessly.

It is important to wait to mention to a pupil a conversation held with a parent until an opportunity has been made to get to the bottom of the parent's concern. This does not mean being disingenuous with a child you teach, but restricting information to what you have agreed you will say. Telling a child what a parent has said about them may not be appropriate. Ask the parent if their child knows they have rung, and if the child agrees there is a problem. Wait to decide what to share with the pupil until you and the parent have agreed on the most helpful approach.

The role a teacher can play is that of an interested friend, an adult who cares but does not experience the same intensity of feeling. If the teacher feels his/her composure is failing in a discussion with a parent, the embarrassment may be enough to worry that his/her authority will be reduced with the pupil, who may well hear of the exchange. As secondary teachers are well aware, authority in the face of adolescence is a tall order at the best of times. Your insecurity could turn into a desire to reassure the child after a difficult conversation. It is useful in difficult relationships with awkward adolescents to have a common enemy, but the desire must be resisted. By communicating a disagreement with a parent to their child, the child is given mixed messages from the different adult carers in their life and then both teachers and parents may experience the consequences in ongoing day-to-day behaviour problems. Divided opinion about the best course of action puts the pupil in the position of choosing the easiest option. The resilience of a united front is a better strategy to prevent a teenager from taking an easy route out of a problem.

There are other dimensions to a parent's expression of emotion to a teacher. Firstly, parents are familiar with strongly expressed emotion within their role at home. But strength of feeling may be off-putting when expressed in what to teachers is a professional environment. They half expect or need a parent to ask questions in a professional way, without losing their temper or raising their voice. In other words, they wish parents were in a more uniform and boundaried role, like themselves, which would help to control their anger and any antisocial feelings in the same way that is expected of the pupils and the staff. This is understandable given the immense discomfort that can be caused when a parent's intimate anxiety is communicated suddenly to teachers. It can be much harder to deal with than the anxiety of the children.

Secondly, from the teacher's perspective, it can feel inappropriate to be too communicative themselves with parents, given that the teacher's impartial role in the classroom must be preserved. A key challenge to school staff is therefore to respond to parents in a way which allows frank conversation but preserves the boundaries of their teaching role when they are back in a classroom situation with the child. It may also be necessary to identify the most appropriate party in the school to hold the discussion with the parent if that person was not the first person they rang. They may have lighted on the Biology project, for example, simply because they came home one day and found that was the latest example of a sequence of difficulties, rather than the most difficult.

Thirdly, it is likely that cultural differences may be highlighted in stressful communications. If a parent is from a community where emotion is frequently or openly expressed, where others tend to sympathise and feel familiar with the language used because they are of the same background, this parent may feel pushed out or misunderstood by a less sympathetic reaction from a teacher of a different cultural background to their own. Sensitivity to this sort of cultural difference can increase from learning about the community. Cultural sensitivity may need to encompass community values, or the history of the family's experience in the UK. Asking others from relevant backgrounds in the staff team may help. Gaps in understanding the cultures of families represented in the school community should be highlighted and influence the recruitment of new teaching staff and other posts for which particular knowledge or community languages are required. This will increase the skill base of adults in school who can work with parents in difficult situations.

■■■ An unhappy ending

> Mrs Desai personally visited the school and spoke to a senior manager there. The person she met had begun to ask different subject teachers for reports, which showed underachievement, but they explained that it was considered to be a matter for her to deal with. She expressed her strong feeling that she could not do any more and asked for help as a single parent. They finally agreed that disciplinary measures could be taken at school – but did nothing for some time. Although school staff had been the first to raise concerns, the pupil was put on report more than a year after any problem had been aired and six months after the school had agreed they would act on the parent's concerns.

This example was chosen because it is representative of the type of unresolved dissatisfactions aired by parents in the course of researching this book. Territorial conflict and personal anxieties are not in general acknowledged or dealt with in the best interests of the child. From the parent's perspective, the school in question complained on one occasion about late homework at a Year 8 parents' evening, but took no coordinated action to help the boy to become more attentive. The homework book provided was not filled in by the pupil and never checked by a tutor. There were no guidelines produced on homework or coursework, so parents did not know what to expect or how to help by planning time for homework in family schedules. The parent in question gave her son a ticking off and the issue disappeared in a vacuum of communication between home and school until the following year. Of all the different adults responsible for the boy at school, none knew his mother well enough to feel they could pick up the phone to discuss ongoing problems with her. When his mother took this step, she felt that the particular Year 9 staff member concerned gave her an inadequate response. She had given it much thought and then had made the effort to overcome her nervousness of talking with a teacher. She felt her concern warranted serious attention.

When Mrs Desai subsequently described her attempts to take action, the vivid feelings she had had at each stage re-emerged, illustrating what an unspoken battle is still being fought between parents and teachers. The way she presented the experience showed she had decided that the school was entirely responsible for the problem and its lack of resolution. No common ground had emerged, despite a face-to-face meeting, on which to negotiate how to tackle the problem together. When the school, prompted by the parent's visit, finally threatened the boy within the disciplinary system, no action followed for many months. The report card was too little, too late, even if it offered a useful method for communication between home and school for a week.

A period of delayed reaction in response to a parent's intervention is typical, but the parent was not told how long it would take and with hindsight it did not benefit the child to have a one-off, delayed reaction. The parent in this case felt the disciplinary response was appropriate in its nature, but that the delay had caused her son's attitude towards school to deteriorate quite seriously. She ended up blaming the inadequacy of the school as a whole and its child-centred but ineffectual disciplinary systems. This conclusion was unproductive and may have been ill-founded, but there were no records of action taken, and no apologies for the inadequacy of the response. The school had probably tried different approaches and not communicated them to her. Letters home may never have arrived. The pupil was put in the position of choosing his options without the necessary joint support of home and school. Both sides had cause for complaint, but neither achieved a dialogue that would address this pupil's developmental difficulties through a sustained effort over a period of time, as pupils often need.

The snatched conversational exchange epitomises the problems created by poor home–school relations. Brevity in communications with parents itself betrays the fact that relations are fraught. They are squeezed around the edges of lessons and breaks, or, like parents' evenings, appointments are too short and pressurised. This prevents discussion developing into a clear and honest exchange of views. At parents' evenings and on the telephone, a teacher's besieged mentality can find greater expression than their ability to find a constructive solution. If a parent is not silenced by the initial response, the school's action can be so delayed that the effect of any agreement to act in partnership with a parent is watered down and ultimately nullified. Obstacles to good communication between home and school can thus result in missed opportunities for pupils and the school alike. School staff need to be more aware of how barriers have developed to discussing both behaviour and academic progress with parents, and why they persist.

The 'public' boarding school

The evolution of the teaching profession must not be forgotten; the foundations on which state education was built did not include a spirit of partnership with parents. The British tradition of the institutional boarding school demanded military-style allegiances from children, as if seeking to transfer their affections from the private realm of the family to the public realm of society – epitomised in the name given to 'public schools'. Parents were replaced rather brutally:

> 'Finding a young pupil weeping miserably, James Boyer, the famous nineteenth-century boarding-school Headmaster ... questioned the boy. When he was told that the misery was because he missed his parents, Boyer declared: 'Boy! The school is your father! Boy! The school is your mother ... your brother ... your sister ... and all the rest of your relations!'

(Marland, 1984, p.45)

State education in the UK was partly modelled on the independent system, so it is not perhaps surprising that teachers take over parents' roles more easily than in other parts of Europe, where there are higher rates of personal contact between teachers and parents (Macbeth et al., 1984). History has had an impact on general expectations, leading to a prevailing 'leave it to the professionals' attitude, especially amongst the non-professional classes. The classification of children into different schools gave parents particular reason to resent schools in the more recent past. We are emerging from the effects of a selective education system that downgraded a whole generation of parents. Through the eleven-plus, they were labelled as not academic and were basically told they were not as capable as others. Their antipathy to the remembered secondary-school culture may show in ways that would encourage their children to identify with an anti-education stance and serve to demotivate them. Teachers may then justifiably prefer to focus their efforts on the children instead of tackling entrenched family attitudes.

Family control versus the state

The power that parents have over their children's development is diminished by the very existence of state education. Teachers, perceived as the agents of the government, take children away from their parents to a secluded environment in order to take care of them and educate them. This model is so established worldwide that the loss it generates within a family is largely ignored. With younger children the loss is mainly felt to be emotional, a healthy part of letting go, but with older children it can cause financial hardship for no apparent good reason. The impact of compulsory education on the life of an impoverished family is still revealed through poor school attendance in poor countries. Even here, since the raising of the school leaving age, capable adolescents have not been allowed to earn a wage for the family or look after younger siblings, which withholds a certain amount of recognition for their life skills.

Families have also discovered how divisive education can be to maintaining a common language and reliable kinship bonds. Many pupils from working class families, for example, have realised that, by going to university, they stepped over a dividing line between them and others with their background who 'stayed at home'. Sometimes they have cut emotional and cultural ties without any intention to do so. Adults may not have much power to influence the choices the younger generation will make, at the most they may choose *not* to recommend a university education. But those who have least benefited from this atomisation of the family and the new privileges of a good education may not be very supportive of children currently at school. Parents may also find it hard to accept social limits such as the fact that it is against the law for their children to work more than a certain number of hours in paid employment.

Although compulsory education is broadly accepted and the wealth of post-industrial nations has silenced all but a few overtly dissenting voices, in areas of high unemployment teachers may still be battling against serious disaffection amongst parents and whole families. The social value attached to education suggests it will be a key to getting a job without explanation about the many small steps necessary beyond school. Succeeding in terms that sound beneficial to one's family or community might also be important. Schools may be held responsible for better prospects for the child as an individual as well as a member of their particular community, than if the child left at sixteen to get a job. But school education no longer guarantees jobs immediately as it did in the past; more education or training is needed to develop skill levels to higher and higher standards. Including examples in the school prospectus of how diverse cultures feature in lesson content, or mother tongue Saturday schools, will show that as a school you define education broadly and do not exclude parents' definitions of a good education for their children. These parents may also need to be convinced that schooling will result in some sort of success. Including interviews with young people from the area who have made it to a paid job, however many years after school, with descriptions of how they did it, might give both parents and children a more positive attitude towards the benefits of a school education.

▓▓ A factory model of education

Problematic communication between teachers and parents is in many ways simply a vestige of an industrial tradition in the education system. The large numbers of children and adults involved in a school community can lead to a depersonalisation of the educational experience, as if education is a factory production line with a clear division of labour between teachers and parents. In this model, the adults who supervise a child's learning are producing different mental outputs, through different methods and processes, and are responsible for different dimensions of a child's industriousness and learning. Their responsibilities are defined and limited to the sites of production – the home and the school. Yet we know in fact that children's behaviour and learning cannot be so neatly compartmentalised. The inter-relation between what they learn in different environments is as lively as their habits of mind. Their assimilation of learning from different environments leads to overall improvements in an individual's quality of thinking. The curriculum content cannot, unlike a factory product, be separated from its production, delivery, and new ownership.

Trying to put home influences out of the classroom can be confused with trying to teach concentration in a purely academic or cerebral way. Learning is a mental process requiring the ability to think about new information rather than taking it as read. Thinking takes place over a longer period of time than the actual lesson in which it is stimulated, so a child needs to be able to feel free to think and discuss ideas both at home and at school. Learning begins by being able to concentrate and take in information from each individual teacher and children who 'like' their teachers are more likely to learn in their classes. So teaching and learning are about good relationships as much as parenting is. 'Liking a teacher' conveys the significance that a child has attached to a lesson, in which it is difficult to separate the power of the relationship from the attraction of a method of working or a particular subject.

Territory

It is not surprising, given our habit of thinking of school and home as separate worlds, that territorial conflicts emerge when parents and teachers meet. We try to think of the child's experience in each environment as very different. When we come into direct contact with each other, the conceptual flaw in the supposed divide of territory becomes apparent. Different adults responsible for the same child each have a sense of responsibility for the child's whole development. The same child is learning different things at home and at school, but unless we are specific about what to discuss, it quickly becomes obvious that the child in question cannot be described from both perspectives at once. Rather than trying to turn the conversation to the child's advantage, parents and teachers may either seek to agree with the other, or to score points. A teacher may experience the interest of a parent as a threat. It can be strange for the parent, too, to discuss a personal family issue with someone outside the family. Working together calls into question the professional autonomy of a teacher and the private autonomy of the parent. Teachers will resist a request by a parent that appears to question a professional decision because it can feel as if a parent is telling them how to do their job.

It is important to recognise that, just as parenting is an intensely personal experience, dedicated teachers have a very great personal attachment to the children they teach too. The intensity of teaching and learning creates a special relationship within the school that is hard to share. It can feel as if a teacher's loyalty to a pupil is being challenged by a parent's perspective, and when this happens territorial feelings give licence to the human tendency (when things are difficult) to push them away. Naming the particular qualities a teacher finds in a pupil's work and attitude can be an important first step towards acknowledging the importance of their learning to both teacher and parent.

Parents have seen their children with other adults and are aware that all carers may teach the child habitual mechanisms of communication, emotional defences and coping strategies as well as knowledge and beliefs. Parents can provide clues to the child's perception and inform the school how their child learns best, but not unless they feel they have a right to comment on the child's progress. A child may care so much about school teachers, whether subject teachers or a pastoral tutor, that their perspective of adults at home and at school becomes interdependent. Many parents feel conscious that it would be developmentally unhelpful to contradict a child's teachers, no matter what their children say about them. Conflict or emotional distance between caring adults disintegrates the support network for the child's security and conflicting spheres of influence can be immensely unhelpful. Parents also comment on their reticence to teach children themselves out of a fear of creating conflict in their child's process of learning. They do not wish to confuse their children by presenting information in a way that will contradict their teachers.

Adults who play any kind of educational role need children to listen to them and believe that what they have to say might be beneficial. When they are not working together and especially if they distrust the other parties, they might try to achieve this 'despite' the others, pushing them out. Ignorance about home life can also result in missed opportunities for learning. This happens clumsily when teachers are not aware of home factors, as illustrated by the discovery that certain homework tasks are not straightforward in an Asian or Jewish home. It happens offensively when teachers do not give a thought to a child's home situation at all, or so fear making a mistake if details about home life are sought that they fail to find out crucial information such as a recent bereavement. It can be embarrassing for a child to mention their home situation – foster care, for example – so unless teachers remember the different circumstances of children in their classes this completely different life context may not be thought about. A regular exchange of information between home and school, about the child's learning, behaviour and friendships, relies on both teachers and parents accepting a joint role. Presenting information honestly to each other, agreeing what both parties will do and reporting back after the initial conversation is far from standard practice.

Power bases

The traditional home–school divide has created power bases that dissuade both parties from communicating in the best interests of pupils.

It is often argued that the exclusion of each other's influence is beneficial for pupils because it allows mutual compensation for difficulties. For teachers, the difference between the two environments may be perceived as beneficial so that the pupils with difficult home environments can grow in the liberal progressive school environment as individuals in their own right. The assumption that school is better than home is fundamental for this proposed compensatory effect, which is value-ridden. Maintaining rigidly separate worlds similarly enables parents to dismiss secondary schools as awful places from which home life is a welcome relief. When parents and teachers talk, the danger is that they will both be trying to preserve their superiority.

Professionals versus non-professionals

Both teachers and parents seem unaware how much respect they command from the other.

> 'Teachers dread parents' evenings and even seeing a parent coming in your direction causes stomachs to sink. Whatever happened to respect for teachers and their professionalism?'

(ATL, 2000b, p.4)

To an extent, a feeling of superiority is encouraged by virtue of being a professional. A perception of oneself as a member of a professional class, a group with a particular training and identity, automatically implies a boundary outside which those without this training are amateurs or less skilled, with less power and knowledge.

Some parents share this perception, seeing teachers as different and better placed than they are 'to know best'. Parents can feel misunderstood and undervalued. This presents a real obstacle to the development of partnership in home–school relations. Teachers may overcome it if they can incorporate into their professionalism the ability to discuss issues in a sensitive and friendly way with parents. Professionalism can otherwise get in the way of being an ordinary human being with whom a parent can have a confiding relationship. Professional parents like Mrs Desai in the example above can still be undermined and feel incapable of working with teachers to solve a problem, because they are not talking to the teacher as another professional but with all the emotion of a concerned mother. As Bernard Shaw said, 'All professions are conspiracies against the laity.' (The Doctor's Dilemma, Act 1)

■■■ **Status issues**

'When we are face to face with a man, woman or child ... , we are reduced to two human beings of equal status.'

(Winnicott in Philips, 1995)

All teachers, but especially senior managers in schools, have to understand the way they are sometimes perceived – as inspiring figures of authority in their own right. Until parents see a public figure as being an ordinary 'person' with humanity, their authority can prevent real communication. Teachers' words are imbued with a professional value that both teachers and parents have elevated above the value of an amateur carer and educator of children such as a parent, which militates against close and equal partnership.

Teachers still feel 'above' criticism and so they resent it when parents have independent views. There is a problematic tendency, reinforced by sensationalist media images of parents, to blame parents while still demanding respect from them:

'Too often parents 'think' they know how to teach and encourage learning better than the teachers. Society at large has run down the role of good quality teachers and then blamed these teachers for the ills in society which should rest with parents. Respect runs both ways – or at least it should.'

(ATL, 2000b, p.4)

Parents have become confused in teachers' minds with 'the public', when in fact the majority of local parents, when asked, praise their local schools and defend the teachers. This sort of defensiveness distracts from what teachers and parents could do if they worked together in a trusting way. It is more likely to be a powerful media story that downgrades professionals than parents of children at your school.

Improving communication with parents requires finding methods of discussion that free both teachers and parents to explain their different perspectives without implying one is better or more powerful than the other. Given education has been endorsed worldwide with social value and status, this is difficult. Many parents have unspoken expectations of teachers and often their feelings contain mixed dynamics of respect and resentment. The relationship is far from straightforward. In silence, a parent may be deferential, or may be withholding information. Parents can feel dependent on the school – for childcare if they are working, for example – which may make them afraid to speak up until such a point that their self-control cracks. Some parents who seem quiet and reasonable suddenly become overtly angry because of an incident involving their child. Demanding parents, who are assertive or confident and aware of their rights, or provoked to rudeness, can elicit intolerant emotions in the member of staff dealing with them. New teachers understandably cannot cope with being confronted by people whom they feel do not truly understand education or the school. Why should parents understand education? Teachers sometimes need to stand on their status because parents have a powerful agenda, the children for whom the school exists, which can appear to threaten teacher power. So perhaps they are expecting a kind of understanding from parents that only another teacher could really give.

These invisible barriers between professionals and non-professionals, between those inside schools and those outside schools, reinforce the unhelpful feeling that a teacher occupies a position little understood by parents. Effective interpersonal communication is prevented by the persistence of mutual suspicion. A school can reduce the distance by challenging teachers' attitudes towards parents that are revealed in misrepresentations of parents and the social groups to which they belong.

Attitudes towards parents

'The existence of old attitudes frequently persist long after they are no longer openly expressed or legitimised. So it is best to be cautious before getting carried away with examples of good practice.'

(Brighouse, 1993, p.176)

Even those teachers who most support state education for all exacerbate the divide between parents and schools through negative attitudes towards parents. Some of the most caring and experienced teachers express views about parents which prove, upon reflection, to be prejudiced and exclusive. Parents are still classified in staffroom conversations as sharing unpleasant characteristics – they are inadequate or pushy, neglectful or interfering. Teachers' attitudes are conveyed in references to parents in these generalised terms that if applied to any other group of people would be properly challenged. They are labelled too quickly and the power of stereotyping is that it accentuates difference and minimises connections between people. A lack of connection or empathy and a feeling of not knowing where to start become somehow justifiable.

It is common to feel false confidence about what a 'good' parent or teacher is like. This confidence arises because almost everyone has had a parent themselves, just as everyone has been to school and therefore feels justified in 'understanding' the role of a teacher. In addition, teacher confidence increases from being professionals on the inside of a purpose-built state institution, while parental confidence does not have a reason to increase. Parents who never attend a one-off annual meeting make teachers think they do not care about their children, and a parent who even once does not show absolute engagement with their child's education gets tarred with the same brush.

In other words, prejudice abounds because of the lack of real contact with people who occupy a role that is different yet similar to our own and whose authority over children gives them threatening power. The IMPACT home–school project has been working in this field since 1987. The project founders have observed the pattern of dynamics between parents and teachers gravitating towards the development of stereotypes:

> 'Through the construction of boundaries, with the concomitant notions of insid-
> erness and outsiderness, particular forms of 'otherness' are construed and cre-
> ated. The use of generalization and universalizing descriptions assist in the
> formation and maintenance of stereotypical positionings. Thus statements of the
> type, 'Parents like that won't/can't help their child with maths ...' both create a
> position and simultaneously force its occupation upon those who might otherwise
> cause disruption.'

(Merttens and Vass, 1993, p.11)

Stereotypical attitudes can change by understanding why bad feeling manifests itself in this sort of group-blaming way. It is generated by insecurity, such as that created in a teacher's mind when imagining the enormity of the role they would have to assume in order to work with parents. Each teacher, whether man or woman, parent or not, has to work on their own style of communication when discussing progress with parents, which is a very individual challenge. This is a particularly difficult task as many of our dealings with parents are isolated from other colleagues and are responding to a problem that has developed over time. There is no support or training for this sort of meeting and no body of experience on which to draw. The fact that most of the encounters between home and school involve mothers introduces gen- der- and role-specific issues into the conversation. But the most acute factor in a teacher's anxiety about working with parents is the aware- ness of how different 'we' are to 'them'. There is a chronic lack of iden- tification between parents and schoolteachers, which is promoted by the difference in their roles as well as individual differences in person- ality, culture and life experience.

The anxiety voiced by many teachers seems particularly acute when they consider the prospect of working with the poorest, least educated parents and they fear or feel guilty about the gulf that may be created by socio-economic and class differences. Most commonly, a split is imagined between the well-off teacher and the badly-off parent. Those who most need to improve their children's educational chances and to speak with a teacher are likely to have been labelled already as inadequate. Differences are accentuated between teachers and the more articulate parents by seeing these parents as only interested in their child. Parents' voices are heard and ignored when they are perceived to be selfish or prompted by interest in a mere individual child. A teacher can easily take the school's side against the parent's with the justification that this is fairer to the majority of pupils. Parents also try to take sides by seeing teachers as insensitive to their individual children's feelings.

What is not understood about parents is much more obvious than what teachers do understand about parenthood. Although many teachers are parents themselves, being a parent becomes difficult to remember once a teacher enters their role at school and puts their personal life out of their mind. Role boundaries are helpful in building specialised skills in a work environment. But traditionally work is separate from the home domain, so although 70% of teachers are female, we get used to putting on our work hats in the morning. This means that the experience of being a parent may not enter into discussions in role unless a point is made of it. It is therefore important, at the earliest opportunity, to identify teachers who are parents themselves amongst the staff and show through discussion how common worries about one's child at school are. Labels on the basis of brief meetings should be avoided, as parental confidence varies with the ups and downs of family life. Teachers who are parents themselves will be aware how a stray observer will make them feel or say: 'You must think I'm an awful parent but ... '. Even other parents cannot really understand how your many-layered relationship with your child works, or the various strategies you employ to take care of them. Experience of longer conversations with individual parents will belittle most stereotypes.

Teachers with little experience of parenting themselves will also be able to make a valuable contribution. As colleagues, they will bring a teacher's perspective to the debate even once teachers who are parents have started to talk from a parent's point of view. They might bring rational thinking to the often-emotional debate within the staffroom about working with parents. They may, in meetings with parents, be better at listening to a parent talking about their child without experiencing feelings of competition or trying to introduce into a conversation their own approach to parenting. Clarity of thinking will also ensure that foster carers, step-parents and those who are not the birth parents do not get forgotten in strategies that embrace the majority of parents.

▰ The home backgrounds argument

Phrases heard in the staffroom, such as 'What can we achieve of any significance given their starting point and their life outside school', betray a feeling of impotence and a fear of failure that dangerously write off certain children without regard to their individual potential and strengths. Obvious class, parenting and cultural differences appear to provide evidence for the fact that working with some parents will prove difficult, if not impossible, and the emotional experience of trying to find common ground with a parent whose attitudes are completely incomprehensible leads teachers to make extreme judgements and feel a sense of resignation – 'With parents like that no wonder!' Brief meetings with the worst off in society are likely to create great feelings of hopelessness, despair and anger, on behalf of the children about whom most teachers care greatly. Discussions about home life can too easily acquire an atmosphere of taboo, or create the worry amongst teachers that disadvantaged pupils who have less emotional support than others in the school will be embarrassed by contact between school and home.

There is an obvious relation between poverty and under-achievement, but valid observations of cultural and class differences become oppressive when they are assumed to apply to every individual in that group. Rhetoric regarding the influence of home backgrounds on the ability of children to learn is an expression of stereotypical attitudes towards disadvantaged families. Bernstein (1970) was ahead of his time in rejecting compensatory education models that implied the home upbringings of working-class children were lacking. His definition of education as an introduction to 'public forms of thought' and his insistence that there have to be links between a child's social experience and 'the total culture of the school' acknowledged the middle-class roots that make education exclusive if teachers do not understand the cultures of the children they teach.

Class awareness in itself does not help to improve communication between home and school. It can accentuate middle-class guilt, and working-class resentment:

> *'It is easy to misuse sociological information, especially analyses of the characteristics of social class ... This knowledge can be misused to create an oversimplified kind of 'determinism', which is allowed to trap pupils in their current plight: 'You can't expect high literacy standards. Look at their homes', or 'There's nothing relevant in the curriculum for them, so naturally they aren't motivated to do homework.' Such attitudes ... are dangerous if they lead us to treat pupils as if school had nothing but sympathy to offer.'*

(Marland, 1993, pp.12 –13)

Similarly, it is wrong to assume that parents will only want sympathy when their lives are hard. Caring about their children's education will come across as helpful, and they will respect teachers who do not give up on them because of their lives, and who do not patronise them out of embarrassment at the vast social inequalities that of course exist. Teachers need support when facing the extreme social disadvantage they see in some communities and all children and families need to be treated with respect. An appreciation of difference therefore needs to be balanced by an appreciation of our fundamental right to be treated as equals. Humility and compassion are needed to bridge power differences which are not easy qualities to acquire.

A sense of fatalism that is applied to children's potential harks back to debates in the 1960s and 1970s about the impact of school on a child. Researchers at that time attempted to propose a predominant power in a child's life. Deterministic views tallied with the emphasis placed by them on hereditary factors (nature), family environment (nurture), or class (social economy). The concepts of joint ownership, power-sharing, and partnership were not then as important as they have become.

When national education policy incorporated the selective eleven-plus examination, generalisations about children in terms of their likely delinquency or the compensatory education they would require were common. The tendency to label a child for life has thankfully greatly reduced, and it is also no longer quite so acceptable in special education to underestimate the future of whole cohorts of children, to the extent that inclusive policies have started to create truly comprehensive school communities. But the complaint that certain parents and children will not be 'helpable' still arises frequently. It usually takes the form of a despairing and emotional comment that tries to keep professional insecurity at bay. As the home backgrounds argument still has credibility today, it is important to examine relevant research and to encourage a higher level of debate amongst staff so that they question this block to working with all parents regardless of their socio-economic background. The convincing nature of the cry comes from a truth taken out of context and put to the service of simplistic thinking. Teachers know from experience that there is some basis for their views but that this cannot be the whole story.

Michael Rutter (1989) in his longitudinal exploration of the continuities and discontinuities between childhood and adulthood showed that there are many influences on the course of individual development. The idea that deprivation while very young has an impact throughout the rest of life had over-simplified the real complex picture:

'The process of development is concerned with change and it is not reasonable to suppose that the pattern will be set in early life. ... However, continuities will occur because children carry with them the results of earlier learning and of earlier structural and functional change.'

(Rutter, 1989, p.26)

Rutter concurs with the view that people change a good deal over the course of development and that the outcome following early adversities is quite diverse, with long-term effects dependent on the nature of subsequent life experiences. Home, school, personality and environment all combine in different ways in different individuals to determine their progress. Arguing for one to have supreme influence is denying the permeable and unpredictable nature of child development, although early experiences should be kept in mind if they prove to have an enduring influence.

Rutter pinpoints the fact that although attainment levels can be projected from earlier life, progress at school is also open to influence. So predicting the *final achievement levels* of children on the basis of their home lives can be accurate but will also condemn a child to low expectations by suggesting their educational fate is predetermined. The *process* of improvement and the value of belonging to a social group, learning to function well in society, are overshadowed when teachers reduce the worth of all their daily efforts to limited predictions on the basis of social class or entry levels. Even heads of schools in the poorest areas insist on high expectations and have proven most successful when aiming high, which shows a basic belief in every pupil's potential.

Limited expectations will be all the more powerful if shared by the parents. Parents and children themselves are as observant as teachers about their lot in life. Many recognise the level which is comfortable or right for them, with an almost Buddhist sense of acceptance, and their expectations too need to be both realistic and higher than the minimum. In discussion with them, hearing their views, school staff need to work sensitively to promote realism and ambition. If teachers are trying to remain too buoyantly ambitious on behalf of the children they teach, a different view to their own can incur their wrath – what would be the point of education or believing passionately in individual potential if we had an allotted place in life? Feeling outraged that home backgrounds 'hold children back' can be equally unhelpful.

Blaming home backgrounds is a common defence against criticism, an instinctive rather than a substantiated theory. It is often a fear of failure that turns our minds to find a cause for the problem that does not implicate ourselves. One of the first tasks to consider is therefore the development of an intellectual culture amongst staff and governors of your school so that discussions do not rely purely on received wisdom with its untested conclusions. A programme of seminars with invited speakers can contribute to professional development. Discussing targets and achievements will show differences in expectations between departments or individual staff within a department. Tracking pupil achievement carefully will reveal strengths and weaknesses in teaching and will bring greater confidence in the process of improvement. The home backgrounds argument needs to be challenged so that it does not legitimise staff feelings of hopelessness. Good home–school strategies will back up the service being provided by teachers by encouraging joint responsibility with parents or carers, so that teachers do not need to resort to a deterministic ideology to justify difficulties with both behaviour and achievement.

▓▓▓ The school effectiveness debate

Rutter (1989) referred in his research to the evidence that school can make an enormous difference – despite problems at home. He refers to the effects of 'poor schooling':

> 'The children who went to less effective schools were twice as likely as other children to show poor school attendance; poor attenders were twice as likely to leave school early without sitting national examinations ...'

(Rutter, 1989, p.31)

and so the effects compound. The chain of circumstances could equally be positive:

> 'Those who had good [school] experiences were three times as likely to show planning in their choice of careers and of marriage partner. This meant that they were much more likely to marry for positive reasons ... the presence of such marital support greatly increased the likelihood that they would show good social functioning and good parenting as a young adult.'

(Rutter, 1989, p.33)

A compensatory effect is acknowledged, particularly in the case of children living in children's homes.

In the last two decades, the debate about the factors that vary from school to school has become more sophisticated. The argument that schooling does not make much difference in the face of extreme social disadvantage has been replaced by the conviction that indeed it does. Schools have recognised the importance of realistic planning and high expectations. Parental involvement in education and extra-curricular projects are re-emerging to fill some of the gaps between teaching at school and care at home. At the start of the twenty-first century, there is a clear belief in the value of education for all children regardless of their social background, and particular community schools who foster relations with parents to maximise this effect are achieving prominence in the public eye.

A vision of riches

When one child in three lives in poverty, what can schools do to raise expectations? In Portsmouth, primary head Colin Harris is determined his pupils will fulfil their potential. **Stephanie Northen** reports

More than half of Harris's pupils have special needs and 40 per cent claim free school meals. Most would number among the 4 million children growing up poor in the UK ... Early deprivation is still the strongest indicator of an adult life dogged by ill-health, debt, depression, and disaffection. Colin Harris – like the present Government, which has vowed to eradicate child poverty within 20 years – believes children can break out of the vicious circle.

Mr Harris says their success depends on them believing in themselves... Mr Harris has set up a breakfast club and an after-school club... There are children on the premises from 7am until 6pm every day. They have discos, they go bowling, they go skating, they have sleepovers – all organised through the school. In other words, they do all the things normal children do... They also do their homework – or they and their parents are in trouble.

For schools in deprived areas, parents are often the key. They have to back up their children's efforts... Before Colin Harris arrived at Warren Park, the tendency was to shut parents out. 'I went against the grain,' he says. 'I said 'Open the gates, I want them all in.' I want the confrontation, because every confrontation gives me a chance to put my message across.' Proof of the distance he and they have travelled came about 18 months ago. Five parents came to see a classroom teacher. Their problem? They wanted advice on how to support their children now their children knew more than they did.

(TES), Friday 30 June 2000)

Equitable strategies

A major reason why teachers in state schools in particular have not taken up the home–school challenge whole-heartedly is the perceived inequity of existing approaches. It is widely felt that middle-class, more advantaged children get the most out of good work with parents. Many teachers feel irritated that articulate parents are the ones who manage to get through the protective walls of a school and put the teacher in a difficult position of defending their practice or policies. Resentment is often voiced against 'the middle-class parents' – as if their advantages in life disqualify them from resources from state schools. Teachers often use this as a reason not to increase work with parents, yet simultaneously claim they never see the parents they need to see. In other words, those most in need seem uninterested and those most willing are not welcomed by the school, beyond existing activities and events which in many cases are attended by the determined few.

There are several fallacies in the perception that the parents who are committed to education are middle class. Firstly many parents, not just the better-off, need and even expect more information and advice than state schools have historically anticipated. To assume parents will not be interested if they are not successful 'types' is a kind of class prejudice.

Secondly, if a school discovers there is truth in the staff's feeling that only the middle-class ones make themselves heard, then this does not mean they are the only ones interested. The inequity in current arrangements for meeting and talking with parents is often caused by *ad hoc* arrangements that derive from an era when parents were deemed to have few rights in a school. All parents are entitled to more information if they need it, regardless of their class. Schools need to address the number of parents who attempt an enquiry and are put off. The frustrating reality of the experience of too many parents, regardless of their own level of education or wealth, when they attempt to address secondary school problems, have come to light through detailed academic study (Teacher–Parent Interviews, 1983; MacLure and Walker, 1999, 2000). Class and economic differences between parents might show in a certain confidence or courage to keep on trying to get involved, and if so, the small number that succeed will make it seem unfair to devote one's time only to them. They may be expressing problems that all parents face in communicating with the school.

As for inequity in current meetings with parents, the dialogues featured in Chapter 6 show that the voices of parents are commonly hastily suppressed, whatever the social strata they come from, when the subject is a child's progress. Research by Martin, Ranson and Vincent (2000) confirms the likelihood that professionals or managers, 'Class 1' parents, will perceive responsibility for their children's education to be shared with teachers rather than handing their own influence over to the school during the day. They describe it as 'managed trust', in contrast with the less advantaged cohorts of parents who display 'partial trust' or, further down the scale, 'forced' or 'given trust'. This refutes the perception that improved communication will only benefit the better-off pupils. Brief communications will evidently discriminate against certain pupils by discouraging certain parents even further from talking with teachers. But parents of all classes are likely to raise issues rather than to be trusted by teachers who then discuss these issues with them. Even once a parent has spoken with a teacher, results can fail to materialise or, if they do, they may go unnoticed. Without changing a school's whole approach to working with parents, increased communication with parents will be of limited benefit, and will only reinforce their current perceptions. So in the case of those who are actually better-off, their parental *monitoring* will improve without the actual relationship with school improving. For relations to improve, a school has to aim at reversing the current lack of trust with most parents, through methods of communication and reforming meetings so that teachers can create and build personal trust with parents across the social range.

In addition, it must not be forgotten that the majority of parents involved in schools are mothers. This fact, even in modern society, increases the likelihood that they will internalise their resentment rather than fighting openly on behalf of their children. Many caring mothers think their children would suffer in school from having a 'complaining parent'. Even those parents who are middle class do not tend to express their dissatisfaction openly:

> 'The dominant picture drawn from transcripts is one where parents' interactions with the school are touched by uncertainty, of trying out strategies, of compromise. The mother quoted here describes her daughter's struggle to do a particular advanced level course in the school's sixth form consortium,

> 'The AS level maths doesn't seem to be offered now even though it was advertised, so we are actually taking this up with the school, because if necessary she will do this independently [with a private tutor, the family have employed in the past] [.......] My husband left a message on [the voice mail system] for him to be contacted at his school or at home, this must be two weeks ago now, we haven't had a reply to that, so now we shall write in because we're obviously losing time on this.' (Dora)

> In this example, the family clearly have the resources with which to compensate for the possible lack of provision, but it is interesting that Dora's immediate

response to the situation is to establish a fall-back position, to obtain the syllabus so that her daughter can follow the course privately. She speaks only of clarifying the situation with the school, of finding out whether the course is available, rather than displaying any anger or determination to get her daughter taught within the sixth form consortium.'

(Vincent and Martin, 2000, pp.471–2)

Comprehensive parental involvement

My hypothesis is that a school is unlikely to be truly comprehensive while disaffected parents are ignored. If it has become acceptable in your school to reject vocal middle-class parents, over a number of years this attitude will covertly discourage a certain section of the population. Parents of all backgrounds choose when to withdraw resources – whether their time, energy or thought-provoking comments – from state schools. When parents are given the opportunity to be involved in school life in some way, whether by fund-raising, organising social events or a more active involvement on site, at least the minority with time and confidence are allowed access to judge whether their faith in the school is justified. Unless the school is felt to be meeting their children's needs, which is very much a matter of individual negotiation about what is possible and fair, parents with a strong will have the power to move school, or to give up on the school as the centre of their child's learning and invest more in home activities or supplementary education. Most will ask other parents and then adjust their expectations of the school rather than move schools given the family upheaval a school move causes. Private tutoring and Saturday schools are chosen by parents who are careful to respect the limitations of the state school. So it is important for headteachers to become alert to the existence of a silent constituency of parents who use alternative and supplementary education. Trace the roots of their private, quiet, low expectations of your school.

Some parents will shout or protest, which may express their distress or how much they value education, neither of which are class-specific. The invisible barriers described in this chapter dissuade all but the most confident or the most desperate. It is a mistake to think that social status is the whole story. The value placed on education shows equally through respect by minority ethnic families who exert their influence outside the school. John Bastiani quotes a study of family practices of high achieving pupils in which minority parents who value education undertake complementary activities *outside* the school (Wolfendale and Bastiani, 2000). They may value education highly but feel compelled to occupy the 'forced trust' position of outsiders. They need to know that their way of supporting education is relevant, how much time to make for homework, and when it might help to talk about a school topic with their child. Parents can be of great support to teachers if they hear about school lessons and activities. Mainstream schools might feel parents need to be told 'how' to help, but this is not always necessary. Parents have imagination and may be stimulated by topics if they hear what pupils are doing. Strategies cannot all be concentrated on parents who contact the school.

Furthermore, the fact that the parent or carer is an advocate for an individual child can feel like a challenge to the group culture in schools. Most home–school strategies will improve a school's ability to identify a need for support in the case of individuals. It may be unfamiliar territory deliberately to benefit individuals rather than form groups, but individual planning is a crucial dimension in modern comprehensive education. The challenge is how to address a level of deprivation in particular homes that is harmful to a child's education, while a school is trying to provide an equally valuable education for all.

Unequal resources are necessary as some children need more help, and schools should not discriminate against those who are in need, however silent their parents are. Relating tracking reports to work with parents should reveal who is benefiting and for how long support tends to be needed. Allowing differentiation in work with parents is as important as whole school approaches. Special public resources will need to be prioritised for the most disadvantaged families on relevant criteria, such as poor attendance or completion of homework. Cultural awareness can be identified amongst minority ethnic parents and brought into the school. Extension activities involving parents, volunteers or teaching assistants might boost a whole form by preventing behaviour difficulties amongst more able children and allowing more teacher time for those in most need of specialist help.

Some school staff members express real resistance to addressing the problems with parents, but by doing nothing, gaps between children will only increase. Schools that do not improve parent–teacher relations are likely to perpetuate educational inequalities because schools that do not reform their work with parents will preserve the social *status quo*. A low level of contact between home and school is likely to perpetuate educational disadvantage and reinforce socio-economic divisions between pupils. School staff need to become more aware of how a lack of communication and dysfunctional relations with parents preserve a power imbalance between parents and teachers and thus between children in different socio-economic groups (Martin and Vincent, 1999; Vincent and Martin, 2000). The generally accepted belief in promoting equal opportunities seems to be forgotten with regard to work with parents.

▓▓ Conclusion

Attempts to improve home and secondary school relations often fail, or seem unsatisfactory, foundering in hidden struggles between parents and teachers. Pre-existing attitudes of both teachers and parents lead to unhelpful assumptions on both sides that are reflected in the communication, or lack of it, between them. In a school where the starting point is that parents rarely contact the school, when a parent takes the initiative to do so, they are bound to encounter surprise and discomfort. The teacher's energy can be focused on minimising the implication that something is wrong by virtue of the fact that a parent is commenting at all. Oppression results, in which the professional autonomy of teachers is considered sacrosanct, and parents' voices are excluded or silenced to protect the expert's educational judgement. Once secondary schools have overcome these historical and psychological barriers to work with parents, practical solutions will be much longer-lasting. Changes and improvements in home–school strategies now have precedents.

2 AUDITING YOUR CURRENT COMMUNICATION WITH PARENTS

An audit of the effectiveness of parent–teacher communication can focus the attention of staff and governors onto the relevant issues. A hallmark of good communication is its sustainability, so a snapshot view will not give a complete picture. The senior management team needs information that will enable a consideration of home–school partnership in a range of situations, over periods of time, before proposing a plan for specific changes.

Procedures for home–school communication that are already established can create inertia, as they suggest that there is an active dialogue, hiding the real difficulties. A seminar or staff discussion on problems in communication that currently occur may make it more apparent that there is a need in the school for improvement. After discussion with a small number of staff, it will be necessary to present specific examples of problems, to observe communication in process and to discuss more openly the reasons for the need to introduce a new strategy, or to review an old one. If there is enough interest in this sort of exercise, a working group dedicated to an audit of existing communication with parents can help to focus minds and energies. Planning the audit requires leadership. The chair of this group needs to be given the authority to ask questions of a wide range of staff.

Ensuring that both teaching and non-teaching staff representatives belong to the Audit Working Group is important and personal experience of parenting must also be recognised in this group. An audit aims to gather relevant information without hastening to practical solutions. Although members will all be practitioners in school with the ability to propose initial solutions to what is found, information gathered from the first consultation and observation stage of the audit should be shared widely in the staff team rather than progressing too swiftly to action. This will address the fact that staff attitudes have such a large part to play in the success of any new work. An audit exercise should also include a consideration of school policies that relate to home–

school work but are not directly aimed at parents. A comprehensive review of a school's communication with parents will lead to behaviour, assessment and curriculum policies being reviewed with parents in mind as well as the more obvious issues of homework and primary–secondary transition.

Aims of an audit of your school's communication with parents

- To assess what current home–school contact achieves.

- To note long-term gaps in communication and frustrations amongst both teachers and parents.

- To report how inclusive the school's current methods of communication are.

- To inform yourself about the lives of the parents who the school will be addressing.

- To identify areas for skill improvement amongst staff.

- To contribute to some proper organisation of the work which will include defining the tasks that are needed, and the staff who could achieve them.

Audit questions

Each aim will attract a number of possible questions. The audit's breadth and depth need to be decided in advance and the questions it is seeking to answer clarified.

- Assess the level and quality of relations with parents of the school.

All communications – on the telephone, in writing and in person – are the vehicle for home–school relationships. How much communicating goes on? What is the level of satisfaction with it? This is quite a different exercise from asking parents and teachers what they want for children at the school or how much should be expected of the school in general. In meetings with parents, the aim of that particular meeting from the teacher's point of view could be noted and then reviewed. Questioning parents before they leave a parents' evening can yield informative results about whether the issues they brought were dealt with over the course of the evening.

Letters and other written communications may never reach home if 'pupil post' is used. A suitable audit question on this issue would be: How often on average do parents receive what is sent via pupils?

Teachers may also be able to report on their satisfaction after conversations with parents. If all tutors chose five examples of situations where parents were involved, how many worked to prevent the escalation of a problem over time, how many only contacted parents at a late stage, and how many encountered difficulties communicating with responsible family members?

- Discover ways in which current links promote or prevent equal opportunities.

If there are any patterns in parental involvement over the years, you may find that certain groups of pupils miss out on the benefits of current home–school dialogue. Which children benefit the most from your current level of contact and why?

You may only be able to uncover inequity in whole school approaches by making links with the socio-economic status of families, which will need to be recorded confidentially. Minority families should not be excluded by current strategies. Minority issues, such as single parenthood, ethnicity and children living with step-families or grandparents, will have to be taken into account when devising effective strategies for communication with parents and carers.

- Inform yourself about the real people whom the school will be addressing.

A realistic plan for improvement will take into account who your particular parents are, in terms of the nature of their occupations, their cultures and their economic status. Parents differ in each school, change over time and may have working lives or domestic issues particular to your local community. Parents are sometimes seen as one amorphous group – a coherent community on the outside with a great investment in the school and a forceful agenda. They can also be perceived to be a collection of individuals who all wish to discuss with teachers the interests of one pupil, which would not be practical. Both these extreme perceptions need to be moderated by information about parents' actual lifestyles, so that meetings can be arranged to suit the average parent's situation, and about their expectations of contact with school staff. The collection of information about the parents is essential to cater for parents in groups, such as all those who do shift work, as well as for individuals whose needs will be the exception not the rule. A school will then be in a better position to cater for the average type of enquiry in its systems and staffing choices, while aiming at an increasingly individual response.

- Identify areas of strength amongst the staff and within current school systems.

Who deals with parents the most? If it is front-office staff, they will themselves be a source of information about how often parents speak to the teacher they are seeking. If there is no telephone in every part of the school, how do messages get through?

Which members of staff are involved in discussions and family meetings? In individual meetings, which staff have a good rapport with parents? Where did they gain relevant experience for this kind of work?

Teachers may be parents themselves, with the ability to draw on their life experiences. How many of your staff are parents and which teachers say they use this experience in their work with parents of pupils at the school?

The audit should record how the range of pupil needs in your school is currently addressed in work with parents, whether on a small or large scale.

Rare or regular home-school contact

The role of the audit is to develop a full picture of parent–teacher communication at times when nothing is apparently going wrong as well as keeping records of the inevitable difficulties, such as during the exclusion process. One approach is to develop enough information over a term or more, in order to predict how current communication over a period of time will lead to a good or bad outcome for the child concerned. Forms should be used to record communication about particular issues or even documenting the progress of work with particular pupils and their parents.

The audit of the quality of parents' contact with the school needs to uncover any veiled frustration on the part of parents, as well as asking them if teachers manage to respond to them. When there is a clear problem and they are asked to contact the school, the school can monitor whether parents attempt this and how easily arrangements can be made to talk about the problem. Teachers sometimes express shock and disbelief that parents do not appear to care about their children enough to make an effort on the rare occasion they are contacted. The rarity may be the problem. If it is a complaint, it causes the anguish of uncertainty, raising the spectre of an enormous problem in the child's and possibly parent's mind. This can create an automatically negative association with the school in a parent's experience. One part of your audit should be to note the level of contact made with parents for negative and positive reasons (and for information only which might be classified as 'neutral'). When a school has resilient and healthy relations with parents, communicating good news about their children starts to balance the bad news, in a more realistic mix.

An audit of home–school communication has to look at the effectiveness of existing letters, conversations and meetings but also include methods that gather information about how misunderstandings develop. When things go wrong, it is understandable that there will be mutual blaming and unhappiness. Teachers can feel that parents are at fault, whereas parents are predictably likely to be wary of an unknown teacher who is merely a representative of an impersonal institution, even if they have the ability to imagine the situation is their child's responsibility. The working party needs to ask for examples from both sides and make it clear that the aim is to find solutions and prevent the same happening to others, ensuring anonymity within their report at the end of the exercise.

Focus areas

One or two members of the senior management team will usually initiate the audit of communications with parents. It may be necessary for them to recommend how the Audit Working Group should proceed, as it can be difficult to develop a clear view of the starting point of the whole school at any one time. A more manageable process could involve an analysis of the strengths and weaknesses of your school's current approach in one specific focus area at a time. It may be useful to think about the parental dimension to existing priorities within the school, identify the focus areas and then choose which method is suitable for the audit in these areas.

Focus areas with suggested audit methods

School priority	Parental role	School/teacher role	Audit focus area	Audit method chosen
New pupils	Visit school; Sign home–school agreement	Guided tour of school; Meet all new parents	Letters of invitation; First meeting at school; Copies and number of signed home–school agreements	Letter to be reviewed by Parents' Association; Observe meetings in July; Records of meetings with mid-year entrants
Homework	Read and sign homework diaries; Understand expectations of the school	Homework policy – define expectations according to age/year; Communicate key points to parents	Records of homework set; Diaries; How marks are fed back to parents	Sample of diaries for examination by working group; Telephone survey of parents views, one form group per year
Punctuality (Same Day Response)	8.30am – 9.30am – ring in if child is late	9.30am – 11.30am – ring them if pupil does not arrive	Telephone call records, notes in registers	Look at notes in registers and check times/dates
Attendance	Understand school rules on attendance; Notify absence in advance, in writing	Inform parents if absence will be authorised or not; Form tutors remind pupils of rules	Year 7 parents' meeting attendance; Records of authorisation and pupil attendance	Look at registers and notes from parents; Ask those who attended what they understood
Behaviour	Contact school if cause for concern, e.g. divorce; Respond to school concern	Respond to parents' contact within one day; Telephone parent if minor concern; Write if major concern	Records of telephone and in person discussions; Detention lists; Check telephone numbers are updated	Form tutor survey; Year meetings discussion; Compare in-house disciplinary measures with records of contact with parents
Curriculum	Monitor if child is coping in range of subjects, via homework; Contact form tutor if not, or if work is too easy	Subject teachers – respond at parents' evenings; Form tutors – telephone in response to particular concerns; SEN department – contact home if any sign of repeated difficulty; Tutors, heads of year or heads of department meet parents if necessary	Parents' evenings Years 7, 8 and 9; Tutor records and response times; SEN records; Meeting records	Survey of parents' views by Year 11 pupils; Report on staff experience of contact with parents at parents' evenings and informally; Interviews by non-teaching assistants of parents with children with SEN – deputy head (Pastoral) to devise questions
Equipment/uniform	Obtain correct uniform and kit as necessary; Write or telephone 8.30am – 9.30am with the reason if there is a problem	PE dept. issue guidance to parents, record problems and liaise with tutors; Tutors pass uniform detentions to year heads	PE letters and leaflet; Tutor records on PE kit problems; Year head – uniform and detention records	Review user-friendliness of letters and leaflet – A.N. Other (Consultant); PE and pastoral staff surveys; Consult parents if necessary

▨ Good practice in conducting an audit

▨ Ask difficult questions that teachers may not want to ask.

There is still a perceptible resistance in schools to seeing parents as well as children as the community served by the school. Asking questions about the 'service provided' seems to make teachers feel judged rather than seeing the results as an important part of an ongoing relationship. A non-judgemental approach, which seeks to illustrate the complexity of meeting the needs of teachers as well as parents, can be helpful when surveying the extent to which current communications are of a desirable standard.

▨ Listen to parents and teachers without your teaching hat on.

It is essential that concerns and suggestions from parents and teachers are heard properly by a neutral skilled third party, as both may need to adjust their expectations, their views or their current methods of communicating. Senior or middle managers can occupy a middle ground in the interests of partnership with parents. They can also manage and lead this drive for partnership in the interests of all children at a school. Staff who can show teachers and parents that they are able to hear both sides equally should ask the questions, in a non-teacherly manner.

▨ Build collective wisdom on the basis of evidence, not received wisdom.

Check views from a wide cross-section of parents and teachers against actual practice in the school. Are teachers' views influenced by occasional bad experiences with parents? Are parents' views based on actual experience in your school or their own experience of schooling? Is there any evidence that supports received opinions?

Research done by the Centre for Successful Schools at Keele University in 1994 indicated that the majority of parents hold conservative, positive views about their local school that are in fact based on blissful ignorance. Michael Barber writes,

> 'When parents are asked about education, schools and standards in general they are victims like everyone else of the media portrayal of falling standards and poor state schools. When asked about the school they know their views shift from concern to what can only be described as complacency.'

(Barber, 1994, p.3)

The majority in each school would not change much, or would not know what to change. Why is this? Information provided to them about the actual school attended by one or more of their children may never get to them, or may not be presented in an accessible form. There may not yet be up-to-date leaflets on the curriculum and schemes of work recently developed. Secondary teachers may not wish to complicate life in the classroom by taking into account the influence on children's minds of their cultures or families outside. Or staff may perceive parents' views as irreconcilable with their own. It is common to blame a reason outside the school for a difficult problem, and the home may be the nearest target.

Methods

Choosing the best method for reviewing each area is important. Consultation is necessary to get first-hand opinions but observation will also be needed of how teachers, office staff and learning assistants communicate with parents. Another main source will be existing information, such as attendance at parents' evenings and other events, or lists of the jobs that parents are doing so that meeting times and contact arrangements can be reviewed for likely effectiveness. Where many parents do shift work or both parents in many families commute back after work, schools will have to make arrangements that accommodate these restrictions.

Consulting

Consultation does not necessarily mean asking everyone. It involves asking appropriate people so that your questions are answered. The number asked would only be significant with additional information on why you chose this group. Some managers worry about the representative nature of the sample chosen, and others pay attention to statistical significance. Whatever your concerns, your first step should be to think about what your aims are in each part of the audit, where consultation is really necessary and which methods will give you reliable results and a true cross-section of views. Asking large numbers is pointless if you can predict a low engagement rate with the method used.

Consider the following options.

Structured surveys

To check that the questions you have designed will yield useful answers, test them on a small number of people first. Questionnaires tend to get poor response rates if sent in the post, so devise a format that can be used in person or on the telephone. Use written questionnaires with a captive, literate audience (like evaluation forms that have to be filled in before people can leave a training event or a meeting). You can also plan two stages in the survey. For example, if you were considering changing the times of the school day, you may find a first stage of consultation useful to request constructive suggestions that would contribute to the final plan proposed. Parents of one year group in both Upper and Lower schools might be included at the initial stage, before a full formal consultation. Pupils in these year groups could perhaps interview parents or carers as homework of relevance to English or citizenship, and give their own and their parents' views recorded on a questionnaire. Year 10–12 pupils can be trusted, with a little supervision, to interview adults who attend school events – this is ideal for times when parents or teachers have to wait, such as at parents' evenings.

Designing surveys

You need to know who your parents are in order to assess whether you have gained a cross-section of views – how many parents do not have a telephone, how many are parents of children with severe learning difficulties, or are many parents single mothers working full-time? If 5% are parents who do not speak English, they should be invited to attend a meeting with an interpreter or a community worker.

Include some open questions starting 'what', 'why', 'how' or 'how much', rather than a series of closed questions that ask for yes/no answers.

Break down responses into five categories if you wish to work out mean scores. In the choice of 'very much' 'a lot' 'quite a lot' 'not much' and 'not at all', the middle 'quite a lot' will score 3 and indicate neutrality, above or below indicates agreement scoring 4 or 5, or disagreement scoring 1 or 2.

Survey of parents' views July 2001					
Please tick one box for each question	Extremely	Very much	Quite a lot	Not much	Not at all
I agree with the school's anti-bullying policy					
Staff seem concerned about the safety of my child					
It is clear who to contact in the event of a problem at school					
When I visited the school I felt welcome					
Your comments:					

▣ Helpful others

■ A local market research company may be a good partner during the audit – their expertise in broad surveys could fill a gap in yours. Similarly, a local college of higher education may run courses in social work and education from which pupils could be invited to help to observe meetings and record them.

■ Auditing written communications might be best achieved through review by an individual who is not familiar with the school, and has the relevant skills, or by some current parents.

▣ Small 'focus' group discussions

These are suitable for contentious issues such as drugs education in schools, where all the adults involved at home and at school would have to co-operate for an initiative to work. A great deal of effort will go into organising these, so it would be advisable to enlist the help of a few parents to convene the event and to employ a skilled interviewer if possible. If you can video the event, the time will be more worthwhile – make it clear the tape will not be used without every individual's permission. Provide refreshments too, and have several issues to discuss.

With teachers, focus group discussions are more straightforward as they can be organised for an INSET day or Year meetings.

ARCHWAY COMMUNITY COMPREHENSIVE SCHOOL

Parents' views on drugs education

Consent form – recorded interview – to be kept with tape serial no.: . . . .

I consent to the recording of a discussion amongst parents about drugs education. I understand it will be kept on tape/videotape and may be used for purposes of evaluating school policy, informing staff, governors and other parents, and promoting our work. If the tape is to be heard/seen out of school or for other purposes, the school will consult and take my views into account first.

NAMES OF ALL THOSE APPEARING ON THE RECORDING	Age (if under 18)	SIGNATURE (at conclusion of recording)
. . . .	. . . .	. . . .
. . . .	. . . .	. . . .
. . . .	. . . .	. . . .
. . . .	. . . .	. . . .
Name of group facilitator		SIGNATURE
. . . .		. . . .

▓▓▓▓ Consulting parents

Modern public services have started to take on board the standards of service expected by the general public. Previous neglect may have implied a prevalent 'welfare' attitude to beneficiaries of free services, as if they were lucky to be helped rather than entitled to a state service. Schools have often escaped norms of adult public services. Consultation is the first respectful step towards the need to include parents in decisions made about their children.

It is worth remembering that parents can be prejudiced, like any group of human beings, especially when they do not know the people they are commenting on. One headteacher invited parents to discuss their views with her frankly and discovered that racism was endemic. Understandably, there was a fear of racial discrimination amongst minority parents and families which she had to counter publicly in order to forge trust and emotional investment in the school. Parents, like any group in the public, will include individuals with unpalatable views and school leaders are often forced to take a contrary position, in the interests of the cohesion of the school community. The audit consultation can therefore be valuable in creating the desired ethos of a school.

Do you need to assess general satisfaction with the school among parents? The function of general consultations of parental opinion will not necessarily be to improve the school's communication with the majority of parents. Nevertheless, they will show that the school is serious about listening to parents, and views given may well contribute to school planning and other future activities. You may not wish to give rise to a series of self-interested complaints, such as requests for extra-curricular activities with no intention of supporting the school in any new venture. However, an honest attempt to consult parents should not shy away from the uncomfortable reality of parents' views about approaching and raising issues with the school – this is an area of real experience, so they could give examples rather than opinion. With their support, teaching could be less problematic.

Activities that acknowledge the value of parental opinion have developed alongside a national debate regarding parental participation in both primary and secondary schools. It is increasingly recognised that the involvement of the majority of parents is important but difficult to achieve in practice. Parental involvement was taken literally in the legislation on parent governors in schools, and equally literally many primary schools have brought parents into the school to help with reading and other curriculum initiatives. At secondary level, home-school projects have discovered that the role of parents is much less tangible. The

The first section of a four-part questionnaire

Doing A Home-School Audit

PARENTS' QUESTIONNAIRE

1) What stage in the school is your child/are your children at? Please tick.

P1 ☐ P2 ☐ P3 ☐ P4 ☐ P5 ☐ P6 ☐ P7 ☐

2) What languages do you speak at home apart from English?

Please indicate your view with a tick. For instance, if you think that your child always enjoys school put a tick in the 'always' column. If you have more than one child please choose one of them and answer all the questions in respect of that individual child.

MY CHILD	always	most of the time	some of the time	never
enjoys being at school				
finds school work interesting				
gets an appropriate amount of homework				
is encouraged to work to the best of his/her ability				
gets to talk to teachers about his/her homework				
is treated fairly by teachers				
respects his/her teachers				
is respected by his/her teachers				

Please indicate below whether or not you agree, or don't know, for each of the statements.

COMMUNICATION AND INFORMATION	YES	NO	DONT KNOW
School reports give me an accurate and helpful picture of my child's progress			
I get regular information about my child's progress			
The school has explained its homework policy to me			
The school has explained to me what part I can play in my child's education			
The P.T.A. is good at keeping me in touch with school matters			
Letters from school are friendly and welcoming			

kind of moral, emotional and practical support provided to secondary age pupils by their parents takes place largely outside school. This may create a conviction amongst secondary school staff that little can be easily done to influence the way in which parents provide this support. In fact, the support that parents provide is greatly influenced by the

Doing A Home-School Audit

SECTION TWO

Please indicate below whether or not you agree, or don't know, for each of the statements

PARENTS AND THE SCHOOL	YES	NO	DON'T KNOW
Most parents show support for the school			
Teachers are good at letting you know about your child's strengths and weaknesses			
I am happy about the kinds of things my child is learning			
Parents' evenings apart, the only time I would contact teachers would be to sort out a problem			
I am confident that if I complain about something I will get a sympathetic hearing			
The school Board seems to be a useful thing for the school			
I know that if my child is having difficulty he/she will be helped			
I think that parents should be involved in classroom activity			

SECTION THREE

This part is about meetings where parents visit the school, usually in the evening, to talk with individual teachers about their children's progress

FORMAL PARENT-TEACHER MEETINGS	always	usually	some-times	never
Meetings are arranged at a time which suits me				
The event is well structured and organised				
I feel welcome and know where to go				
I am treated like a partner in my child's education				
I get a chance to speak honestly about what concerns me				
Teachers are frank with me				
I come away feeling I have learned something useful				

(Alexander *et al.*, 1995, pp. 27–8)

school's expectations of them from the time their child enters a new school.

The points where parents have contact with the school are crucially important, as these brief interactions quickly convey what the school would like from parents of their pupils. The extent to which parents

CANTONIAN HIGH SCHOOL
Fairwater Road,
Fairwater,
Cardiff CF5 3JR
Tel: 564598, 561810, 564501

PARENTS' EVENING SURVEY

Please help us to improve our Parents' Evening arrangements by answering the questions below, and return your Survey Form to Mrs. G. Williams, through your child's Form Tutor, or place the Form in the Box provided in the Reception Area.

Name of Pupil: _____ Reg.Group ___

	Your answer
1. When did you receive notification of this parents' evening?	
2. Did this give you enough time to make arrangements to attend?	
3. Did you see all the teachers you had planned to see?	
4. Were the discussions you had with teachers helpful?	
5. Have you made contact with the school prior to this parents' evening concerning your child?	
6. How long has your visit taken this evening?	
7. Did you have to take time off from work to attend?	
8. Do you expect to attend any further parents' evenings to discuss your child's progress?	
9. Can you suggest ways in which the arrangements might be improved?	

Is there anything else you would like to say about your child's progress, the Reporting arrangements or arrangements for the Parents' Evening that you have not had the opportunity to express this evening?

_____

_____

manage to sustain confidence in an open and communicative relationship with the school depends on their experience of trying to ask questions of school staff and trying to make their views heard. Where there are regular opportunities to communicate, success can at least be assessed, if not scientifically measured. Parents are rarely requested to comment specifically on their experience of actual events at their children's secondary school, yet organising a consultation exercise of this nature is relatively simple. In Cardiff in 1994, Cantonian High School conducted a Parents' Evening Survey which found improvements were needed in the timing, venue and even the furniture being used. The teacher who summarised the results noticed a gender pattern in those children represented at the event. He finished his report with another important point: *'I think we should survey the non-attenders to ask their*

Report on survey results

2.   I have looked at the main survey forms so far received and while most parents were satisfied with the arrangements, those commenting mentioned:

Timing: would prefer later in the evening or more time to be allowed for the large number (sic!) of parents attending. Work problems were mentioned. This might be a reason for the low turn-out as many of our parents cannot get time off without losing pay.

Appointments: some complained that the appointments system does not work. We are well aware of the reasons for this. However, a longer time-span for the whole session would spread parents out more.

"Visibility" of Staff: For new parents especially it is difficult to see who is where. How about:

(a)   Other rooms to be used as well as the Hall, clearly signposted, so that more room can be allowed: this will assist visibility as well as provide more space for parents and staff. The Science Labs in A Block could be used for Science subjects (as they are in St. Cyres, for example). Perhaps we could use the Dining Room if we can negotiate a night when the Bowls Club don't meet?.

(b)   Tables (not the horrid exam desks) to be used for interviews. More space would make this reasonable.

(c)   "Sign-posts" to be manufactured by Craft Department, comprising a pole on a pedestal, surmounted with a card bearing the subject area in large letters, to be placed strategically at the set of tables where those subject teachers are seated.

(d)   A clearly drawn and marked plan to be located in the Entrance area showing where various subjects/teachers are situated.

(I may be in a minority, but I still favour a good half-hour interview with a Form Tutor, certainly in Year 7 and 8. If our communications between Teaching Staff and Form Tutors are not good enough, they should be improved - after all, **we all perform both roles**. At least then we could guarantee parents a time and a good over-view of their children's performance.)

I think we should survey the non-attenders to ask their opinions about re-arranging the evening.

A. Geldart.

opinions about re-arranging the evening.' This survey was followed by one of both staff and parents' views after three years. Parents preferred the new system although staff could not comment on the benefits, so the new system was kept for Years 10 and 11.

Consultation need not involve parents coming to the school to have their say. At New Heys Community Comprehensive School, Merseyside, a home–school worker conducted a survey by telephone across the school in order to talk with parents about why they did or did not attend parents' evenings. It is significant that the Cardiff parents noted the number of parents attending – they evidently felt the size of the event was quite large enough already whereas schools expect high percentages all on the same night, ignoring the unpleasantness of such an occasion.

If you have an active Parents' Association, remember 'the best person to ask a parent is another parent'. Find out where parents meet outside the school, for example at a certain pub, or in cultural community groups if you have any parents with English as a second language. You can then ask a parent to ask others in this environment and get them to let you know the range of views expressed.

▰ Using existing opportunities for consultation

There are opportunities to consult parents if they are visiting the school for other reasons:

- New parents' guided tours, open classrooms in the summer term.

- Information evenings about how schools work today.

- Homework meetings once a year as part of an annual review of homework policy.

- Reading and writing meetings once a term, 'how to help your child at home' evenings.

- Hosting a cultural group's annual festival and inviting some staff and youth workers to meet community group leaders.

- PTA or PA participation in assemblies, PSE lessons, parents' room discussions.

- Having a 'branded' project in the school around a home activity, e.g. Real books project/'reading is fun' lunch-time club.

Home/workplace visits may need to be undertaken with a very small number of parents who would otherwise be disenfranchised. If you know local services where workers visit parents in the community, they may be able to help here.

▰ Working with parent governors

You may find it useful to work with your parent governors to consult parents, whether in person at parents' evenings or at Parents' Association meetings. In planning their involvement, keep in mind that it would be helpful to state to parents how the parent governors will use the information to exercise their role. As Alistair Macbeth points out, parent governors can be representatives of the parents at the school or trustees of decision-making on behalf of parents (Macbeth, 1989). The headteacher will know from governing body meetings if they give a parental view in discussions among governors and what this is based on. If they claim to be representatives, do they attend PTA meetings or how do they communicate with other parents to gain a wide section of views? Are any guidelines laid down that they have to follow? This is crucial for an audit because information they could collect will be influential.

Consulting the governing body

The governors may well support improvements in home–school relations because they are in a position to see the environment outside school and make connections between parents' and teachers' views. A discussion about parental involvement can be used to clarify the thinking behind the need for an audit. Contacting individual governors and then presenting the results of the audit at a full meeting is an alternative route for engaging the governing body. The views of governors will be useful in presentations to both parents and staff of the reasons and need for an audit and a new policy on communicating with parents. Other contextual factors are also important, such as supportive legislation, local interest groups and the reputation of the school amongst primary pupils.

Parent governors in a full meeting of the governing body may be able to report on their involvement in the consultation if you have worked with them separately. Otherwise, make it clear that they are being asked to endorse this initiative as a whole governing body; you are not expecting them to turn to the parent governors and say 'over to you'.

Consulting staff

You will get a good impression of teachers' attitudes towards parents from the audit and you could also question how these attitudes have been formed. Informal chats may result in disproportionate views from those comfortable in their dealings with parents, or those who reflect the class or culture of those asking the questions. They are, however, a good method to discover the best way to ask certain questions, or to work out practicalities to get the range of views you need.

Do you have an overview of the actual level of contact teachers currently have with parents of children of different abilities? If not, it will be necessary to conduct a survey of the current level of communication and if possible the quality of relations between staff and parents.

It is common for teachers to spend the most time with the most difficult parents. This often leads to an unbalanced view because teachers do not, in general, meet a broad cross-section of parents and understand the range of views they hold. Senior managers have more opportunity to meet parents. In contrast, subject teachers are often reactive rather than proactive and do not have the time to talk properly with parents. Discussion should include teachers' own feelings when they are in the role of being a parent – what do they expect and need with their own children? If they are assuming parents of the school's tough pupils are different, is this an over-generalising (prejudiced) view? Do they partly know who to contact in their children's schools because they can imagine how a school works?

Form tutor surveying can give an overview of current workloads – how many parents do you know well, where you understand their circumstances, and feel they would ring you? – Why? – Is it weighted towards those whose children have behaviour problems? If so, these may be reactive relationships. Is it mainly those seen at parents' evenings? If so, are they high or middle achievers who would enjoy hearing the reports about their child from several different teachers? Is it something to do with understanding the culture of the family because of the individual teacher's background?

You will become aware of which staff are interested in the issue and who sustains good relations. Keep in mind the future need to train other staff, perhaps asking staff interested in middle management positions to devise this training.

How staff will respond to the consultation will depend on:

- their positive thinking. Is it worth establishing a time-limited working group? Often, positive thinkers are the busiest people. A balance of realism and ambition is useful.

- where your school is on the school improvement continuum. Are staff familiar with processes of change?

- The number of staff who are parents themselves and can suggest better standards in communicating with parents.

Views and attitudes of school managers

An important factor in the future success of home–school communication will be the attitude of key senior management team members to this area of work. Asking these managers for their views should be part of the audit. Do you, individually, think that working with parents is likely to be satisfying, difficult, worthwhile or inconclusive? Do you feel generally positive or negative about the benefits of parent–teacher relations? How has your attitude and those of other senior managers been formed? The experience of other schools could influence your view.

I recently asked two headteachers about particular home–school strategies. The first was a new secondary head in an inner-city school. I asked him whether he had considered the Same Day Response scheme that the Secretary of State for Education had advocated that morning on the Radio 4 Today programme. It involved notifying parents as soon as children were late that morning so they knew they had not arrived at school. His response – 'It's not our job' – was basically defensive. His thoughts were not about the principles behind the scheme, such as child safety, nor did he see the possibility that the school reputation could be enhanced, and the responsibility for welfare could be clarified as that of the parents not the school. He must have experienced the suggestion as reminiscent of media attacks on overloaded teachers rather than a proposal that would reduce their load in the longer term by taking action in the short term.

Asking this sort of question can nevertheless be a first step in debating the value of work with parents, and articulating how, in this example, a response to problems with punctuality can be an opportunity to involve parents by identifying their interest in the relevant improvement.

On another occasion, a well-established head at a primary school was describing some of the special needs of pupils at her school to me. When I enquired if she thought there might be some solutions to the problems they showed in school, she declared it was their 'home backgrounds' so there was little a school could do to make a real difference. Child development research proves that this is not the case by any means. Despite the importance of early years relationships with parents and carers, studies show that events and people at any stage of life can make an enormous difference to prospects and well-being. Michael Rutter names positive experiences at school as exactly the kind of influence that can make a difference in the future, compensating for a troubled start in life (Rutter, 1989). That home backgrounds are still blamed for underachievement illustrates the fatalism you may encounter when trying to improve liaison with parents. The fact is that some children will not get to university, or even get many GCSEs, but to see end results as a valid indication of their success is buying into simplistic thinking that does not take into account learning distance travelled or added value. Schools have also commonly confused pupils' results with their total achievements, which does not fit most definitions of education or its value, but makes teachers feel defensive and likely to try to find something else to blame when feeling insecure. It is essential, when discussing people's views, to quote the evidence in research that shows the importance of high expectations of pupils. This might convey to the member of staff that although their view has been formed from real experience, over time such views can limit a pupil's opportunities in life, by labelling them as destined to fail too early in their school career and restricting the second chances they are given. As the 'home backgrounds' argument is such a common response, a detailed exploration of this issue is given in the next chapter. If the member of staff who holds this view is a senior manager, parent governors may need to be involved in order to create the political will within the leadership of the school to carry forward changes.

Real time observations

A consultation exercise about home–school communication differs from a full report in which senior and middle managers plan to gather comprehensive information and views about your school's current level and quality of contact with parents. Skilled observations of current parent–teacher interactions will ensure your report can go beyond the subjective experience of teachers and parents and the personal views expressed by them. Real time observations will illustrate communication skills in meetings, levels of confidence among staff and parents and the ability to develop good relations over a period of time. These features cannot be reliably assessed purely by those involved. You could suggest that teachers write down the first five minutes of their meetings almost verbatim and then discuss them with colleagues. You will then get feedback about the kinds of situations arising, while they improve their skills through discussion with an experienced staff member. Teachers on MEd courses can use video, which has the advantage of being private. Ask them to view the video on their own and record whether they achieved the objectives both parties had at the start of the meeting.

Auditing written communications

The first priority in considering the ways in which parents keep in touch with school life is a review of the information they get about the school.

Pupils are their first port of call for information. If they do not say much about school, or parents cannot tell staff what their children are saying about it, this may indicate the distance to be travelled in projecting the work of the school.

If the school newsletter gets home, is it read? How do you know? How often does it come out and what sorts of issues does it feature? Do leaflets become paper darts in the playground? It seems shocking that many parents of children in secondary schools do not read or remember letters home. Some never arrive, or they stay at the bottom of the school bag, or they are not read properly. Many schools fail to imagine how busy parents are and how little time they may have to read. I have spoken with parents who do not even know the school has a new head-teacher. Sending out standard, wordy or impersonal letters can be the problem, in which case a review of letters and other written materials can make a quick difference. In Chapter 4, you will find examples of re-worded letters. Presentation does count for something, so check the standard of what is sent to parents.

Outcomes of an audit

You should have the information to show the following:

- The level of satisfaction and comfort amongst teachers and parents in their current communications – in writing, on the telephone and in person.

Secondary schools have, in general, greatly improved the standards of written reports and information given to new parents, such as the prospectus, whereas face-to-face meetings can still be a source of tension. Few schools monitor the standards of response that parents receive when they telephone or write to the school. Few schools offer training to teachers on how to deal better with parents. You should gain a realistically mixed picture. An audit is likely to result in some positive recognition of the work you already do as well as some unpleasant facts. You will be able to use both the positives and the negatives.

- An overview of the quality of current home–school relations with relevant statistics to illustrate general points, details of particular situations that have arisen to illustrate any problems in your school and conclusions on the equity of current communications.

Giving the detail of the work done with a particular family may focus thinking on the amount of work carried out on certain issues, such as behaviour or drug use, and how effective this work is felt to be by staff. Listing attendance at parents' evenings over the last three years, set against ability groupings of pupils, would show any trend towards catering for the higher ability families exclusively.

■ Possible obvious areas for action and improvement.

It may be possible to take certain action immediately, e.g. recording information – you could introduce forms to record telephone conversations, and outcomes of meetings, which would help to prevent misunderstandings and gather more information about contacts over the next term. Selecting areas for improvement will involve discussion in the school regarding the desirable nature, quality and cost of home–school relations in the future, e.g. improving informal communication may involve introducing a new telephone system with voicemail for every tutor. Improving formal communication may require a review of written reports, or co-ordination of marking or set homework, followed by information for parents on new policies. These initial areas should be written into the school development plan. The priorities you have identified will contribute to a review of the school's policy on communicating with parents.

■ Ways of describing the attitude held by the majority of teachers towards parents. This contributes to the atmosphere surrounding all communications with parents and will be a key consideration when deciding on your strategic priorities.

Generalisations by teachers about parents may be commonly accepted in the staffroom. Beware of prejudice. Are you stereotyping parents as a group when in fact they are as diverse in personality and culture as the children you teach? You may need to challenge existing, established views among staff and parents quite regularly in order to stimulate thoughtful debate about the needs of each group and valid approaches to working together. It can help to show your genuine understanding of strong feeling, such as the helplessness teachers may experience in the face of the powerful influence of home backgrounds. The problems a child and their family bring into school cannot necessarily be solved by lone teachers – a team strategy with a framework of policies and the whole school approach should help individual staff to continue giving children the second chances they need throughout their time in school.

■ Areas where more information is needed in order to form a view.

A lack of common causes for complaint or a lack of information can frustrate efforts to devise appropriate strategies for improvement. If parents have not replied to questionnaires, does this mean that they do not see the point of visiting the school and are happy with their child's progress, or does it mean that they are not engaged in their child's education and are unlikely to help the school and the child appropriately? Patterns for inadequate responses can sometimes be traced through the methods used, such as when pupils are responsible for 'posting' which can be reliable in primary schools when schoolbags are prepared by parents, but unreliable later on. But if the net has been cast wide enough, you are sure to have gathered useful information: the detail of the progress or deterioration of a relationship with a parent, or a summary of contact in sequence with a parent or family from first contact to the most recent, can be as valuable. Subjective descriptions of a meeting can indicate clearly some initial areas where staff would appreciate further training and clarification.

The audit will generate tasks based on the information collected over a limited period of time, so further consultation or monitoring will be necessary, even when a large audit has been undertaken. Once parents' views are known, the level of information that has nourished these views must be examined. In parallel with the development of accurate ways to generalise helpfully about parents of your particular school, it is important to remember the basis of the generalisation so it can be re-examined regularly, rather than becoming received wisdom which prevents change and renewal in the future.

If certain groups, such as parents without a telephone, have been excluded from the audit, consultation with them needs to be built into the first action plan. State gaps in any written report on the audit exercise so that they do not get forgotten.

▓▓▓ The next step

Once a school has an overview of home–school contact, the quality and effectiveness of communication between teachers and parents needs to be assessed by reflecting more deeply on the experience of the participants. The records and observations made during an audit will provide material for discussion. Firstly, it is important to ask whether objectives of both parents and teachers are met through the strategies currently adopted. The intentions and hopes, as well as the rewards and disappointments, of staff and parents can be monitored over a longer period of time if this is not yet clear. Secondly, the equity of your current approach must be summarised. If some parents are getting a better response from the school, it should become a deliberate strategy to target those most in need, rather than a matter of chance. It is important not to reject parents who do contact the school, even if they are the more confident ones. They will give you valuable information about how welcoming the school is. If resolving problems at your school is difficult, it must be asked why.

Conversations between teachers and parents give clear signs of the current effectiveness of communication. The problems that they attribute to the other's environment are frequently not aired or explored, and are quickly forgotten. Sensitivity to the dynamics of recent conversations will help staff to form a view regarding the extent to which your school prevents problems developing and creates opportunities for parents and teachers to talk effectively.

The work done so far will enable you to develop priorities in the improvement of home–school work. These will be chosen by having a picture of the kind of communication you would like to promote between parents and teachers. It is encouraging that in some secondary schools, including pressurised inner-city schools, teachers have managed to create an ethos in which parents are trusted and appreciated by the school community rather than regarded as a threat. Where teachers' attitudes have changed, they experience the benefits for the whole school community of this openness of mind.

3 STARTING STRATEGIES: FROM REFLECTION TO ACTION

In schools where home–school work has become a priority, it is easier to assess the extent to which you achieve good communication with parents – good in the sense that it functions to prevent most crises, supports individual pupil achievement, and maintains parental confidence in the school. In other schools, however unintentionally, parents are easily ignored unless they clamour to be heard. Here, the separation of the two environments has become problematic and epitomises outdated concepts of how education as a whole should be delivered. It is not surprising, given the history of education and traditional barriers between teachers and parents, that many schools have remained remote from parents. It is time to review attitudes and to update existing practice.

The days of keeping parents at arms' length, asking them not to teach their children to read and telling them not to cross lines in the playground, are over. But as the first chapter described, invisible barriers still exist. Staff can be inherently critical of parents, seeing them as unfortunate necessities, and finding their worries, hopes and sentiments unhelpful. These teachers might feel that parents do not understand, and where this century-old, deprecating British attitude lingers on, teachers find it difficult to work with parents even when a pupil's future is at stake. Parents feel threatened when schools are not overtly welcoming and do not have the courage to complain on their own. The arrival of a group of complaining parents is horribly familiar in schools where parents are afraid to venture. Even if parents are more clearly welcome, they also have higher expectations, such as wanting to know the extent of their involvement in a child's learning at home. Without accessible information about appropriate involvement, parents may expect more than a school can give.

Even in successful schools, the pressure of meeting with parents can be unevenly shared amongst the staff team, or the culture of respecting parents as part of the school community can be held by a key senior figure in the school who becomes fundamental to its continuation. Pupil behaviour and progress can dip without proper discussion with parents, until the situation has gone beyond redemption, because standard procedures that would facilitate communication between home and school over a period of time are non-existent. Welfare issues, such as bullying, that generate anxiety amongst teachers might be quickly resolved, but parents' questions are easily considered uninformed or a nuisance.

In addition to the required shift in teachers' attitudes, parents too need to learn about a new school. They need information in order to form realistic expectations and know where their child should be aiming each year. This will involve changing the expectations that they formed during the primary phase and shifting gradually to a different relationship with the secondary school's teaching staff based on an understanding of the new learning environment. The first year is a crucial one to give them opportunities to learn and to develop skills in negotiating about aspects of their child's learning and integration into the new school.

Transitions

The needs of the pupils and parents in a school community are particularly acute at times of transition into a new phase. Every family with a child at the school will be involved in some way with the excitement or anxiety of a life event. Secondary schools should aim to start to prepare parents a year in advance of any change of teachers, school sites or curriculum key stage. Transitions provide an opportunity to focus on communication with parents in Years 6 and 7, 9, and 11. Changes in how the school relates to parents are also easier to introduce at these key points. In this chapter, successful strategies to establish good contact at two major times of transition are described, with the support of information from secondary schools that have introduced them.

Primary-secondary transition

The primary–secondary transition dramatically embodies a large step up from childhood towards adulthood. It is also the first transition where interaction with parents can make a lasting difference and this contact can be formative for appropriate parental involvement in later years.

The fact that the school system requires children to move *en masse* is a clear signal to parents as well as to teachers that they are meant to help children to leap up into a different, more adult environment. The transition to secondary school may coincide with a time when, within many families, the parents are expecting a child to become more independent. Parents under stress may welcome the step in the hope that their children will not need them as much. The emerging maturity of children is often reflected in changes in their family, as parents turn their minds back to their own lives and work. If the new school conveys that parents are not particularly needed, the sudden change of phase may encourage these parents to let go equally suddenly, forgetting their responsibilities or expecting the school to take over completely. Unless their involvement is clearly defined, they may do little more than try to take an interest in any work brought home and facilitate their child's attendance.

The structured, less intimate environment of a secondary school symbolises an adult world to which children will belong. The transition can appear frightening to children and Year 6 pupils often predict there will be bullying or other frightening problems. They anticipate without relish the prospect of being the youngest in an unfamiliar environment instead of the oldest in their primary school. But they need to learn how to face and prepare for life changes and transitions. Making this step is part of their learning about how to adapt to change in life; facing and learning from it is part of their learning process. Although some children seem to manage the new experience without too many problems, and many are excited by it, the move is rarely smooth. The time-defined suddenness of the change can put children in a sink or swim situation, with all the accompanying feelings of panic and desperation. Careful teachers as well as parents may anticipate these feelings, showing their foresight in the preparations, while the child is still at a primary school, for a move to a new school.

Secondary teachers make special arrangements for Year 6 pupils and often organise events at the new school, such as group visits to Year 7 classes for incoming primary pupils. It is equally important to make arrangements for parents, so that they are not left out of the move to the new secondary school. Most of the schools mentioned in this book demonstrate an emphasis on working with new parents that places an importance on the first meeting truly befitting the magnitude of starting a new school. Because parents of new pupils are conscious of their lack of understanding about the new environment, the secondary school has an opportunity to educate them about how many things have changed since they were at school. To do so in a way that does not undermine their confidence or reinforce their inevitable feelings of helplessness requires skill. Primary schools should be guiding parents and involving secondary staff in this work.

New parents are particularly receptive to information from the school and new pupils are not yet in a position to translate school messages into home language, so communication with their parents at this stage needs special attention. However, a school's enthusiasm to work with parents cannot be channelled purely into giving them information, as if they were going to study extensive manuals or policy handbooks. Like most members of the public, they will probably read short written communications and try to keep large documents for reference later on if the need arises. If new parents are given too much written information by the school, or are only invited to very large events, rather than being given a real opportunity to ask questions, they are likely to assume an increasingly passive position.

> *'Meetings need to have clear and well-publicised aims, but also include a space in which parents can raise queries and concerns.'*

> (Martin, Ranson and Vincent, 2000, p.25)

A brief presentation about the school will create space to imagine their children in the new place and air any concerns, such as what the rules are, or the school's response to bullying and racist remarks. After talking openly about the culture and ethos of the school, allow the opportunity and enough time for questions. The aim is that parents experience the enrolment as a step they are helping their child to make in which their role is active and supportive. Otherwise, they may see the change as inevitable, determined by forces beyond their control. By inviting prospective parents of Year 6 pupils to meet a Year 7 teacher, an opportunity is created for them to imagine their child's move to the new school well in advance. Such a meeting can even be held on the primary site, before coming into the secondary school.

Visiting the school

Most parents who are intending sending their child to your school will want to visit so that they can imagine what sort of place they will be attending. The impact of a visit has to be acknowledged. Although the most common reason for choosing a secondary school is its location, the policy of parental choice creates a feeling that there are some options at this early stage:

> *'Sixty-one per cent of parents state that they chose the secondary school for their child because it was the nearest school to their home. Fifty-two per cent chose the secondary school because they believed their child would be happy there. Forty-six percent made the decision following attendance at a school's open evening.'*

> (Barber, 1994, p.6)

School staff should start by considering how they will make parents feel comfortable and relaxed. Measures taken for new parents will benefit all new visitors to the school. Signs and guides need regular review, and staff should be involved in seeing the school from the point of view of newcomers. Parents still fear large schools and do not see them as places where they would feel comfortable, even if they were welcome. Many schools have already improved the layout of reception areas and signs to find key rooms and people. Most still have a list of concrete improvements they would like to make. A checklist follows:

- Can a person who is completely new to the school find their way to reception from the entrances or car park without needing to ask anyone the way? The size, number and location of signs needs regular review (Marland and Rogers, 1991).

- Are entranceways secure but attractive so that parents know their children are safe and visitors do not feel like intruders? Lockable security doors should not obscure eye contact with the receptionist if relations are good.

- Do the displays convey the spirit and beauty of your school?

- Is there a 'Welcome' banner in the community languages spoken at the school? This implies an inclusive ethos.

- Are the facilities, such as a visitor's toilet, clean and tidy? Are they checked regularly and easy to find?

Small meetings

- Is it standard to offer tea or coffee to visitors?

- Is there a quiet area where parents do not have to wait in a corridor? *'Such a waiting area needs to be adjacent to reception, so that ... the visitors are not left to feel abandoned.'* (ibid., p.83)

- Is there a neutral, tidy room available for private meetings, near to reception?

Tours of the school for new parents

A child and their parents are often invited to walk round the school with a pupil as a guide. A tour shows them what the school is like and if it is post-enrolment, it can also be used to show them how they can keep in touch. Pupils or staff can introduce them to the important rooms and people, always starting with the front office staff with whom they are likely to have the most frequent contact. The guides need to know enough to answer questions, so it is worth training older pupils and support staff so that they know what sort of questions to expect. If any parents express a desire to help the school, for example, the response should show thoughtfulness so that their interest is evidently valued. Learning Support Assistants may also be popular guides and some of them have more contact with parents than teaching staff. As the Manchester research project quoted here suggests, consider inviting parents in small groups as lack of familiarity can make a tour of a big school quite overwhelming. They should leave feeling they know the sort of place the school is, not feeling bewildered by the size of it or the number of different people they have met.

The Link Project on parents and communication

'I was hit by the enormity of the school. It was new and scary, you don't know anybody. You get lost and those feelings stay with you throughout the school.'

The size of secondary schools is intimidating and memories from the past are triggered by initial visits.

'I was expecting it to be packed (Year 6 transition evening) and it wasn't. They took us round the buildings in small groups ... We all felt it was a family thing.'

(Beresford, Botcherby and McNamara, 2000, p.8)

An observant guide will notice first impressions when showing parents around the school and respond to them on the spot. They could talk with them about the activities their children will be doing, give them some brief history of the school and share some of the problems as well as promoting the school. This will start relations on a realistic footing. In one school where parents suffered particular urban poverty, I showed them the library to enable them to visualise where the literacy project would take place. They supported their children's membership of the project even more gladly when they saw they would have somewhere bright and warm to sit during lunch-break once a week. This was part of the service to be offered to their child and I was pleased to show them a modern quality resource. Humility should not lead guides to play down clear benefits for their child which will generate positive thinking towards the school as a whole.

It was evident from subsequent questions that one or two individuals were slightly overwhelmed by the amount of resources a public institution can have, and did not understand how resources were allocated as a result. I knew how many books were still needed and felt slightly embarrassed to have portrayed the school as well off. Their attitude reminded me of the dependency that parents feel on their child's school, particularly when they have stressful lives and do not feel they have given the particular school much thought before their child starts. Importantly, their impression that the school would be a great provider of books needed to be corrected. If a school cannot afford to lend text-books to every child for their homework, parents need to be told this so they can imagine the value of an after-school homework club, or understand the point of visiting a local library.

The creation of smaller groups of parents visiting the school can be extended to other activities, for example by encouraging form tutors to hold tutor group meetings of parents once every term, rather than expecting a whole year group of parents to discuss any issue thoroughly at one large meeting.

Transition activities for pupils

Activities at the secondary school offer new parents a means of getting to know the big school gradually. Langdon School mainly takes children from five primary schools and organises an annual programme of events for Year 6 staff, children and parents. During the summer holidays, the two-week Summer Learning Scheme is attended by local children from the age of 9. A Year 6 Saturday school started in 1998 which runs for 30 weeks, with a Junior school ethos and a focus on numeracy, literacy, science and IT. The Primary–Secondary Co-ordinator attends these activities and has met most of the parents by the time their child starts at the school. The Instep Project in Castlebrae High School organises a series of summer preparatory activities that take into account information on the abilities of pupils from their primary school.

Langdon School facilitates visits in small groups, where parents and children meet pupils and one or two members of staff who become familiar to them. In October, parents and children are invited to visit with the choice of six daytime slots and one open evening. Informal conversations with parents enable teachers to communicate that parents will definitely have a role when their child starts at the new school. Parents need to be told that they have the power to influence the child's attitude even though their child will grow up and appear independent.

Individual meetings with new parents

It is a huge step from having one main teacher in the primary school to having a number of secondary teachers who will not know their child in the same way. This difference alone makes parents reluctant to contact secondary schools. Schools need to prepare parents by introducing them to the person or people who will be responsible for their queries and by explaining how to contact them during the day. At Langdon School, in the Summer Term, twenty-minute interviews are conducted with parents and the child together, with the following aims:

Primary–Secondary Links: Interviews

The primary purpose of the interview is to welcome the student and their parents/carers to Langdon.

Our procedure helps to collect and collate background information on each of our new intake, so that we can build an individual profile on each student ...

The interviewing process involves the parents or carers, with their children who are due to join Langdon in September. They are met by one of our staff on a one-to-one basis. During these visits further relevant information regarding the students and the School is exchanged. All those attending are invited to discuss and sign the Langdon Achievement Contract ...

The purpose of these visits is to introduce the prospective students to the school, to confirm information held and to clarify our procedures, thereby ensuring an effective transition in September and the basis of a sound relationship between the family and the School over the coming years.

(Langdon School Staff Handbook, 2000, 8.1, p.2)

A gradual change (that mirrors preparations for new pupils) has occurred in schools that work effectively with new parents. Instead of seeing the first meeting as inevitable and letting it follow the child's settling in period, senior managers and year heads arrange to meet the parents or carers individually before the child starts at the school. They explore non-judgementally the issues their child will be bringing to the school, whether special needs, special interests, high intelligence or low attendance. This is valuable whenever there is a new arrival during the year, so year heads may hold this duty as a matter of policy. Pupil mobility, especially in schools with high levels of social deprivation, is such that these initial individual meetings will be necessary throughout the year (DfEE, 1999b).

There should be a tangible difference between the atmosphere in this sort of meeting and the dynamics of selection interviews; indeed, parents can be told directly that the purpose is not to test them or their children. It may be interesting to hear why they wish to attend this school to understand their ambitions and ideas, and similarly valuable for the parent to hear a teacher's description of the ethos and culture of the school. The earlier the range of needs amongst pupils is understood, the better the school's planning of educational provision will be. A personal approach enables the parent to tell the school about any difficulties that might be predicted and prevented, rather than suddenly discovering a child cannot participate in school life in September because no-one has addressed their need, for example, for a hearing loop or for English lessons. The Education (Pupil Information) (England) Regulations 2000 specify the information that must be sent as a minimum on each pupil when they change schools. Although records are transferred from school to school, it can prove unhelpful to await the arrival of a file when a personal meeting would give you crucial information as well as forging a relationship with the family that will set the individual pupil record in context. We are moving away from an institutional factory model of education into a more personal, interactive style of accommodating both children and parents as individuals.

Llanedeyrn High School holds individual meetings with all parents of pupils due to start in the following term, discussing the home–school agreement and ensuring the details on the pupil personal information form are correct.

▇▇▇▇ Home-school agreements

It is helpful, after initial contact, to spell out the terms of the relationship rather than landing teachers and parents suddenly in the uncharted territory of home–school relations without a framework or anchor once a problem has developed, as often otherwise happens. It will clearly contribute to the school's aims to cultivate a feeling of partnership with parents rather than distance, by defining what the school will contribute over time. Making clear what you will bring to every child prevents parents from perceiving schooling as a one-sided imposition and makes requirements of them less personal, putting demands in the context of what a functioning school community needs.

A systematic approach ensures all parents are included, not just those who can attend one particular meeting or who feel comfortable talking with teachers. The Taylor Report in 1977 suggested a letter. The School Standards and Framework Act 1998 made it a requirement that every parent signs a home–school agreement. Good practice demands more thought and action than the statutory minimum. An agreement simply provides a convenient focus for the need for every parent to have some kind of relationship with their child's new school. Discussing the rather impersonal terms needs to be woven into a welcoming, getting-to-

<u>LLANEDEYRN HIGH SCHOOL</u>
<u>PUPIL PERSONAL INFORMATION DOCUMENT - CONFIDENTIAL</u>

Please complete this form in BLOCK CAPITALS or by ticking the appropriate box

CHILD'S SURNAME		CHILD'S FORENAMES	
ADDRESS			

POSTCODE		HOME TELEPHONE		DATE OF BIRTH	

SEX	M		F		FORM		

ETHNIC ORIGIN		LANGUAGE NORMALLY SPOKEN AT HOME		RELIGION	
Bangladesh		Bengali		Not Known	
British		Cantonese		Anglican	
China/Hong Kong		English		Baptist	
East African		Greek		Christian	
Ghana/Sierra Leone		Gudjurathi		Hindu	
India / Sri Lanka		Hindi		Jewish	
Italy		Italian		Methodist	
Jamaica/Trinidad		Punjabi		Muslim	
Malaysia		Portuguese		No religion	
Pakistan		Spanish		Other	
Other Comonwealth		Turkish		Roman Catholic	
Other European		Urdu		Sikh	
Other Non-British		Welsh		Unclassified	
		Other		United Reform Church	
				Jehovah's witness	

	PARENT/GUARDIAN	PARENT/GUARDIAN
TITLE (MR/MRS/MS/REV/DR/ETC)		
FIRST NAME		
SURNAME		
ADDRESS (If different from above)		
POSTCODE		
TELEPHONE		
OCCUPATION		
RELATIONSHIP TO CHILD (Mother/Father/Grandparent /etc)		

know-each-other type of meeting, so that its apparently official nature does not get the relationship off on the wrong foot.

A 'public' agreement can make home–school relations more tangible, especially at secondary level. It can capture how secondary teachers try to co-ordinate school life under the banners of behaviour policies, school codes and school rules. Many schools now print their rules and requirements into the pupil planner and school newsletter. But over time, the role of the parent in helping their child to stick to these rules can become rather invisible. If they find the role difficult, they are more likely to fall silent than share their difficulties, unless they have met at least one teacher at the school with a positive, non-judgemental attitude. When adults are new to each other, there is a need to establish a foundation for a dialogue before it will be possible to graduate onto

BROTHERS/SISTERS ALSO AT LLANEDEYRN HIGH SCHOOL:	FORM
1.	
2.	
3.	
4.	

EMERGENCY CONTACTS	FIRST CONTACT	SECOND CONTACT	THIRD CONTACT
NAME			
STATUS (NEIGHBOUR, AUNT, ETC.)			
ADDRESS			
TELEPHONE			

NAME OF FAMILY DOCTOR	
PRACTICE	
SURGERY ADDRESS	
SURGERY TELEPHONE	

DETAILS OF ANY PARTICULAR DISABILITY, ALLERGY, MEDICAL HISTORY, ETC. OF WHICH THE SCHOOL SHOULD BE AWARE (e.g.ASTHMA, ALLERGY TO PENICILLIN etc.)

USUAL LUNCH TIME ARRANGEMENTS (PLEASE TICK):

SCHOOL LUNCH		PACKED LUNCH		HOME FOR LUNCH	

PREVIOUS SCHOOL(S)	

NOTE: ALL PUPILS ARE EXPECTED TO REMAIN ON THE SCHOOL SITE AT LUNCH TIME UNLESS SPECIFIC PERMISSION IS GIVEN - IN WRITING - FOR ALTERNATIVE ARRANGEMENTS TO BE MADE.

I AGREE TO ABIDE BY THE SCHOOL UNIFORM CODE AS STATED IN THE CURRENT PROSPECTUS.

SIGNED: _____ (Parent/Guardian)   DATE: _____

more informed and sophisticated discussions about homework, the curriculum and subject choices. There is no one-off or quick method for developing good relationships where trust and goodwill play such an enormous part over a long period of time.

Meetings to sign home–school agreements

Home–school agreements are at the centre of an initial personal meeting with parents in all three schools featured in this chapter. The piece of paper itself should merely record and mark that a discussion has taken place. Purely asking parents to sign an agreement without meeting them is a wasted opportunity. Face-to-face contact will lay the foundation stones of a long relationship with parents, and often with whole families. As was suggested in the chapter on auditing, schools will need quite detailed information about the cultures and backgrounds of pupils to ensure home–school strategies are equitable, so meeting all parents in person provides an opportunity for teachers to learn about the community they serve.

Parents too need to overcome trepidation to visit the school, and learn to recognise a member of staff who they can ask for if it should be necessary. The 'terms' of the agreement define the boundaries and expectations for this relationship and establish the fact that the parents' main relationship to the education system is via the individual school. Choosing who should meet them to sign it is crucial, as this person will both represent the school and should be in a position subsequently to offer open communication with parents in order to answer any early queries. This responsibility currently often lies with members of the senior management team but it is also being delegated to a middle management level (heads of year and other pastoral co-ordinators). The person who meets the parents is making a crucial first contact, so their responsibilities should include sustaining communication after the meeting.

Wording your agreement

The exact wording of an agreement is usually discussed by governors, teachers, and any Parents' Association as well as with pupils themselves, so that everyone involved feels their perspective has been acknowledged. The changes to the first draft, after consultation, reflect shared ownership of the principles and meaning of the agreement, so it is important to let go of your initial text and strive to reflect the collective spirit in the wording. A clear introduction should express the purpose of the agreement.

Llanedeyrn High School in Roundwood, Cardiff has been using its Home–School Agreement for five years as part of the primary–secondary transition strategy. The three sections for parent, teacher and child to sign represent the secondary pupil's growing autonomy – their power and responsibility to decide to keep to rules and their independent commitment to do so.

When the Deputy Head, David Jordan, first introduced the agreements in 1995, he met scepticism from other schools where heads felt that it would not be signed or that parents might use it to sue the school if the school's commitments were so clearly stated. Such a climate of distrust and suspicion reflected the need at that time for home–school relations to enter a new era of partnership in more than merely name.

▨ Presentation

Attention to the appearance of written materials that are presented to parents is a graphic illustration of the fact that they are entrusting their children to a capable, professional environment in which the written word is taken seriously. Poor photocopies may give the impression that the school is not thinking about its communications with parents, or that teachers do not care about their audience. A high standard of presentation will in turn attract greater respect and support for the school. In the past, some schools have excused tatty materials, either blaming the lack of resources or claiming to make a political point of denying appearances are important; this was thought to contribute to egalitarianism. Unfortunately, appearances have been neglected when they could be making the equally valid egalitarian point that all children and parents deserve respect and high standards of care and education, regardless of their background or abilities. In order to appeal to your audience, make the agreement aesthetically attractive. In this age of word processing sophistication and low printing costs, it is no longer

Facing the Challenge

LLANEDEYRN HIGH SCHOOL

Home – School Agreement

The Llanedeyrn High School Home – School Agreement

Dear Parents

This agreement is designed to help your child to mature and develop in supportive surroundings, both at school and at home, so that he/she can make the most of the opportunities which will occur during his/her time at school.

This agreement is a way in which we can all commit ourselves to working together during the next few vital years.

We hope that by signing this agreement we will forge a partnership between home and school which will lead to a better understanding of our responsibilities and that your child will feel the benefits of our joint pledge for the future.

We look forward to a long and happy partnership with you.

Staff of Llanedeyrn High School

THE LLANEDEYRN HIGH SCHOOL
Home – School Agreement

AS TEACHERS AT THE SCHOOL WE WILL DO OUR BEST TO –

- *Care for your child's safety and happiness*
- *Achieve high standards of work and behaviour from your child*
- *Provide a balanced curriculum to meet the needs of your child*

- *Develop your child's talents and abilities as fully as possible*
- *Keep you informed about your child's progress in particular, and about school matters in general*
- *Help your child leave school well-equipped to make the most of the career opportunities available*

AS A PARENT I WILL DO MY BEST TO –

- *Ensure that my child attends school regularly, on time and properly equipped*
- *Take an active and supportive interest in my child's work and progress, including homework*
- *Attend Parents' Evenings and other discussions about my child's progress*

- *Let the school know of any concerns or problems that might affect my child's work or behaviour*
- *Support the authority and discipline of the school including the wearing of correct school uniform.*
- *Get to know about my child's life at the school*

AS A PUPIL OF THE SCHOOL I WILL DO MY BEST TO –

- *Attend school regularly and on time*
- *Bring all the equipment and kit that I need for every day*
- *Wear the correct school uniform and be tidy in appearance*
- *Complete all my classwork and homework as well as I can*

- *Be respectful, be polite and be helpful to other pupils and the teachers*
- *Care for the school environment and help to keep the school free from litter and graffiti*

necessary to give illegible or fuzzy documents to those new to the school.

Design

A strong design can communicate several things to parents and pupils. The school logo or emblem and traditional motto communicate that the school has a clear distinctive identity and a pride in its achievements and reputation. A very small investment at the start of production reduces costs later on, as a good design can be photocopied rather than needing to print materials. If a colour can be afforded, the graphic designer can use the school colours. At secondary level, this can reinforce the fact that the environment is a working community in which unity is important. Llanedeyrn High School used a colour emblem on its printed agreements in the first few years, and then moved to black and white photocopies very effectively. The standard of design and reproduction have been maintained without increasing costs. The colour of both their emblem and their school uniform is red. The colour version of their emblem is used on their headed notepaper and report cards, putting the same piece of inexpensive design work to extensive use.

Signing the agreement

At Llanedeyrn High School, the agreements are signed over a month in the summer term, once the list of new pupils has been drawn up. Every new parent is invited to the school to meet a senior member of staff, a head of year, head of department or member of the senior management team, with individual appointment times. It is made clear that signing the agreement is not a condition of entry, nor is it a legal contract. In the first four years of introducing the agreements, only half a dozen parents objected to signing it. Some of those who initially seemed resistant expressed the reason for their fear – a distrust of signing anything which made them think of legal contracts. They all responded to a conversation about it, proving the importance of a personal meeting at the start to build trust.

The next stage of transition: years 9 to 10

The next major transition on the horizon in terms of the education and development of young people is when pupils are preparing to move towards the final years of compulsory education, with the accompanying choices of subject options and examination courses. Teachers are aware that this transition is a fundamental one for pupils but may wonder why schools need to work with their parents at this particular point.

Year 9 commonly coincides with mid-adolescence for many pupils; they enter a process of preparation for independence which focuses their turbulent energy. Growing up involves finding one's own identity, which preoccupies the teenage child increasingly and shuts their parents out, together with many others in the older adult world. They may be keeping others out to protect their growing independent self quite naturally. The child psychiatrist D. W. Winnicott commented that *'preservation of personal isolation is part of the search for identity, and for the establishment of a personal technique for communicating ...'* (Winnicott, 1965, p.190). In the meantime, the responsible adults have to find a way to communicate with them and with each other that does not intrude on their privacy. Their apparent self-sufficiency has to be complemented by the school's awareness of the world beyond the individualistic mentality of adolescence. Options provide an opportunity for the pupil to express their growing identity, both from the act of choosing and from considering where different options will lead. The developmental change is expressed in the questions, 'Who am I now?', 'What sort of person do I want to be?', 'What am I interested in?' and then, 'How will this be expressed in my life?', or 'What should I do to get there?' Beyond the immediate and absorbing task of choosing options lies the future, an expanse of time that few pupils have imagined realistically.

Parents obviously have a great emotional investment in their offspring's future, even if they respect the burgeoning adult life that will increasingly reduce the part they play in their child's decisions. A three-year government research project on parental involvement found that *'all the parents wanted some involvement in the decision'* about subject options even if this meant just being kept informed about what their child was being asked to decide (Jowett and Baginsky, 1991). Research about parents' experiences of careers services after children had completed Year 11 revealed that 52% wanted more frequent contact during secondary school:

'The main reasons given by parents for wanting more contact are given below, in order of frequency of mention:

■ *parents need to be more involved with their children's thoughts/decisions;*

■ *it takes time for children to know what they want to do;*

■ *[it] avoids situation where child deals completely independently with the careers service and doesn't tell parents what is happening;*

■ *having a goal helps children to study, helps 'A' level or other educational choices and stops them drifting;*

■ *emergency options need to be discussed if things go wrong.'*

(DfEE, 1998b, p.42)

Schools also have to inform parents about options because often pupils of this age cannot articulate the process to people outside schools, even within their own families. They may not understand the need to do so, or they may not yet be mature enough to assume responsibility for informing their parents appropriately. Schools vary considerably in the flexibility of subject combinations they offer, and if the choice is limited, it creates anxiety and uncertainty that is difficult to resolve unless a pupil knows exactly what they want to do after school. It is preferable to create blocks of options after the pupils have made their choices, rather than presenting a narrower choice from the start that creates even more emphasis on the importance of particular qualifications for future routes of study or work.

The transition in young people's relationship with their parents will be reflected in how they discuss the choices being made with each other, and schools have a role to play in ensuring that both have the information they need for the discussion, which will mainly take place at home. A large event featuring subject options early in Year 9 can provide adequate information for the majority of parents, freeing staff time to offer more personal communication or involvement with associated issues in private. The Options Evening and booklet devised by the Philip Morant School is set within a sequence of opportunities for both pupils and parents to be informed at this important time.

▓▓▓▓ The Philip Morant School: Options Evenings

At the Philip Morant School, a large event is part of an interesting process of parental involvement with their child's choice of subject options in Year 9. This large school offers 21 options and has developed a paced process with both Year 9 pupils and parents to enable them to choose the right options at this important stage. Staff have won the confidence of the pupils in their teachers' abilities to deliver information directly to their parents. In some ways, they model how pupils themselves will keep their parents informed in the future. The teachers' efforts are rewarded by a consistently high level of interest and communication with parents at this time.

Presentations to pupils

The process starts early in December when options are presented to Year 9 pupils by subject specialists in assemblies over two months. The core subjects are presented first. Staff also discuss which options to choose in careers and PSE lessons. There are no option blocks in this school, so pupils have a free choice of subjects, providing enough pupils sign up for

each class. As this complicates the timetable considerably, the options have to be chosen by early March
which creates time for staff responsible for the
timetable and for pupils who have to change their first
choices.

Year 9 options schedule	
End November/ early December	Presentations in assemblies and PSE/Careers
January	Parents' Evenings (choice of two dates)
End January	Options Evening
Early February	Options Booklet and choice forms sent home
February	Individual consultations
Early March	Options forms returned

Parents' evenings

Parents' Consultation Evenings are held on two dates
in January. These give reports on all subjects in the traditional format of a parents' evening. The timing is
intended to feed reports on current progress into the
pupil's decision-making about future directions, providing information directly to the parent as well as their
child.

Options Evening

These activities are followed swiftly, within a few weeks,
by a special Options Evening at which up to five members of staff speak.

Presentation skills

The Philip Morant School is a Technology College so computer and
visual aids contribute to a high-tech presentation. The other key aspect,
not dependent on resources, is the team work between four members of
staff in the school who specialise in giving presentations and have

developed the necessary skills together. They include the Deputy Head, who has a degree in Theatre Studies and enjoys this sort of activity. She confidently uses a simple software package (Powerpoint) to project information directly onto a big screen behind her, while she faces the audience and is able to look directly at them. Transparencies are only needed as a back-up. The Headteacher speaks first, then the Deputy, and then two or three specific issues are highlighted by other staff to show parents what their children will be facing that year, such as Key Stage Standard Assessment tests or 'pupil responsibilities in the school' at this age. The Deputy Head reported:

> *Options Booklet*
>
> The accompanying 42-page booklet illustrates the ability of staff to make the descriptions accessible and clear. It is sent home after this evening with the pupils who, in the main, are now adequately prepared to make their choices for Year 10. The A4 size booklet is aimed at parents but designed so that it can be read by both parents and pupils.
>
> *Individual options counselling*
>
> In order to be sure that everyone has made appropriate choices, parents and pupils are invited to request individual fifteen-minute counselling appointments with a member of the senior management team, to help them with any difficulties.

When the school first introduced this approach six years ago, about 70% made individual appointments. As the staff have become more experienced, they have started the process earlier, preparing the pupils from the first term of Year 9 and arranging parents' evenings and the distribution of the booklet in a logical sequence. After three years of refining their approach, only 21% (60 pupils out of a year group of 280) needed an individual consultation. Those responsible for options at this school have thus shown how intensive work with the pupils and a well-organised process of informing the majority of parents can lessen the time-consuming nature of individual work.

Involving both parents and pupils

The school in the case study does not exclude parents from discussions about the important decisions pupils are making. But simultaneously, a thorough process of preparation of pupils over a six-month period acknowledges that as they grow up they will increasingly make this

Mathematics

YOU MAY NOT HAVE A CHOICE
<u>BUT</u>
YOU CAN STILL ENJOY IT !!

All students will follow a programme of study based upon the National Curriculum for Mathematics (including Number, Algebra, Shape & Space and Data Handling).

The syllabus used is provided by the EdExcel Foundation and the following will apply :

- © 20%   Coursework
- © 80%   Two Examinations at the end of Year 11.

<u>Statistics</u> (Southern Examining Group)

Many students in Mathematics will study an extended statistics course in order to gain an extra GCSE. These students will study for this course during normal Mathematics lessons tackling **<u>one</u>** piece of coursework in both subjects. The subject stipulates a weighting of :

- © 20%   Coursework
- © 80%   One examination at the end of Year 11.

Head of Faculty : Mr.A.Maydon

sort of decision for themselves. Both pupils and parents are given several opportunities to ask any questions they may have, on different occasions.

Year 11 and school leaving

A large event could also be developed for families to attend together when they are deciding when to move on from secondary school. The National Record of Achievement provides a useful focus for

Science

The Science Faculty at The Philip Morant School offers its students THREE different options at GCSE level, each option being administered through the London Examination Group.

ä   Combined Science   (Double award)
ä   Modular Science   (Double award)
ä   Triple Science   (Triple award)

Combine

This cour
arise fro
as machi
the stude
world. Th
between
even thou

At all
*   tern*

Assessn

ä   75%
    thr
ä   25%
    Inv

Students
(Double A
TWO

Science

Do you understand why some metals corrode ?
What is a healthy balanced diet ?
Do you know how it's best to insulate your home ?
Can you wire a three pin plug correctly ?
Can you decide how best to grow your plants ?
Why are antioxidants added to food ?
What is a renewable source of energy ?

These are just a few questions that everyone
should have some knowledge of.

SCIENCE IS FOR ALL NOT JUST FOR THOSE
PEOPLE IN WHITE COATS.

and remember

We all live in a technological age.

Head of Faculty : Mr.K.Blanchard

achievements at 16. The Instep Project in Scotland has found that the interest of parents increases strongly as they look beyond school to the wider world, even amongst those previously completely uninvolved with their child's education. The choice at this stage, whether academic or technical, may be even narrower than in Year 9, or appear so. Pupils who do not have a tradition of work within their family will need guidance and a relevant work placement to give them valuable experience. Working parents of a school can help to find placements in their industry, or encourage their employers to provide information at a careers evening. Good careers services may be able to help to organise events on behalf of the school, inviting employers to speak, advertising the event, and sending out personalised letters of invitation. They also, in some areas, work closely with parents beyond school, bridging the step onto colleges of further education and provision further afield, especially where a young person has special needs (DfEE, 1998b).

Large events at times of transition

Occasions on which parents are invited to the school to visit in large numbers will already feature in most schools' annual calendars. A public occasion can have symbolic value in its apparent openness and inclusiveness. Teachers may simply desire an event to show the importance of the information that the school is trying to get across. School staff who have a sense of urgency to meet all parents without ensuring any immediate concrete benefit to pupils tend to be disappointed by parents' attendance. Annual Meetings are notoriously unsuccessful in this regard, particularly if they focus on the management of the school instead of the children. In fact, the attraction of a large event may be merely practical in that it can be organised using familiar school procedures and several staff will concentrate on making it happen despite their competing priorities.

It appears odd to many secondary teachers that *all* parents do not prioritise events organised for them at their children's schools, often interpreted to imply neglect of parental care and responsibility. Teachers also often express despair at attendance by the same parents each time. Influential factors outside the school are easy to blame, when it would be more interesting to examine the motivation of parents to stay away, or the way in which the event is organised. The accusation that some parents do not care often reflects the fact that teachers have pigeonholed certain parents, and are assuming that these parents' attitude towards education is symbolised by not attending certain events. A sense of parental responsibility can in fact be the reason for not attending an evening event at the school – because parents need to care for other children or work late, for example. As parents also have competing responsibilities, it takes some resolve and a long-term view on their part to decide to attend a school event. Schools can make it easier for parents to attend by giving a choice of times or dates, by keeping in mind transport used by parents to get to the school, and not limiting attendance by other children and adults. A crèche and activities or videos for children of different ages should always be offered on site. Events for parents could be timed to coincide with a youth club, or they can be designed to include pupils as in the examples of academic reviews in Chapter 7, if it is done carefully.

Teachers who judge parents as uncaring are also perhaps forgetting the off-putting nature of large events in an unfamiliar and often uncomfortable environment. Teachers spend most of their working day controlling large groups and learn to deal with performing to a large audience, whereas adults in other workplaces in the UK develop completely different skills and often work in small teams. Most parents will feel comfortable only on their own territory, while teachers are already on familiar ground. New parents are sure to compare the larger more formal secondary school with the primary schools their children have attended, and being invited by standard letter without knowing anyone in particular will automatically dampen the parents' potential interest.

Aiming at very high attendance at an impersonal type of event is unrealistic. Parents might imagine a cold Victorian school hall, or a daunting atmosphere that evokes their memories of being a new pupil themselves thirty years ago. Parents of older children may feel wary of the situation they remember from their first visit – they will not be noticed by anyone in particular, while feeling self-conscious as they walk into a large room. If a concerted promotional effort is made, high numbers of parents will attend, but unless it is a positive memorable experience, even more effort will be needed for the next invitation to the same group of parents.

Inviting parents into the school *en masse* may not, therefore, seem a very attractive option, but large events can work if they are organised to maximise the personal dimension. This personal dimension is captured at times of transition because children are all facing a new phase of life and their development is mirrored by the external public world of the school at these times. A large annual event before a transition helps parents to see that they are in a common situation, creating a sense of community, in contrast with their separate experiences of parenthood. Parenting today is often very isolated, and parents often move on into longer hours of employment as their children progress through the education system, so they will appreciate social events at which they can meet other parents informally. Open Evenings for prospective parents should always include some social time. Teachers will also find this time useful because it gives them the chance to be more personal and friendly.

The presentation can be made more rewarding by ensuring that at least one part of the evening is organised in very small groups with other parents. The parents can be asked to sit in tutor groups so that they gradually get to know each other. Using the opportunity for consultation can be incorporated into the aims of the event. The consultation exercise can reinforce messages given during the presentation. An event to introduce a new homework project, for example, could create an opportunity to consult parents effectively about the school's homework policy.

New events in a school's annual calendar are bound to need a few trials in order to get them right, and if the event is designed to happen once per year, this may mean that it takes three years to become standard practice. Exchanging information with other schools who have already introduced similar initiatives is therefore important when planning a new activity or event, to save time. Large events and annual activities develop a place in the schedule by using experience from the past to influence the decision on the best time of year for them.

▨ Objectives

The objectives of the event need to be worked out beforehand, to be clear whether the main purpose of the invitation is purely to inform parents or to facilitate a discussion or consultation. If a large event has to be planned at your school with the sole aim to inform or teach parents something, remember the following:

- ▨ Any newcomer or relative outsider to a school will imagine the likely value of the meeting and how welcome they will feel from the information provided, and will consider the practicality of attending in the light of their other commitments.

- ▨ If the objectives have been clearly stated in the letter of invitation and they understand how their child might benefit, they are more likely to come than if the purpose is assumed to be obvious.

- ▨ Pupils are good ambassadors if the event seems worthwhile to them, so discussing the purposes in tutor meetings can reinforce the message.

- Staff appreciate a reminder of the objectives just before the meeting.

▨ Promotion

- Limit invitations to parents for a large event to essential times when they are most likely to be able to imagine the value of coming in for a meeting.

- Send written invitations in the post if the event is really important. 'Pupil post' is so unreliable that it can be worth the cost, especially if there is no other way parents will hear of the event. Weigh up the cost, too, of an advertisement in a free local newspaper that would get people talking about the event.

- Summarise the key aims and messages and prepare pupils in advance so they can answer questions their parents ask at home about the event.

▨ Delivery

Some teachers may enjoy presenting to an adult audience and might use skills that will be valuable if they are interested in gaining experience of training adults. Methods of presentation need to stretch beyond presenting the facts, as even adults remember only a fraction of a lecture compared to their retention when they can actively use the new information themselves. A presentation that aims to impart information should be followed by more active participation or an exercise in small groups or pairs. The audience is then much more likely really to learn something – often remembered in lesson planning but forgotten with parents.

- Design an evening that will be useful, informative, friendly and engaging to parents.

- Ushers from sixth form or college courses could be recruited with the clear responsibility to welcome parents on these occasions, and they should be paid at least the minimum wage.

- Ask colleagues to rate the presentation and small group exercise.

- Tell parents clearly who to speak to afterwards, e.g. 'Talk with Mrs Dawson, wearing the red shirt, about homework, Mr Khan in the blue suit about uniform, and come to me with any other issues.' Do not assume they will remember names.

- Include some social time in the programme.

Concentrating events and activities for parents at transitions will contribute towards a more comprehensive home–school approach. A match can be made at these times between the needs of parents to learn and the school's plan to meet and inform them in person. The likelihood of success with the majority can create time to meet more effectively with the minority who may otherwise find a whole school approach too impersonal.

Events and activities organised for parents can be only a part of a whole school strategy to improve home–school relations. The next step may be to consider the systems of communication used when parents are *not* visiting the school and the effectiveness of these systems in sustaining the home–school relationship. Your strategy needs to include procedures that make communication possible with parents once normal everyday life reasserts itself.

4 OPEN CHANNELS OF COMMUNICATION

At its best, good communication between arranged meetings at the school will enable parents and particular members of staff to sort out minor problems before they have a real impact on a child's education. These informal interactions, whether on the telephone or in the form of written notes, build positive and constructive relations with particular members of school staff. Communication channels need to be designed to maintain an exchange of information and to create a clear and efficient route for messages and conversations.

Creating more open channels of communication will encourage parents to contact staff and develop trusting relations, including those who are less confident about approaching the school. During the research for this book, school managers expressed their dissatisfaction that those parents they wanted to see rarely wanted to see them. As sociological research shows that less-educated parents are likely to need the most encouragement (Vincent and Martin, 2000). Equitable procedures are needed. It is unlikely to be effective if schools make general vague appeals to parents such as 'Contact the school with any queries', without ensuring that parents will get a prompt and friendly reception.

Key findings from the Manchester Link Research Project

- *If parents had concerns they contacted schools on average once a term. 30% maintained they never contacted schools.*

- *There were wide variations across schools regarding who parents said they knew best. On average, 27% of parents claimed to know no one in the school well.*

- *Substantial difficulties in contacting individual teachers were experienced by nearly 20% of parents.*

'I do think it would be a good idea to sort out getting through to people when you ring. The office is not manned after school and there is no voicemail for the staff.'

Comment from parent.
(Beresford, Botcherby and McNamara, 2000, pp.7–8)

▨ Improving telephone contact

The telephone is still, in general, underused in home–school work. Many secondary staff find it a frustrating means of communication simply because administrative systems have never been updated. A parent may telephone on several occasions and fail to make contact with the appropriate staff member. The telephone is, however, a good way to establish a rapport and is much more personal than a note. It may in fact be the only way that a parent could imagine having an informal yet relatively private conversation with a secondary teacher. The Manchester Link Project research shows the frequency with which those parents who try to speak with a teacher find it too problematic.

Difficulties in communicating by phone deserve careful attention as even minor problems have an effect on the beginnings of home–school relations. The fact that parents are aware how busy teachers are helps to reduce the workload of stressed teachers, but puts obstacles in the way of powerful parental support. If parents get the impression that the school does not have time for them, they may feel that they are not valued. Bad experiences will increase the likelihood that they will try to address a problem by other means more within their control, such as private tutoring if the issue is felt to be with a particular subject, for example. An inadequate response can discourage parents from trying to talk about issues that will then snowball into resentments and problems. The stage is then set for a fraught conversation when a parent and teacher finally manage to speak.

Parents and carers have immense motivation to help their child and the vast majority respect teachers automatically. Research has shown that interest and goodwill towards the school do not depend on social class, whereas the ability to intervene on behalf of their child is class-related (Martin, Ranson and Vincent, 2000). According to national surveys, over 90% of parents believe that their children are well cared for at school without knowing that much about school life (Barber, 1994). An unconditional regard for teachers or the school is a good starting point to build a relationship. But, perhaps *because of* the unrealistically positive image that many parents have of schools, research also indicates that parents are far too easily put off by single incidents (Beresford, Botcherby, and McNamara, 2000). The deflation of unrealistically high expectations appears to lead them to leave the school to its own resources too quickly. This disappointment can be avoided by improving the efficiency of channels of frontline communication.

Access to the right person

When parents telephone a school, it is rare that they will be able to talk to a subject teacher immediately. Explaining the teacher's timetable on the day of the call can help. However, people outside schools are not used to school bells and other environments do not run to the minute, so they may not easily ring back keeping the exact minute of school breaks in mind. Even between lessons, it is extremely hard to find a particular teacher – office staff might try several places: 'I'll try the staffroom for you,' or, 'She might be in her office.' Or the receptionist might not have time to do this, and so promise a reply without naming who is responsible: 'I'll get someone to get back to you.' This is the kind of situation in which response standards would make an immediate difference – agreed guidelines so that everyone knows how soon to expect a reply. They will also act as a counterbalance to the stresses of the moment which, despite the school and the receptionist's equitable principles, might give an advantage to some callers over others.

It is at a very early stage when parents are forming a view about whether to try to work with a teacher on a problem or go it alone that the school's insularity will be tested. The parent may not know who to talk to or even how to name the problem in school language. If, for example, their child is put on the first stage of the SEN Code of Practice and the Special Educational Needs Co-ordinator writes to inform parents about this, they may feel they need to speak to someone quite urgently on receipt of the letter. The name of the person who wrote the letter may be different from the form tutor or a senior manager they have met. They may ask for any of these people if they ring, or may just say that they have received a letter about their child. The administrator needs to ask what it is concerning and to have a great deal of information – form lists, staff lists, procedures for different issues – in order to know how to deal with this parent promptly on the phone and at least give them the name of the person responsible for their type of inquery.

Agreed standards

Administrative systems around the world have become sophisticated. Modern training and equipment deliver a highly responsive service to the public, but many secondary schools are still using procedures from a bygone age. It is standard to attempt to answer the phone within four rings, with a good telephone manner. At the very least, parents should be able to ring someone at the school with general enquiries and get prompt replies. Out of school hours, an answering machine is essential. Parents in low-paid jobs might not be able to talk for long, but the school can at least offer to ring them back.

If parents' expectations are higher than those of the staff, it must be asked if the school's expectations could be brought to an equivalent level. Parents are often generous, forgiving or polite at first, but keeping people waiting dents their goodwill. The welcome that parents are given, whether at reception or on the telephone, should meet agreed standards. Brief records of enquiries and responses will help to keep track of the quality of service to parents and others who ring. These standards can then be monitored across years and school departments.

It is a valid fear that regular discussions on the telephone with parents could increase expectations of the amount of time a teacher has to talk with them outside direct teaching time. But if calls are unexpected, a parent who rings about a small issue may provoke a teacher to make a strong response, so that the pupil concerned feels it is out of proportion, and the teacher loses respect. Similarly, if teachers rarely call parents, several teachers telling parents in person about a problem at an annual meeting may misfire. A pupil cannot improve overnight and one-off conversations do not help to track progress or resolve the problem. If the problem endures, parents are likely to blame the school.

A dialogue can be sustained providing responsibilities for talking with parents are clearly defined. Once the first line of responsibility for responding to parents has been decided, it will become clearer which staff will be responsible for resolving different types of queries in the longer term too. The times within which telephone calls can be returned, 'response standards', also need to be agreed.

Standard response times from staff with examples of types of queries:

- Non-teaching staff (respond same day if possible) – Office staff: first line for points of information, e.g. What happens if my child is ill?, Did my child arrive safely at school?, Who is my child's form tutor?, How do I arrange lunch vouchers?, Who's who within the school? Support staff (respond within two days): first line for parents of all children on the special needs register, reporting incidents at home, with a worry about homework, or any other general queries.

- Form tutors (respond within a week) – first line for worries about schoolwork, or a child's behaviour, and need to be told what is happening at home, e.g. moving house, separation of parents.

- Heads of department (respond within three days) – first line for queries about test marks, or reports.

- Year heads (respond within two days) – to report bullying, racism, or harassment of any kind, problems with a teacher, first line for formal complaints and queries about school policies.

- Deputy head (respond within 24 hours) – any emergency or if a parent needs a quicker reply than general.

If a parent needs an immediate reply:

- Put them through to first line staff if possible; if they are not available, tell them by when they will hear back, and ask if it is urgent (if so, refer to nominated senior manager).

If they are reporting a dangerous incident:

- Guarantee that someone will ring them back within 24 hours.

Once standards are agreed, schools should tell parents what they are. The principle can be extended to following up action promised in meetings, within agreed periods of time. All callers should be sent a form to return to evaluate the new system, and to help to draw attention to any delays beyond the stated times.

Procedures for missed appointments

Parenting is a phenomenally pressurised activity, resulting in tiredness on a par with levels experienced by staff in schools! An appointment is usually conducted out of school hours, so re-arranging schedules can be difficult. Some parents are needy and dependent on the school and yet find it very difficult to keep to appointments. Some may arrive an hour and a half late, knowing their child's timetable but with no concept of the secondary school environment and the commitments of the teachers. The chaos of some parents' lives is being transmitted into the school. Strategies that would exclude certain parents but save teachers time may reinforce inequalities counter to the ethos in your school. A non-punitive response is the most helpful, with a procedure agreed with office staff for the reassurance of the parent concerned and encouragement to try again, with clear information about the teacher's availability and a note to the teacher concerned saying what the parent has been told. A guarantee of a standard of service to visitors including parents and non-judgementally recording all attempts by parents and teachers to communicate will allow a coherent response by a senior manager if problems arise.

 If a parent has not got the time or ability to see the value of attending the school to meet with teachers, their child will suffer from this lack of support. This is by no means a problem only for poor parents. Some may appear to be well off, but appearances can be deceptive. The most pressurised parents may need the most resources, regardless of their economic status or job in the world.

▰ School office support for parents

The key roles played by office staff in both giving information directly and relaying information between home and school cannot be underestimated. They need detailed information from teaching staff to be effective in this role, about people in the school, policies and procedures and individual cases, too. Invite them to staff meetings and brief them fully by taking them into your confidence, so that they understand the importance of the part they play in facilitating communication. Contact by receptionists and other non-teaching staff should feature in records alongside teachers' comments, to ensure regular communication between all staff about the parents' relation to the school. They may be sustaining relations on behalf of the school without acknowledgement. Their familiarity with a family could also be helpful when a problem arises.

▰ Sarah Burkin – Annexe Office Manager, Deptford Green School

- Standard school office duties: typing, finance work, first aider, completes Late Book, keeps medical book.

- In addition, handles detentions given by year heads and gives late detentions.

Sarah Burkin has worked for seven years at Deptford Green School. She has become a key home–school liaison figure in the Annexe (420 pupils). She is ideally placed to deal with queries from home and liaise with teachers on behalf of parents because she is available all day. Her office is situated close to the entrance to the Lower School building.

She relays messages to both pastoral and subject teachers in the school. At the start of the day, she receives calls from 8am onwards from worried parents. The newer parents need constant reassurance, which she relates to her own experience as a mother – 'A parent doesn't want to hear an authoritative "I haven't got time", they need a quick response,' she says. Parents who have been asked to ring by their child also telephone her – 'Ring Sarah and tell her I'm late.' A parent whose child has forgotten her lunch money might ring.

Sarah can inform them about school procedures; in this case, there is a voucher scheme for repayment to help when a parent cannot come in with the money.

Parents sometimes need to give their children a message. Or a child might have forgotten to say they would be late home as there is football practice after school. They pop in to see Sarah who makes sure they have enough money for the call and sends them to the phone box. She helps them to remember that they need to bring money for this – 'Don't come in [to my office again] next week!'

'Sometimes a parent wants to tell me about the problem. I can listen and let them let off steam. Then I tell them who they need to speak to.'

When a child has not done their homework and will be given a detention, their parent might call to speak to the relevant teacher or head of year. Sarah's neutrality is important here, 'Have you got the letter in front of you? I need to ask you about it.' Once she knows the department that has given the detention, she can look at the relevant teacher's timetable. 'I'll ask them to call you back.' She might have to say, 'Unfortunately they are teaching all day but they'll get the message you called.' As she deals with detentions herself, she has a list of all those referred and files correspondence on each child. This aspect of her role prevents her being forced to take sides between teachers and parents.

Her role as an intermediary between home and school is as dependent on her personal skills in talking with parents and children as on her administrative efficiency. She receives about 15 calls from parents in a day.

Checklist

- The telephone manner of the receptionist is a crucial part of the school's response to parents. A parent who has plucked up the courage to ring and is feeling very emotional when they call needs the understanding voice of someone who respects their level of anxiety or distress. In most cases, if the first conversations are positive, they will not feel anxious unless there is cause to do so.

- A reliable message service is a basic requirement. If there is no system for relaying the information given, whether in person via reception or with the help of an answering machine or voicemail for that member of staff, parents are likely to get the impression that they are being too demanding.

- Good administrative practice should be defined and monitored by a senior school administrator. Are names recorded correctly on messages? Written messages should show the name of the caller, the time, the date, the name of the staff member to whom they spoke, and if the enquiry is of a confidential nature or not. The person who took the call should record briefly what they told the caller. (The example on page 102 is from INCLUDE's *Welcoming Parents* pack).

- The receptionist needs to be able to explain the process by which they will get a response, the amount of time they are likely to wait and who they will hear from in reply. Or they may prefer to ring the parent back when they have passed the message on. Lists in the office should be kept updated and notes on the responsibilities of staff.

- Appreciate the receptionist's ability to listen and to note the relevant information, which may be dependent on their workload, the environment in which they sit, or their skill level. The receptionist may be told some of the detail of the enquiry or problem which should be recorded on a confidential form and given to the staff member responsible.

- Administrators with the skills to deal with stressed parents on the telephone can help new form tutors and other staff who need to use the telephone for their work. Telephone work can be supervised and supported in open plan offices and through peer support when discussing records made of enquiries.

Technology

Introducing new technology presents an opportunity to reduce the distance between parents and teachers. Telephone systems and new message services can encourage parents to ring, allowing more privacy – for example, they can bypass reception if the extension is known. New telephone 'handsets' enable staff to distinguish between internal and external calls, and to redirect calls if they wish. Menus can offer recorded information about particular issues or forthcoming events. Training when a new system is introduced is essential, as otherwise staff will not use the technology and managers will mistakenly think that the service to callers has improved.

Parental Enquiry Form

Type of Enquiry: _____

Telephone ☐   Visit ☐   Letter ☐

Name of parent/caller: _____

Name of child: _____   School form: _____

Reason for enquiry: _____

_____

Staff member requested: _____

Was he/she available?   YES/NO

Information given to the caller: _____

_____

Action requested of staff member: _____

_____

Response time: _____

Name of person receiving the call: _____

Time: _____

Date: _____

CiS
Turning lives around

▨ Voicemail

Voicemail is an answering service innovation that is particularly appropriate for messages from parents, as it allows recorded messages to be stored on a system for individual members of staff who can access their messages from any phone in the school.

Unfortunately, in some schools where voicemail systems have been introduced, problems have not disappeared. Teachers who do not have time allocated in their timetable for working with parents may not have any time to conduct these conversations. In recent research, a parent is quoted as saying:

New technology

At Willows and Llanrumney High Schools in Cardiff new telephone systems have been introduced which include controlled access by all staff. Willows High School also introduced an easy to remember telephone number. The telephones have been situated in lockable rooms to avoid abuse of resources. Mr Barnfield, Headteacher, commented in a telephone interview: 'These modern telephone systems allow 45 internal extensions and voicemail. All classroom teachers can have access to these features. External calls are limited and every phone has its own bill. The number of provider companies has greatly increased.' He also pointed out that this sort of streamlining can reduce running costs, although it would take some time to assess this saving. Parents increasingly give mobile numbers to schools, so the actual cost of introducing new technology remains to be seen.

'I had a struggle ... because you'd ring up the school and leave messages on their voicemail but they don't listen to them, so days would go by and I'd send one of the other kids in to go to the teacher and say, 'Hey listen to your voicemail'. I was trying to get help for a long while.'

(Vincent and Martin, 2000, p.472)

This is not a reason to avoid new technology, but the school's capacity to use it to the full needs to be monitored by administrative and senior managers.

Use of the telephone to arrange proper time to talk

If possible, the office should be given stated times when each named contact for parents will be available on the phone. They are then in a position to arrange telephone meetings at least, to ensure a particular teacher and parent manage to speak within the response time stated.

- Introduce the concept of telephone meetings to parents in a one-page leaflet at the start of the year.

- At every opportunity, tell them who to contact about their child's work that year and remind them of the phone number, the form or class their child is in, and the school year they are in. Compliments slips with spaces for this information can be produced for all form tutors to use for short notes.

- Define at the start of the conversation how much time you have, without sounding off-putting if possible. Say, when you are calling, if it is purely to inform a parent or if a longer discussion may be needed. If it is not convenient to speak immediately, offer to ring them at a particular time and ask if they will definitely be in at that time.

The pressures currently on schools can mean that meetings to which a parent is invited are dictated rather than offered and negotiated. Parents, like most users of public services, welcome appointment times being made with their timetables in mind. Office staff can ring to make a meeting time rather than just sending them one in the post. This is especially important when the meeting may be of a sensitive nature. Once frontline communication systems have been improved, fewer urgent meetings with parents in person will be necessary, and it will also be easier to arrange meetings.

Arranging meetings about a mentoring scheme

Office staff in Wembley High School in Brent in 1998 helped to make individual appointments of 15 minutes each to meet twenty parents of Year 7 children targeted for a mentoring programme. Arrangements were made by:

1) A home–school worker telling the pupils about the project
2) Sending a letter signed by the project worker and a deputy head with the name of the project and the aims of the meeting clearly stated
3) Office staff arranging the exact meeting times by telephone and encouraging them to come into school.

The pupils who were selected had academic potential (the group had the highest discrepancy between their verbal and non-verbal Cognitive Ability Test scores). But they were also at risk of underachievement and teachers could predict from their experience that they might need extra support in the future. An early relationship with their parents was therefore likely to be especially important. This process achieved 95% attendance by their parents.

 # Surgery

One activity that can help the minority of parents who need to contact a particular teacher with an urgent enquiry is introducing 'surgery'

times in the week. Put a sign on the front door, at the school gates, in the newsletter:

'A Head of Year is available to answer parents' questions – come to school reception Thursday after school. Don't wait for a problem to develop – prevent it.'

Teachers who know they will be staffing a surgery in the coming week can request that parents drop in just to keep in touch and to prevent problems developing further. In practice, only a very small number of parents will use this sort of time, but it provides a back-up to existing channels or overloaded communication systems.

▨ Informing parents by written communications

In any school, parents' expectations will vary according to their background, their level of confidence in dealing with the school and the needs of their particular child. Some parents themselves will have needs and a very tiny number will be neglectful, but a sizeable number will support their child's education behind the scenes without needing to contact the school at all. Those who are rarely in touch with the world of education are still interested in its impact on their children. Many desire greater involvement, but do not know how to go about it (Woods, 1984).

They try to develop an awareness of what their child is being taught, what their child is facing emotionally, and the basic elements of school rules and procedures. While promoting their individual child's interest is rightly their highest priority, they are aware that their children's life at school will be subject to the policies of that particular community. There are limits to how much guidance from education authorities or central government can meet their needs. They like to hear when issues such as uniform and rules for behaviour are being discussed. At the very least, responsible parents will seek to maintain a duty to intervene if they can see where things might go wrong. They are reliant on the quality of direct information from the school.

Secondary schools are very specific environments designed around the organisation of learning in a relatively stable community. The intense delivery of information about the new environment by staff and its absorption by new pupils quickly creates a world of insiders. Once a child or an adult belongs to this community and has become familiar with the kind of interactions that take place in a large institution, it is easy to forget the teething pains of a process of familiarisation. School routines reinforce the process and fact of belonging, quickly eliminating the need to explain to pupils the way a school works from first principles. In contrast, parents need information that translates any reference to the education system and spells out even fundamental educational terms. Good information assumes no prior knowledge and will convey that parents are interested partners in the venture of education.

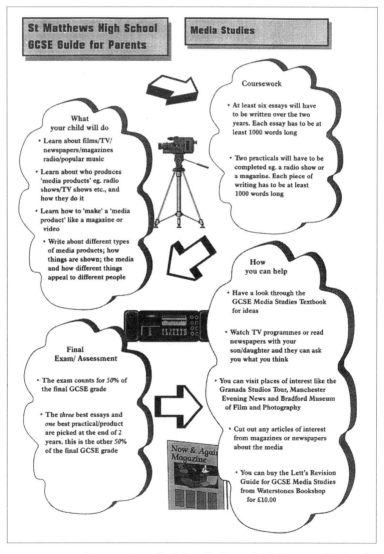

(Source: Beresford, Botcherby and McNamara, 2000, p.25)

■■■ The accessibility of written communications

Do parents receive, read and understand written information given to them? Hardly any parents will become governors or volunteers on site, so the vast majority will not feel connected with the school unless they get regular information about school life. The older their children are, the less they will hear about school. If parents can feel part of school when necessary, they are less likely to need to meet staff in person. Feeling part of things and learning more about the school may be achieved through minor improvements in written communications, ranging from personalised letters to the standard school newsletter.

Most leaflets, brochures and policy documents are written by staff with their school hats on, without taking into account the perspective of the average parent. Written communications need to be reviewed with the limited time and the many distractions of a parent in mind. Teachers are often surprised that much of the language used currently in communication with parents is inaccessible. The task of reaching adult audiences outside the school, including people who are completely unknown to you, may demand new skills.

■■■ Plain language

A standard piece of circular mail elicits an average of 30 seconds' scanning by the recipient. This does not mean that the adult concerned is only capable of this level of reading, but it might mean that this is the amount of time they will initially spend on standard (impersonal) information from the school. Concise letters including key facts are all that is necessary, as these can be supplemented by longer leaflets at a later date, when a parent is interested in that subject.

A fear of being patronising seems to detract from pitching written communications for parents at a realistic level to be digested. It is sensible to take into account the level of language of the average newspaper read by parents. Involving parents themselves in the production of written materials can be one solution. The way in which information is phrased should also be in keeping with the child's age so that the matter can be discussed easily at home when the teacher is not there. When parents read it, they will primarily get supporting information from their children, so pupils' perceptions of the messages you are giving need simultaneous attention – what do they think?

■■■ Using Plain English

The Plain English Campaign has, since its launch in 1979, had a major impact on the wording of documents for the general public. It is not intended to limit personal style and tone. The aim is to create a readable style and to characterise clear communications, eliminating inefficient and unfriendly official language. The short 'teach yourself' course on letter-writing contains some useful techniques that can be applied to most school documents and is available from their website (copyright © Plain English Campaign, 1991).

- Keep your sentences short with an average of 15–20 words. Vary your writing by mixing short sentences with longer ones.

- Use 80–90% active verbs, not passive verbs, e.g. 'We will consider this shortly', not 'The matter will be considered by us shortly.' Too many passives will make the writing dull. Only use when you want to avoid a hostile or accusatory tone, e.g. 'This bill has not been paid,' not 'You have not paid this bill.'

- Cultivate a sense of audience. Imagine that you are your reader, or that you are talking to them in person. Use 'you' and 'we', e.g. 'You must send us ...', not 'Parents must send us ...'. 'You can get advice from ...', not 'Advice is available from ...'.

- Do not use jargon, e.g. 'SATs'. Is it really necessary to teach them? If so, there are guides that can be used to do so effectively. In this chapter, you will find an example of a guide to National Curriculum terms for parents.

- Give clear instructions. 'Please do something' is better than 'Parents should/are requested to do something.'

- Cut out useless words, e.g. 'Parents are required to notify us immediately in the event of their child's unavoidable absence from school for sickness or any other reason and the attached note explains your legal obligations' becomes: 'You must tell us immediately if your child is away from school for sickness or any other reason. The attached note explains what you must do.'

- If you are replying on a difficult matter such as a complaint or an exclusion, put yourself in the reader's shoes. Be professional, not emotional. You may have to give a firm, unwelcome answer, but be as helpful and polite as possible. If you are going to apologise, do so early. If the problem is your fault, say so. Apologise completely but concisely, sympathetically but sincerely. And whether it is your fault or not, try to emphasise what you can do for the other person.

External resources for plain-speaking to parents

The direct provision by the government of clear information for parents, including guidelines on recommended amounts of homework and new guides for parents on the National Curriculum, offers schools an example of how to phrase such information.

The materials featured were produced by local and central government. Their resources for 'translating' information into family-friendly language have not come from particular school budgets. If a school wishes to review their own written communications, it may be possible to enlist sixth form and parent volunteers to review or write the text of booklets and leaflets. Consider negotiating a partnership with a tutor on a local journalism course or with a publicity agency so that these volunteers can call them for advice a few times per year.

Community resources for informing parents

Adequate translations of leaflets and policy documents should be available in home languages, but keep in mind the literacy of adults if they have recently arrived from poor countries where schooling is under-resourced. Tape-recordings are a good alternative and can be loaned from the school office.

Radio is an under-used medium for informing parents about events at the school. Office staff can be asked to inform radio station and local journalists regularly. In multi-ethnic schools, find out if there is a community newspaper where they would feature school information in the home languages of families in your school.

Information and communication technology

A computer terminal in the school reception area and in the parents' room, if you have one, could be provided for parents to send electronic messages to teachers. This sort of arrangement will rely on all teachers also having access to a terminal in their offices or meeting rooms, and receiving ICT training.

Offering parents more extensive use of ICT facilities can be a channel to increase the use of the school site as a centre for community use.

A number of schools are developing the information available to parents, pupils and prospective parents from a school website. Written and visual information can be made available on a range of issues, from school policies on homework and bullying. The privacy of consulting in this way may make the Internet a valuable resource if parents have

English

Why do schools teach English?
English concentrates on four key skills that your child needs to get the most out of all their learning at school—speaking clearly, listening closely, reading carefully and writing fluently. English helps pupils express themselves creatively and boosts their confidence about speaking in public and writing for others. Pupils read classic and contemporary prose and poetry from around the world, look closely at the way writers use language and explore the social and moral issues they raise.

'Learning English has helped me to read literature, analyse it and also write my own creative pieces. I still write creatively when I have a spare moment and I certainly read a lot. I find that I'm writing all the time at work. Learning English language helps you to communicate clearly, both in speech and on paper and literature can bring people together. It crosses boundaries and gets people talking.' Heidi Gilchrist, 24

Teaching for every pupil

Pupils are taught:

Speaking and listening
They speak to different audiences, adapting their style to suit the audience and the purpose of what they are saying. They structure their speaking so that listeners can follow their line of argument clearly, using techniques such as pace, gesture, anecdotes and visual aids to make their speaking colourful and lively. They learn how to listen carefully, picking out the main points of what a speaker is saying as well as the details and any underlying meanings. They play an active and helpful role in group discussions. They learn how to convey different emotions and moods through drama, and write and act in plays. They learn about how language changes in different situations, about the development of the English language and its importance in the world, and about the differences between speech and writing.

12 / 13

Modern foreign languages

Why do schools teach modern foreign languages?
As new technology brings people closer together across the globe, studying a language like French, German or Japanese becomes even more important in preparing pupils for living and working in the 21st century. Learning a new language teaches pupils how people live in other countries and cultures. It gives them insights into our own multicultural society as well as helping them when they go on holiday. Knowing another language can boost their career prospects if they're interested in working for a company with an eye on global markets.

'If you speak a different language you can be a different person—you can interact in a whole different cultural environment. You can go to a country and you can immerse yourself in their culture, their way of thinking. You adopt a different mentality and you learn new concepts and ideas.' Behram Nasir, 19

Teaching for every pupil

Pupils learn at least one modern foreign language. They are taught the basic building blocks of the language, including grammar and vocabulary, and how to pronounce words and phrases properly. Other language skills they learn include how to listen carefully, how to ask and answer questions, how to start conversations and how to read texts for information.

Pupils are taught the skills they need to develop their learning: for example, they are taught how to memorise words and phrases and how to use the language. While learning the language, they also learn about the countries and cultures where the language is spoken. They learn to communicate with native speakers of the language and work with authentic materials – such as newspapers, books and satellite TV programmes – written or spoken in the language they are learning.

They practise using the language in different types of situations: for example, talking with other pupils and with the teacher, writing letters and making phone calls, and reading for personal interest as well as for information.

52 / 53

(*Learning Journey*, DfEE, 2000)

questions about sensitive issues, such as assessments for special educational needs or sex education at the school. The web also presents the opportunity to post reading lists, curriculum material, homework sheets and other learning resources. The same need for quality and accessibility of language applies in this form as in information on paper.

Letters

Standard letters

Many schools fall into routine formal phrasing in standard letters, without testing them to see how the chosen phraseology is understood by the average reader. It may be helpful to compare these standard letters before and after the process of review. The PE department concerned had developed a series of letters for parents, intending to reflect the different stages of needing to contact parents. The review included the recommendation to include an initial letter to all parents so that they were not purely contacted in the event of a problem.

Before the review:

Dear Parent/Guardian,

On behalf of the Physical Education Department, may I welcome your child to our Comprehensive School. The P.E. department is an exciting and stimulating place to work. There are a wide variety of activities available to all pupils. These are designed to improve co-ordination, social skills, fitness and develop a greater understanding of themselves as individuals.

We are especially, committed to teaching all children to swim. Please find enclosed our School P.E. leaflet which is formulated to help you understand what your child can expect to do, what he/she needs, and some of the major policies of the department.

Physical Education is one of the foundation subjects in the National Curriculum and regular attendance and participation is absolutely necessary. In order to have a safe environment we insist on high standards of personal behaviour as can be seen in the leaflet; however, if you have any problems or questions about any of our policies please do not hesitate to contact us.

Hopefully your child will enjoy participating in a wide variety of sporting and recreational activities throughout the year and the department would like to thank you in anticipation of your co-operation.

Please complete the tear off slip below and return to the P.E. department.

Yours sincerely,

Head of Physical Education Department

PE Dept.

Date:

Dear Parents/Guardians,

The Physical Education department are concerned about your child as indicated below:

(a)   attending school for part of the day but not attending
       Physical Education/Games:

(b)   repeated absence from Physical Education Games:

(c)   forgetting to bring his/her Physical Education kit:

(d)   forgetting part of the kit:

(e)   insufficient work completed during lessons:

(f)   lateness.

We would be grateful if you would speak to him/her about this, as the department has very high standards, and we wish to maintain them.

Please return the slip below with your comments.

Thank you for your support.

Yours sincerely,

✄ ....

OUR COMPREHENSIVE SCHOOL   Please reply to the address indicated above.

I have spoken to my child _____ Tutor Group:_____

Comments:

Signed: _____ Parent/Guardian

After the review:

Our Comprehensive School
Any Town
Address

Dear [name if possible]/Parent or Carer,

We are pleased to welcome your child to the Sports and Physical Education (PE) Department at Our Comprehensive School.

In PE lessons we help your child to develop:
- Health and fitness
- Energy
- Co-ordination
- Positive spirit
- Friendships
- And greater awareness of themselves

YOUR CHILD WILL BE ABLE TO ATTEND PE LESSONS IN WHICH THEY GET:

- FREE SWIMMING LESSONS
- GYM CLUB
[list to be completed according to what you offer*]

In addition, outside lesson time we provide equipment for voluntary activities:

- SPORTS CLUB AFTER SCHOOL
- FOOTBALL IN MORNING BREAK-TIME
- VOLLEYBALL AFTER LUNCH
[*ditto above]

Please see the enclosed leaflet for detailed information about what your child will need to bring to school for PE lessons every week. Each activity requires clothing, shoes and/or some washing kit [*]. We need your help as their parent/carer to make sure that they can take part in these activities.

You will also see that in order to keep them and the other children in their class safe, your child must agree to the PE rules. Please make sure your child understands these rules and can see why they are important for their safety and hygiene. If he/she breaks the rules we will let you know.

Please sign and return the enclosed letter saying that you have talked about PE with your child. We are happy to respond to any questions or comments you may have – call us between 1pm and 2pm Monday – Thursday on 01234 567890, or write to us and let us know when we can call you back.

You cannot withdraw your child from PE lessons as the government requires all children to do some exercise in PE lessons. Please help them to make the most of their time with us.

Yours sincerely,

Diane Runner
Head of PE/PE teacher

Sports and Physical Education (PE) Department
Our Comprehensive School

Dear [full name if possible]/Parent or Carer,

Re: Endo Karim – Year 7. Form tutor – Mrs Saigal.

Your child has PE lessons every Thursday at 11am.

For these lessons this term s/he needs: plimsoles shorts swimming costume t-shirt towel.

S/he needs your support at the moment to make sure:

- S/he brings a bag with the above clothes/kit for every PE lesson.
- S/he attends PE every week.
- S/he understands why PE is important.

PE is important because we help your child to develop:

- Health and fitness
- Energy
- Co-ordination
- Positive spirit
- Friendships
- And greater awareness of themselves

Please reply on the enclosed letter to suggest how together we can help your child to improve in PE at school. Or telephone me on [Mondays/Wednesdays at 2pm] to talk about any problems you or your child may have in them attending PE regularly, with the necessary kit.

Thank you.
Yours sincerely,

Diane Runner
Head of PE / PE teacher

Our Comprehensive School

Dear [full name if possible]/Parent or Carer,

Re: Sharon Besant – Year 8. Form tutor – Mr Sadler.

I talked with your child yesterday about the problems s/he is having in Physical Education (PE) lessons at the moment.

The lesson is every: Tuesday at: 11am.

Kit needed: plimsoles t-shirt swimming costume socks towel

Problem: kit/equipment attendance behaviour enjoyment

My suggestion is:

If Sharon forgets to bring her kit, could you drop it at the school before 10am – at front reception of the Burghley Road entrance, with Mrs Lovett – thanks.

Your child needs your support to ensure they can benefit from our lessons. If you would like to discuss the problem please call me on [Monday or Wednesday at 9.30am] on 01234 567890. The telephone number we have for you in the daytime is: 01234 987654. If this number has changed, please let us know.

Yours sincerely,

Diane Runner / Derek Sadler
PE teacher / Form Tutor

Our Comprehensive School

Dear [full name if possible]/Parent or Carer,

Re: Bozo Bunce – Year 9. Form Tutor – Mr Marshall.

As we have not been able to resolve the problems your child is experiencing in PE, I am writing to invite you to meet me to see if we can talk about the problem in person.

Your child is missing out by not being able to attend PE. This appears to be because of problems with enjoyment/attendance/bringing kit/behaviour.

When a pupil cannot attend PE, they are given other work which they do on their own. They miss out on activities with their friends, exercise and relaxation. As the lesson is compulsory (it is a government requirement), they are also given a detention after school and risk more serious disciplinary measures.

Please telephone me at the school on 01234 567890, on Monday or Wednesday at 2pm, so that we can arrange a time to meet. I am sure we can work out a solution together.

Yours sincerely,

Head of PE / Form Tutor / Head of Year

An exercise

This letter needs re-phrasing:

Dear Mr and Mrs Mazaraki,

Year 8 Admission – March 2001

Antonia MAZARAKI (5.9.87)

I am pleased to tell you that the Governors are able to offer your daughter a place in our School. If you wish to accept the place, please complete the enclosed acceptance form and return it to me as soon as possible. This offer is, of course, made on the clear understanding that you comply with the regulations made from time to time by the Governing Body of the School concerning uniform, discipline of pupils and related matters.

I am glad we have been able to help in this way and I wish Antonia every success in her studies here.

Yours sincerely,

Headmaster

The process of reviewing standard written communications usually includes a wider consideration of the school's approach to parents. In this example, new parents of children entering mid-year are the target audience. What other forms of communication would you recommend to engage them with your school?

Ideas

- Phone call from the form tutor the week before they start.

- A personalised postcard from the headteacher welcoming their child on their first day of school.

- Printing the home–school agreement into school planners or home–school diaries.

Letters about events

DfEE recommendations to careers services on working with parents and guardians include examples of how public services can work in partnership with schools to inform parents and encourage their involvement. They are advised to post home personal letters of invitation to guidance interviews, to contribute to newsletters and to produce guides for parents and young people.

> *'Careers service senior managers should review current methods of distributing literature and other information to parents. They should ensure that the information is actually reaching its destination.'*

> (DfEE, 1998b, p.32)

The phrasing of letters needs to draw attention to the benefits for pupils of parents attending, which in the case of careers interviews were listed in Chapter 3 (p.83).

Individual letters

Standard letters fail to respond to the individual and personal nature of emerging problems. The more personal the form of communication is, the greater the likelihood of resolving difficulties as the parents feel included. Individual approaches to parents are ideally made in personally signed letters that reflect the personality of the teacher writing them, showing their understanding of the situation.

Examples of individual letters

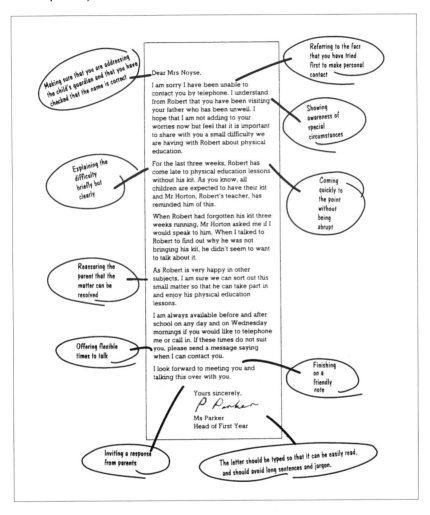

Making sure that you are addressing the child's guardian and that you have checked that the name is correct

Referring to the fact that you have tried first to make personal contact

Showing awareness of special circumstances

Explaining the difficulty briefly but clearly

Coming quickly to the point without being abrupt

Reassuring the parent that the matter can be resolved

Offering flexible times to talk

Finishing on a friendly note

Inviting a response from parents

The letter should be typed so that it can be easily read, and should avoid long sentences and jargon.

Dear Mrs Noyse,

I am sorry I have been unable to contact you by telephone. I understand from Robert that you have been visiting your father who has been unwell. I hope that I am not adding to your worries now but feel that it is important to share with you a small difficulty we are having with Robert about physical education.

For the last three weeks, Robert has come late to physical education lessons without his kit. As you know, all children are expected to have their kit and Mr Horton, Robert's teacher, has reminded him of this.

When Robert had forgotten his kit three weeks running, Mr Horton asked me if I would speak to him. When I talked to Robert to find out why he was not bringing his kit, he didn't seem to want to talk about it.

As Robert is very happy in other subjects, I am sure we can sort out this small matter so that he can take part in and enjoy his physical education lessons.

I am always available before and after school on any day and on Wednesday mornings if you would like to telephone me or call in. If these times do not suit you, please send a message saying when I can contact you.

I look forward to meeting you and talking this over with you.

Yours sincerely,

P Parker

Ms Parker
Head of First Year

(Source: Harding and Pike, 1988)

Ms Ann Christos
55 Fairbairn Court
Jordan Street
London W9 7HG

19 March 2001

Copies: Year Head, Head of Lower School

Dear Ms Christos,

I thought you would wish to know that I was worried about the safety of your son, Mustapha, when he climbed over the pedestrian protective barrier into the roadway and could easily have been knocked down by a car.

He was not meaning to cause trouble, but I thought you would wish me to let you know that he was not looking after himself carefully.

Best wishes.

Yours sincerely,

Frederick Hamilton

Ms Phillips
22 Dorian House
Hampton Street
London N1 8LD

27th May 2001

Copy: Head of Year, Ms Campbell

Dear Ms Phillips

I was delighted to hear from Ms Campbell how pleased she is with how helpful Sam is being.

I do congratulate him, and we look forward to everything going well and his working hard in the future. You will find Ms Campbell extremely supportive and helpful. Please keep in close touch with us.

Best wishes.

Yours sincerely,

Frederick Hamilton

Mr and Mrs Bernat
New Hotel
97 Browns Road,
London NW8 5SD

16th October 2001

Copy: Key Stage 3 Co-ordinator, Mr Charles Smith

Dear Mr and Mrs Bernat,

I am sorry I have been a few days replying to your letter of the 12th October. We are a very well-behaved school, with a strict 'anti-bullying' policy and a very strong programme to teach youngsters how to avoid being bullies themselves and how to avoid being bullied. I am very upset indeed to hear that Khan has not been well treated.

The Key Stage 3 Co-ordinator, Mr Charles Smith, is looking into this vigorously with the Year Head for your son's year, and he will be in touch with you shortly, if he has not been already.

Please be assured that this will be looked into very sensitively and thoroughly.

Best wishes.

Yours sincerely

Frederick Hamilton
Headteacher

Ms Veronica Kendall
12 Denton House
Chartringham Road
London W1 4HF

30th November 2001

cc: Bev Tyrone, Youth Offenders Team, David Hogarth, Education Welfare, Keith Gabadi,
      Client Manager – Behaviour Support

Dear Ms Kendall,

Thank you for welcoming me to your home on Thursday and for your very understanding approach to our discussions of the best way forward for Tony in the present worrying situation. As you know, I am very sorry that you face these difficulties in helping Tony forward, I admire your approach, and I hope that the Action Plan from the Youth Offenders Team and the City's Department of Education can really help him.

As I said, after my further thoughts, discussion with the Youth Offenders Team, consideration of the Pre-Sentence Report, Tony's pleading of guilty, and our telephone conversations, I re-affirmed my October decision (set out in my 20th November letter) that I have converted my initial fixed-term exclusion into a permanent one.

I do understand much of how you must feel, and as a parent as well as a headteacher I deeply sympathise and want to help you. I do believe that the exclusion is not only justified and nec-essary from the school's point of view but also, as indeed you and some other people have said, best for Tony at this moment. I am glad that you liked the arrangements that I am making for study work and the architectural sessions.

In our meeting we went over the next stages of the exclusion procedure in detail. Although I have spelt out all the various technical points and we have agreed them over the telephone and in our meeting, I am setting them out on the attached sheets. I am sorry that these are so long, but I thought it most helpful to give you all the details. Please feel free to ring me, as we agreed, at my home (020 7001 1234) or at school. I look forward to the note you promised by Monday morning, 3rd December, to confirm whether or not you wish to come to the meeting that evening to appeal.

Best wishes,

Yours sincerely,

Frederick Hamilton

Note: Names of members of staff and other professionals outside the school to whom the letter is being circulated should sometimes be included as it enables the family to see the range of people involved in helping. The name and date of birth of the pupil will need to be added by hand to the circulated copies but should not be added to the original sent to the family – 'RE: Charlie Smith d.o.b. 17.01.89' is impersonal and officious.

Newsletters

The small amount of contact that the average parent will have with teachers has to be catered for. They are unlikely to remember informa-tion that they only use once a year. The equivalent situation outside school would be if we were expected to remember the detailed terms of home insurance policies, regardless of the frequency of a need to claim. Only very brief pieces of information might be remembered. Regular opportunities, therefore, have to be developed for giving specific infor-mation, such as an eye-catching school newsletter.

Information provided by secondary schools needs to communicate that parents genuinely have a place in the school community. Only through opening up communication with parents will home–school dialogue start to be characterised by a clear and honest exchange of views.

Ideas for newsletters

- Produce year newsletters in-between the whole school newsletter.
- Explain the most basic terms, such as Form, Class Tutor, or Tutor Group and which year numbers relate to which ages.
- Tell parents the sort of query that can be directed via their child and, if this is not suitable, the type of question that will get an immediate reaction if they contact the school directly. Enclose a little note to stick by the phone with the particular name of their first port of call, such as the school front office manager.
- List brief details of who to contact about what on a copy of the child's timetable with reminder telephone numbers and suggest that parents keep it on a wall close to the telephone.
- Enclose a 'Change of contact details' form regularly:

Change of contact details form

Please give us your new contact details, if they change, or let us know if we have the wrong details on file.

Parent's name: ....
Daytime telephone number: ....
Child/Children's name/s and Form/s:.............................
Address: ....
....
Home telephone number: ....
Mobile: ....

- Summarise the school policy on topics that relate to parents, as on these information sheets produced by Oaklands School (see page 121).

Reports

Report-writing has changed and improved to such an extent that the average school easily keeps parents informed about achievement in class, behaviour and predicted grades. However, the quality and consistency of reports needs to be monitored. Minority parents still

Marking gives your child

detailed information about what has or has not been learnt. It may also offer advice about what should be done to improve such work in the future.

There are two types of marking - effort and attainment.

Effort

E excellent
G good
S satisfactory
U unsatisfactory

Attainment

Either
National Curriculum level

Or
GCSE grade

Or
a numerical mark
18/20, 75%, 4/5

Bullying

* We encourage students to talk to the teachers about any problems they have. If we don't know, we can't do anything to help.
* We look out for any bullying behaviour. There are staff on duty before and after school, at break and lunchtimes.
* We will take action. We will inform parents if their child is being bullied or is bullying. Students have been excluded from school for bullying.
* We write down every incident that is reported to us. Often it is difficult to "catch" bullies. Only by recording every incident can we build up a picture and be able to take action.

Good advice for a student who is being bullied:

Tell an adult you trust what is happening.
Get your friends to say NO to bullies.
Stay with groups of people.
Don't show you're upset.
If you are in real danger, get away.
Fighting back may make matters worse.

Most bullying incidents are "one-off". The important thing is to help the victim to make the bully understand what the effect of their actions has been. Together teachers and parents must try to let students know that they can get along without bullying or harassing others, and that they can gain the confidence to make friends.

Attendance and Punctuality

Good attendance and punctuality is very important if your child is to **learn and achieve** well. Long or frequent absences disrupt learning and it is extremely difficult to catch up on what has been missed.

You have a legal duty to ensure your child attends school. Absence from school can really **only** be justified if s/he is ill.

It is important that you:
- ☐ arrange family holidays during the school holidays
- ☐ make routine appointments for the doctor or dentist outside school hours
- ☐ do not keep your child at home to look after brothers/sisters, do odd jobs or shopping
- ☐ do not keep your child off school because s/he feels unwell and then allow her/him to go out to play or to the shops.

Your child is **must** arrive in school before the warning bells at 8.45am in the morning and 2.15pm in the afternoon. If s/he is more than 10 minutes late we will expect you to give her/him a note stating the reason why.

No child should miss school unless they are seriously ill.

If your child has to miss school you must:
if at all possible telephone the school office immediately on

020 7613 1014

 *on the day s/he returns to school also give her/him **a** note stating clearly the reason for the absence.*

If you are planning a **holiday** that may involve your child missing school you must contact your child's Head of Year to ask for permission. If your child goes on holiday for more than 10 school days her/his place at Oaklands could be lost.

perceive marking and reporting as discriminating against their children and often feel there is no channel for them to check this.

▓▓▓ Informing parents about achievement

The following explanation may be useful as an introduction for parents to assessment and reports. It is derived from the DfEE leaflet (1999), *How is your child doing at school?*

National tests

- The government has set tests for all children aged 7, 11 and 14.
- Schools enter them for these tests when they have completed a course in a few subjects including English and Maths. Courses are partly set by the government through the National Curriculum. Each course takes place over one or two years, called a Key Stage.
- Your child will not be expected to take these tests if their teacher can see they have clearly not reached the right level.
- There are eight levels that show what a child aged 7 to 14 can achieve.

What do the levels mean?

If your child reaches the level expected of them at their age, it means they know and can do as much as, or more than, most other children of the same age.

Your child compared to his or her age group:

	Age 7	Age 11	Age 14
LEVEL 8			E
LEVEL 7			↑
LEVEL 6		E	♣
LEVEL 5		↑	♣
LEVEL 4	E	♣	▽
LEVEL 3	↑	▽	▽
LEVEL 2	♣	▽	
LEVEL 2A	♣	▽	
LEVEL 2B	♣	▽	
LEVEL 2C*	♣	▽	
LEVEL 1	▽		

*Children who are at level 2c when they are 7 may not be able to reach level 4 by the time they are 11.

∇ below expectations
♣ expected level
↑ beyond expectations
E exceptional

7 year olds: Year 2
The tasks and tests given at this age are designed to fit into their normal classroom activities. Everybody involved takes great care to make sure that they are not too stressful and are as fair as possible.
11 year olds: Year 6
At Key Stage 2, children take the tests if they have reached level 3 or above in English, Maths and Science.
14 year olds: Year 9
At Key Stage 3, children take the tests if they have reached level 4 in English and level 3 in Maths and Science.

The tests are not meant to be passed or failed. They help schools to work out how well your child is doing. This will help you and your child's teachers to plan what they need to do next.

Helping your child to deal with low levels of stress will help them to cope with life in the future.

Reports

You will get a written report every year on how your child is doing at school. It will tell you:

- How well your child is doing in the subjects set by the government ('the National Curriculum')

- How well your child is doing in subjects and activities set by the school

- How your child is getting on in general at school

- How well they attend school

- What to do if you want to discuss the report with the school

When your child has taken the national tests, the report will show their test results and the levels they achieved in each part of the subject tested, e.g. reading and writing in English.

Reports show the results of children of the same age as your child at the school. They also show national results for the year before, so that teachers can compare how their pupils are doing with children at other schools.

Examples of reports from Llanedeyrn School

Year 9 update – after Year 9 tests

LLANEDEYRN HIGH SCHOOL

Facing the Challenge

YEAR 9 Update: Spring Term 1999

Name: _____   Tutor Group: 9 _____

Dear Parents,

This Update provides you with an overview of the <u>EFFORT</u> that your child has made in the various subjects studied this year. Please refer to the key for an explanation of the grades. A tick in the column alongside this grade denotes a written comment on the back page.

The teachers have also indicated their suggestions as to the most appropriate level of examination course recommended for study in Year 10. <u>This is intended to act as a starter for discussion.</u> There will be an information meeting about the Year 10 Options on Tuesday 16th March and a Parental Consultation Evening with the teaching staff on Wednesday 24th March. Please book these dates in your diary now.

Should you wish to discuss any aspect of this Update prior to this date, please contact Mr. G. Williams, Year 9 Co-ordinator, or myself.

Yours sincerely

Form Tutor

<u>ATTENDANCE AND PUNCTUALITY - AUTUMN TERM</u>

No. of Sessions:	Authorised Absences:	Unauthorised Absences:	Times Late:

YEAR 9 UPDATE

EFFORT GRADES		SUBJECT RECOMMENDATIONS	
1 =	Outstanding effort has been made.	Z =	Very good GCSE candidate no problems anticipated
2 =	Has worked very hard.	Y =	GCSE candidate should cope reasonably well with the course.
3 =	Working at an acceptable standard.	X =	GCSE candidate but some parts of the course could prove difficult.
4 =	More effort required.	W =	GCSE course possible but candidate will find it very difficult.
5 =	Serious cause for concern - much more effort required.		

SUBJECT	EFFORT	COMMENT OVERLEAF	SUBJECT RECOM	SUBJECT	EFFORT	COMMENT OVERLEAF	SUBJECT RECOM
ENGLISH				GEOGRAPHY			
MATHS				HISTORY			
SCIENCE				MUSIC			
RELIGIOUS EDUCATION				PHYSICAL EDUCATION			
WELSH				DESIGN TECHNOLOGY			
FRENCH				FOOD/ TEXTILES			
ART							

In addition to the subjects listed above, which have been studied in the Lower School, pupils may be able to opt for the additional subjects below.

BUSINESS STUDIES		CHILD DEVELOPMENT	
OFFICE APPLICATION (Computers)		SOCIOLOGY	
INFORMATION SYSTEMS (Computer Studies)			

Year 10

Facing the Challenge

INFORMATION TECHNOLOGY

NAME: FORM: 10

NATURE OF WORK COVERED:

This Information Technology course spanning years 10 and 11 is designed to develop pupils IT confidence and competence in the following areas:

Word Processing: Accuracy in the formatting and presentation of documents.
Databases: Creating a database structure, entering and editing data, searching and sorting, etc.
Spreadsheets: Creating a spreadsheet, editing and manipulating data, use of equations, etc.
The Internet: Use of a search engine for research, cut and paste text and graphics to an application, etc.

STUDENT ASSESSMENT			GENERAL COURSE ASPECTS	STAFF ASSESSMENT		
GOOD CONFIDENT ABOUT THIS	ACCEPTABLE GENERALLY COPING	A NEED TO WORK AT THIS		GOOD CONFIDENT ABOUT THIS	ACCEPTABLE GENERALLY COPING	A NEED TO WORK AT THIS
			Keyboard Skills			
			Completion of Tasks			
			Classroom Behaviour			

STUDENT'S COMMENTS

....
....
....

ACHIEVEMENT				EFFORT			
I have achieved:				I have tried:			
A great deal	Quite a lot	Some success	Not very much	Extremely hard	Quite hard	Hard at times	Not hard enough
STAFF OVERALL GRADE (A-E)				**STAFF OVERALL GRADE (A-E)**			

EXAM RESULT: This is determined by the number of errors made in the examination. Your level of accuracy was:

A high level of accuracy		A satisfactory level of accuracy		A barely acceptable level of accuracy		An unsatisfactory level of accuracy	

TEACHER'S ADVICE: ....
....
....

SIGNED	Student:................................……….
	Teacher:................................………. Date:................................………...

Year 11

These fit into the red National Record of Achievement binders.

SPRING TERM 1999

Name:_____

Form:_____

SUMMARY OF GRADES

A - Very Good   C - Acceptable   E - Cause for Serious Concern
B - Good   D - Insufficient/Below Average

	MATHS	ENGLISH	SCIENCE	P.E.				
ATTAIN								
EFFORT								

ATTENDANCE DETAILS

AUTUMN TERM 1998	Total Number of Sessions : 142 Half days		
Total Attendance	Number of Authorised Absences	Number of Unauthorised Absences	Number of times Late
%			

Form Tutors Comments & Advice
Signed:

Year Co-ordinators Comments & Advice
Signed:

Facing the Challenge

FRENCH COEA

Name: _____

Form: _____

NATURE OF WORK COVERED: **YEAR 11:**		
The content of the syllabus for Year 11 covers :		
Unit 1. Myself and Others	Unit 4. Town and Region	Unit 8. Tourism
Unit 2. Leisure.	Unit 5. The Environment	Unit 9. Living Abroad
Unit 3. Home and School	Unit 6. Food and Health	Unit 10. World Events
	Unit 7. The World of Work	

STUDENT ASSESSMENT			GENERAL COURSE ASPECTS	STAFF ASSESSMENT		
GOOD - CONFIDENT ABOUT THIS	ACCEPTABLE GENERALLY COPING	A NEED TO WORK AT THIS		GOOD - CONFIDENT ABOUT THIS	ACCEPTABLE GENERALLY COPING	A NEED TO WORK AT THIS
			AT1 LISTENING			
			AT2 SPEAKING			
			AT3 READING			
			AT4 WRITING			

STUDENT'S COMMENTS

....

....

....

....

ACHIEVEMENT				EFFORT			
I have achieved:				I have tried:			
A great deal	Quite a lot	Some success	Not very much	Extremely hard	Quite hard	Hard at times	Not hard enough
STAFF OVERALL GRADE (A-E)				STAFF OVERALL GRADE (A-E)			
CONDUCT				HOMEWORK			

TEACHER'S ADVICE:

SIGNED   Student: ....

Teacher: ....   Date: ....

▓▓▓▓ Open communication about progress at school

Parental concerns about academic work are generally more difficult to accommodate than queries about pastoral or welfare issues. Teachers feel territorial about their professional decisions, and parents commonly retreat when they encounter resistance to questions about the curriculum, particularly those who do not identify themselves as belonging to the professional middle classes. An obvious place to start in improving parental understanding and support for school learning is where schoolwork goes home. The next chapter addresses the central home–school issue of homework.

5 PARENTAL INVOLVEMENT IN HOMEWORK

Homework offers an important opportunity to aid and extend learning by setting it into a completely different context. Conversations with adults outside school and other children can spark ideas and debate in a different way to school learning. Research in the local area, at a library, sports centre or cultural centre for minority communities, can open children's and other family members' eyes to resources for learning that are independent of school. These sorts of homework tasks can be kept in mind for weekend homework and homework that can be set at least a week in advance. Work to be done at home offers another dimension because it will contribute to a parent's understanding of their child and the school. It will fulfil very common wishes of parents with regards to their children's education, namely by helping to answer the question: 'How can I see if my child is working and how do I know when she or he is not doing well?'

Most parents want to know more about what is taught in school and how it is taught, including working-class and minority ethnic parents who tend to leave educational decisions to teachers (Woods, 1984; Vincent and Martin, 2000). Parents welcome greater involvement in the subject matter of the classroom, regardless of social class. However, very few secondary schools manage to communicate how families might help to reinforce or extend school learning. Given the inevitable distance of parents from the secondary classroom, it is an undoubted challenge to inform them about schoolwork in such a way that they can support learning confidently, without needing to understand every detail of the syllabus.

Homework is intended to contribute to pupil progress at school. When teachers feel they have little extra time to mark homework, they might limit its use to short tasks and finishing off class work, which pupils find unmotivating (Weston, 1999). Using homework solely to practise and reinforce specific skills also narrows its scope. In recent years, schools have been trying to demonstrate a greater understanding of children's lives after school, providing facilities for homework to be completed informally on the school site instead of at home. This can be necessary, especially when few children can realistically complete homework in the home setting due to family constraints or a lack of educational resources such as books. However, teachers need to be careful that their use of homework is not in fact following low expectations of parents and carers, and that work for completion outside lessons is not merely an impoverished version of work in class.

▨ Illustrating standards and pupil progress

Homework, particularly that completed in exercise books rather than worksheets, provides regular information about what each pupil actually does at school, thus building a picture of their achievements over time. If it is seen before and after being marked, it can portray a pupil's progress and strengths. Ruth Sutton states the importance of the interest of parents in her description of parents and carers as a key audience for assessed work:

> *'We know that parental interest and support make a tremendous difference to children's education. We know too that parental expectations of the child are a key factor in the child's expectations of himself. Anything the school can do to influence positively the self-esteem of children will help them to aspire and to persevere. Focusing on the specific small steps in the improvement of learning, and a continuing dialogue about learning between teacher, child and parent can be assisted by looking at the work itself, not just what we say about it.'*

(Sutton, 1995, p.88)

Homework is the main medium through which work can be regularly seen by parents and carers. This is why schools need parents to understand what is required and why it is important to provide a channel of communication, such as a home–school diary, for an exchange of information about how their children are managing to cope with homework in different subjects, even as pupils grow older. Building a portfolio of assessed work, or completing homework in books rather than on separate worksheets, enables parents, as Ruth Sutton points out, to look at the *development* of the child's abilities over time, so that they form a more complete understanding about their child's standard of work.

▓▓▓ Guidelines and policies

A school with clear guidelines about how much homework to expect at different ages is indicating that teachers are expected to set a certain amount of homework and families are expected to make time for its completion.

At New Heys Community Comprehensive school in Liverpool, homework is timetabled so that the recommended 'one homework per subject per week' can be observed. The homework policy also includes reference to the amount to be expected, and the importance of acknowledgement.

In Llanrumney High School in Cardiff, Mathematics Department staff drew up a policy and guidelines which were distributed with the Department Handbook. Their policy is introduced with a clear statement of the purpose of homework: 'Homework forms an essential part of education and it gives our pupils the chance to practice, consolidate and extend their knowledge and skills in mathematics.' It then includes guidelines on:

- the amount to be set, according to year group
- the extent of the tasks
- how tasks will be specified in schemes of work
- expectations of marking and assessing
- where to record what is set
- where pupils should complete homework
- where parents are to sign
- sanctions for not completing homework.

▓▓▓ The role of parents and carers in homework

Parents need some direction from the school as to what is an appropriate role for them to play, and why they are being asked to take an interest. They can be told plainly that their comments are intended to encourage the child, not make them feel criticised, and that praise and appreciation enhance children's self-esteem. Teachers can ask them to make time for a home perspective to influence the child's view of a topic. Invite them, for example, to add a specific cultural dimension to topics, where this has not been possible in the mainstream school environment. Pupils too need to be reminded that their family might have some involvement; if the topic is rivers, they could find out within the family which rivers run across the county or land of their parents, or for English, they could ask and write about about their family's experience of the host culture.

A description of the parental role can be written into the homework policy, newsletters for parents and homework diaries.

- Helping by providing a suitable environment in which more sociable, team-based methods of completing homework can be used, e.g. inviting friends round after school.

- Taking an interest in tasks set and asking for explanations of the subject or the activity.

- Not knowing about a subject can be valuable, if they question their child and ask them to explain what they have learnt.

- Noticing where general skills, such as reading or writing, are reducing the pupil's ability to complete work independently.

- Observing the qualities of the pupil as they tackle homework – determination, concentration, time management, prioritising according to the urgency of the task.

- Communicating with the teacher how the pupil is coping with homework set.

- Avoiding doing the homework themselves. This rarely happens in practice, at secondary level.

A talking culture

Talking at home about school studies starts to bridge the distance between the world of the school curriculum and the knowledge or understanding that resides in the family. Even basic information about schemes of work and tasks set will allow many parents to discover which subjects appeal to their child and which skills suit their capabilities. Information about topics allows a dialogue at home when something captures their or their parents' imagination. There also needs to be an acknowledgement of the valuable role that family members and others, such as childminders and family friends, can play regardless of whether the child is given homework on that particular topic. In other words, opening a child's mind to other worldviews and perspectives is part of the learning process, and personal opinions or another adult asking about a topic can stimulate a pupil's curiosity, or their desire to explore and to think.

– <u>HOMEWORK INFORMATION FOR PARENTS & CARERS</u>

Homework is an important part of school routine. Research has shown that homework can make a significant contribution to pupil's progress at school.

The Aims of Homework

- To encourage independent learning and self discipline.
- To consolidate and reinforce skills and understanding developed during lessons.
- To encourage and develop planning and research skills.
- To encourage the involvement of parents and carers in supporting pupils' learning.

Type of Homework

Not all homework will involve written tasks, but other types of homework are no less important and will help pupils develop skills to raise their achievement.

Examples of activities which may be given as homework :

Revision	Collecting materials
Drafting	Simple Experiments
Conducting interviews	Projects
Reading	Research
Drawing	Practice – learning by doing.
Essay writing	Designing

Homework Guidelines

Each pupil will be given a timetable with recommended nights for homework for each subject.

In Years 7 & 8 pupils will be expected to do approximately 1 hour per night.
In Year 9 pupils will be expected to do approximately 1 1⁄2 hours per night.
In Years 10 & 11 pupils will be expected to do approximately 1-2 hours per night.

It should be stressed that these are only guidelines. Sometimes it may be inappropriate to set homework on the recommended night and another night could be used. In such cases pupils will be given a reasonable amount of time to complete the task. It may also be necessary to set more homework at certain times particularly as pupils get older and approach examinations.

Completion of Homework

Pupils will find homework easier to complete if there is a reasonably quiet and peaceful place available to do it. This may be at home or pupils are welcome and encouraged to use the Library and Resource Centre at school which is open at the following times after school.

Monday – Friday

Parents and Carers are asked and expected to encourage and check that pupils do complete homework.

Parents will be informed if pupils persistently fail to complete homework.

All completed homework will be acknowledged/marked.
Homework handed in late may not be marked.
Parents will be informed if a pupil persistently fails to complete/hand in homework.

Informing parents

Parents need to be informed about homework, assessment and marking policies, in brief, accessible descriptions about intent and procedures. Schools may not realise that parents make judgements about the school, education and their child's abilities on the basis of how homework is set and marked by teachers. A change in policy needs to be understood by them as well as by the pupils, because otherwise assumptions about the school's standards may be made on face value. These assumptions will then come into play in the school–home relationship when parents experience anxiety and frustration about other matters, especially given the general lack of opportunities for teachers and parents to communicate frequently and openly in secondary schools.

▓▓▓▓ Planners and home–school diaries

On a more regular basis, an information exchange is crucial to ensure homework is being respected by pupils and responsible adults at home. Parents will need to know which subjects are studied on which day, to know when to expect homework in different subjects. Many schools make planners available to pupils where each term's timetable can be filled in and include useful school information is included, as well as the standard space for daily records and weekly notes.

These planners become useful diaries of work and homework set and completed, with space for tutors, staff (including non-teaching staff) and parents to make comments and ask questions. Skilled comments and feedback in homework diaries and on marked homework are likely to increase encouragement for the pupil to work at home.

Langdon School week-to-view

Week Commencing date: 17th July 2000		
Subject	Monday July 17	Time spent
Subject	Tuesday July 18	Time spent
Subject	Wednesday July 19	Time spent
Subject	Thursday July 20	Time spent

Subject	Friday July 21	Time spent

Weekly reading record

Title of book

Writer's name

Pages read: From   To

Teacher/parent/carer notes

Teacher's signature:

Parent / Carer's signature:

Attendance   10

■ How schools have improved pupil diaries

The *Llanedeyrn High School School Planner* includes an introductory section on late procedures.

PUNCTUALITY

...8.40am   School will be open for you to go to your Form Room.

...8.45am   You should be inside your Form Room for the Register to be taken.

...8.50am   If you arrive after this time you will receive a Late Mark from your Form Tutor.

...8.55am   The Register will be returned to the Register Rack. YOU ARE NOW TOO LATE to be marked present by your Form Tutor.

...8.56am   YOU ARE VERY LATE. Go to B5 to receive a Late Mark AND a Late Pass. Go to your Lesson.

...9.30am   YOU ARE EXTREMELY LATE. Go to the Main Office to receive a Late Mark and a Late Pass.

Remember

If you are LATE on 3 occasions you will have to make up the time at 3.15pm School Detention.

LATE ARRIVALS

If you arrive late it is YOUR RESPONSIBILITY to:
I.   obtain a Late Mark.
II.   obtain a Late Slip(s),
III.   pass the slip(s) on to your Subject Teacher and your Form Tutor at the next Registration.

ATTENDANCE

♦   Attendance, like Punctuality, is seen by both the school and prospective employers to be a very important personal quality.
♦   The school rewards with certificates pupils who attend regularly.
♦   If you are not in school there must be a justifiable reason for your absence.
♦   If you are absent from school your Parent/Carer should telephone the school before 9.00am ON THE FIRST DAY OF ABSENCE. If not, school should be notified as soon as possible.
♦   You should bring an absence note from your Parent/Carer the day you return to school.
♦   Whenever possible, family holidays should be arranged OUTSIDE term times. If this is not possible, a written request for absence should be made to the Headteacher IN ADVANCE.

LEAVING SCHOOL DURING THE SCHOOL DAY

Every effort should be made for medical and dental appointments to take place outside school hours. As school finishes at 3.15pm it should be relatively easy to arrange.

If you...
I.   have a medical appointment,
II.   have a dental appointment,

you must bring a note from your Parent/Carer and take it to the Main Office to receive a written Pass which will allow you to leave school.

If you...
III.   feel unwell,

you must go to the Main Office. If you need to go home, your Parent/Carer will be contacted.

UNDER NO CIRCUMSTANCES SHOULD YOU LEAVE SCHOOL WITHOUT PERMISSION

The *Central Foundation Boys' School Student Planner* includes the Daily Timetable, a list of school contacts and form tutors, a reminder of timing in the School Day and the School Calendar for the year.

The School Day

Morning		Afternoon	
8.55	Assembly/ registration	12.55	Lunch
		1.55	Registration
9.05	Period 1	2.05	Period 7
9.40	Period 2	2.40	Period 8
10.15	Period 3	3.15	Period 9– or end of school Mon/Thurs/Fri.
10.50	Period 4		
11.25	Break		
11.45	Period 5	3.50	End of school Tues/Weds.
12.20	Period 6		

Daily Timetable

★Morning Registration/Assembly: 8.55. ★Lunch: 12.55. ★ Afternoon Registration: 1.55★

		Monday	Tuesday	Wednesday	Thursday	Friday
1	9.05					
2	9.40					
3	10.15					
4	10.50					
5	11.45					
6	12.20					
LU	12.55					
7	2.05					
8	2.40					
9	3.15					
AS	3.15/50					

The *Langdon School Student Planner and Homework Diary* includes useful pages for pupils on policies and self-review.

LANGDON SCHOOL
Home-School Partnership Achievement Contract

Langdon sets very high standards for all of its students. We provide equal opportunities for all sectors of the school community and work towards enabling all students to achieve their full potential. We believe that education is a partnership between parents/carers, students and the school and believe that our high standards can only be attained through the co-operation and support of all three parties.

We endeavour to continue to provide a broad and balanced curriculum for your child and will endeavour to provide a secure environment which will enable him/her to reach his/her potential.

At Langdon we recognise and value the contribution which you can make to your child's achievement and we ask you to continue to work with us to support your daughter/son in the following areas:

1. Regular attendance and good punctuality.
2. High standards of uniform and dress, and acceptance of the school's rules.
3. Acceptance of Langdon's Behaviour Policy, encouraging good behaviour both in school and in the local community.
4. Regular checking and signing of Homework Diaries, ensuring that homework is complete.
5. Supporting your child's learning by:
   - encouraging the use of facilities for individual study such as the Study Centre
   - encouraging the use of the Langdon Words books
   - attending Parents' Evenings to discuss your child's progress
   - ensuring that your child has the correct equipment.

We look forward to a happy and successful partnership and ask you to sign this contract with us as the first step in our working together.

(Parent/Carer) .... (Student) ....

(School Representative) .... (Date) ....

Translations

اگر آپ کو اس کتابچہ کے کسی حصے کی اُردو میں ترجمہ کی ضرورت ہے تو آپ سکول سے رابطہ قائم کریں۔

ਜੇ ਤੁਹਾਨੂੰ ਇਸ ਕਿਤਾਬਚੇ ਦੇ ਕਿਸੇ ਹਿੱਸੇ ਦਾ ਪੰਜਾਬੀ ਵਿਚ ਤਰਜਮਾ ਚਾਹੀਦਾ ਹੈ ਤਾਂ ਸਕੂਲ ਨੂੰ ਪਤਾ ਕਰੋ।

যদি অাপ কো ইস কিতাবচে কে কিসী আংশ কী হিন্দী মে জরূরত হে তো অাপ স্কুল সে পতা করে।

যদি এই প্রয়োজন হয় তবে স্কুল থেকে জানাবেন।

यदि आप को इस किताबचे के किसी भाग की हिन्दी में जरूरत है तो आप स्कूल से पता करें।

આ ચોપડા નો કોઈ ભાગ ભાગ ને આપને ગુજરાતી ભાષામાં જોઈએ તો મહેરબાની કરી સ્કૂલ માં સમ્પર્ક કરો.

இந் புத்தகத்தின் இருந்து ஏதாவது பகுதியை வேண்டுமென்று தமிழ் மொழியில் நீங்கள் விரும்பினால் பள்ளியை கம்பந்தப்படி தொடர்பு கொள்ளவும்.

Reviewing Progress

HALF-TERM 1

These pages are designed to help you think about how well you have done in the last half-term and plan your progress in the next. Give honest answers and set realistic targets. Your tutor will help you with this.
Circle the answer which best describes your performance.

CLASSWORK

I am positively involved in class activities
Never — Sometimes — Usually — Mostly — Always

I make positive contributions to class discussions
Never — Sometimes — Usually — Mostly — Always

I use my class time properly
Never — Sometimes — Usually — Mostly — Always

I put maximum effort into my work
Never — Sometimes — Usually — Mostly — Always

My work is presentable
Never — Sometimes — Usually — Mostly — Always

HOMEWORK

I write my homework in my diary
Never — Sometimes — Usually — Mostly — Always

I use my diary to help plan study time
Never — Sometimes — Usually — Mostly — Always

I hand my homework in on time
Never — Sometimes — Usually — Mostly — Always

ATTENDANCE & PUNCTUALITY
Achieved last half-term: Attendance .... %
Punctuality .... %

Planning for Success

HALF-TERM 1

ATTENDANCE & PUNCTUALITY
Targets this half-term: Attendance .... %
Punctuality .... %

PERSONAL TARGETS | **Review**

1. ....
No Progress — Some Progress — Achieved
Comment:

2. ....
No Progress — Some Progress — Achieved
Comment:

3. ....
No Progress — Some Progress — Achieved
Comment:

Parents' Signature: ....
Tutors' Signature: ....

Planning homework assignments

There is often felt to be a tension between planning homework assignments alongside schemes of work and setting tasks on the spur of the moment that reflect how each class has responded to a particular lesson. It can also be complicated to differentiate homework tasks for different pupil levels as carefully as lesson activities, and even more so when there has been no advance planning at all. Penelope Weston comments on the basis of her research:

> 'The argument about planning versus flexibility could be seen most clearly in relation to SEN pupils and their work. Undoubtedly, such pupils would be penalised by any system which expected them to keep up with a set of pre-planned class assignments, and flexibility was needed in setting work appropriate for individuals. But SENCOs who were able to work closely with subject departments saw the answer in more careful planning, rather than a flexible ad hoc approach.'

(Weston, 1999, p.30)

Departmental resource banks of differentiated assignments linked to topics due to be covered every year can be helpful, allowing teachers to select from a range of activities whose purpose or function has already been identified.

▬ Implementation

There is often a gap between homework policies and practice that is difficult to measure without a specific in-house review. Similarly, the role for parents described in school literature needs to be put into practice, which requires all teachers to take parental and family involvement in homework seriously over a period of time. Once guidelines have been introduced, some form of monitoring will need to be introduced to assess if a broad interpretation of the purposes of homework is being practised in reality. Departmental policies can be useful, so that assessment procedures can integrate the assessment of homework on a subject-by-subject basis. Agreed standards on marking and assessment levels will reduce the burden for teachers, and each school also needs to agree how quickly homework will be marked. If too little time is allowed, the quality of the marking will suffer; if too much time is taken, feedback will not be as effective for the pupil concerned.

▬ Giving and receiving feedback

Marks give an honest snapshot picture of one's abilities and allow comparison with others and with average standards nationally. Children will take each mark extremely seriously, and so too will their parents. Without marks, pupils and parents may never develop a realistic picture of their abilities. But the stark nature of grades and percentages provokes a strongly emotional response; they need to be complemented by more descriptive comments. Some teachers may find it helpful to practise writing and giving feedback with each other in order to try ways of phrasing constructive praise and suggestions for improvement. Pupils can also benefit from a discussion about receiving feedback on their work – the sort of subject that form tutors might consider including in the pastoral curriculum.

Giving

- *Be clear and honest.* Giving feedback is a big responsibility.

- *Couple positives and negatives.* A positive statement gives encouragement and something to build on, e.g. 'I like the detail you give here. It would be even more poetic if you could use punctuation to adjust the length and rhythm of your sentences.'

- *Be specific.* General comments such as 'Good' are useless unless skills or behaviours can be named too, e.g. 'Good range of vocabulary', 'Your spelling has improved', 'This clear introduction engages the reader immediately.'

Receiving

- *Listen to feedback rather than immediately rejecting or arguing with it.* You have the choice whether to act or not on feedback you have received. Before putting it on one side, think why it was given to you.

- *Check you understand what is being said.* Paraphrasing or repeating criticism can be useful. If you become immediately defensive, you may be offered less feedback in the future.

- *Check it out with others.* Ask for feedback on a particular point from a range of people.

- *Ask for feedback.* Seek out those who will give you feedback in aspects which you think are important.

- *Thank the person who gives you valuable feedback.* Giving feedback is not easy.

Two examples of active parental involvement

The expectation that homework will be a major channel by which pupils develop the capacity for independent study can stop teachers from considering how parents or other family members could be included. If teachers set work without reference to the context in which it will be completed, they are assuming that homework will only ever be a subsection of class work. The idea that homework is best completed on one's own, in a quiet room, in quasi-examination conditions is losing credibility. It is now considered more realistic to set a range of homework tasks, specifying which require the pupil to work on their own and which require them to take the initiative with others around them to achieve the homework goals. If a task requires active research and planning, the ability of pupils to find appropriate resources in the community or at home will obviously need to be specified. There is no educational disadvantage in the involvement of others, and in the classroom, teachers commonly advocate methods of extending learning such as discussion in small groups and the use of resources outside those provided by teachers. The difference is that pupils are expected to take the initiative in homework activities, whether with adults or friends or on their own. An emphasis on pupil-led learning needs to be clarified in many homework policies, and conjointly the acknowledgement made that work done out of school is likely to be done with others in close proximity.

If any staff are interested in involving parents or carers more actively in homework activities, there is experience in other secondary schools that can take parental involvement a step further. The two examples that follow show different approaches to a more active involvement of parents with their children's work, using short-term projects run by particular departments within the school. They have proved popular and effective with both parents and pupils. Projects for active parental involvement in homework introduce parents to the curriculum, and give them an idea of the child's and the school's standards. They will become more invested in the teacher's assessment and marking of the work, so teachers will need to ensure some consistency in their assessments.

In the first example, the project leaders give contextual information for the development of homework activities. Their exploration of wider issues in school than setting homework *per se* introduces the importance of related school activities, such as curriculum planning, without which a dialogue with parents will not be sustainable. One common objection voiced by staff in setting homework regularly is that some children will benefit more than others, and those who are worst off will suffer disproportionately. Initiatives that benefit mixed groups and classes are homework projects that involve parents practically while allowing flexibility in the amount of involvement they choose to have. Most homework tasks that require discussion can be completed with any interested adult, and older siblings will often also prove a source of useful help at home.

▓▓▓ Dialogue with parents – the IMPACT project

The following case study of curriculum change has been contributed by Patricia Alexander and Lin Taylor of the IMPACT project at the University of North London.

Time required: 12 weeks/one term

Resources: Parent's Help sheets – developed by or in partnership with teachers.

The IMPACT project, based at the University of North London, has long been involved with enhancing parental involvement in primary school mathematics by developing a structure for shared learning. We have, since 1998, been looking at ways of extending this to secondary schools. We were interested in developing a model of supporting parents to help children with the mathematics that was going on in the classroom. Specifically, given that homework functions as an interface between home and school, and that teacher, pupils and parents have a shared goal, how could homework be given a structure that supports dialogue among the parties involved?

At present, the homework experience for parents is not genuinely a mutual exchange of information about the nature of the homework, roles and expectations, or about how pupils' school-based learning can be reinforced in the home. At most secondary schools, pupils are supplied with homework diaries for parents to sign and make comments in, but the diaries often serve merely as evidence of homework being set, not necessarily completed. Despite many schools having a Homework Policy that declares shared expectations based on notions of partnership, parental participation does not often go beyond monitoring and surveillance. Homework can be said to be a representative sample of the school curriculum available for inspection in the home. Parents should be enabled to make informed judgements about their child's achievement and to have a realistic assessment of their child's attainment. In relation to the curriculum, this form of parental involvement entails a radical departure from the ways in which information concerning what is being taught is communicated to the home, and how learning is supported.

Parental involvement can be a crucial factor in a child's success. Parents should be enabled to take a more active part in their child's education, and thereby gain an insight into their child's learning. At the very least, parents should be given the choice whether to be involved. Schools have a role in facilitating this process by making genuine efforts to strengthen links with the home, and actively to seek to promote partnership, based on mutual respect and reciprocity.

Schools seriously intending to improve relationships with the home cannot afford to relegate their partnership with parents to the margins. They must posit parental involvement central to the School Development Plan. This will inevitably lead to a major reappraisal of whole school policies, including homework. The senior management team must acknowledge that critical to the move towards greater parental involvement will be how the staff are supported individually in terms of time management. Teachers need time to review the aims and objectives of their Homework Policy, to consult with colleagues, and to produce homework resources.

A curriculum audit

In some schools, responsibility is given to a member of the SMT to co-ordinate staff development, and to liaise with heads of department and parents. The obvious advantage in a 'top-down' approach is that it provides an overall picture that can be more effectively monitored and evaluated. Curriculum change takes time; department and whole school meetings will need to be allocated for the development of materials and the dissemination of good practice. Prioritising homework will require senior managers to create space on departmental meeting agendas for teachers to devise homework activities that suit particular schemes of work. Teaching staff can only share a sense of ownership, a vision, with parents, where there is a personal engagement with the issue of how parents are valued by the school. Creative departmental discussions will feed into the school's long- and short-term plans in the area of homework.

While the potential for improved relations between the school and home remains a justification for curriculum change, the challenge common to senior management team-led initiatives is at the point of implementation, where limitations will have to be addressed. One obstacle is the mismatch between teachers' and parents' views about what should be the purpose of homework. Also, the purpose is often not stated in ways that are explicit to pupils. A curriculum audit can provide a focus for whole school discussions about the purpose of homework, and the potential for pupils' learning at home.

As long ago as 1935, an HMI report identified different types of homework set by teachers: giving pupils practice in particular operations; verbal memorising; revision of previous work and preparation for the next lesson. Our initial findings suggest that these continue to represent much of the range of secondary school homework tasks (Singh and Taylor, 1998). A curriculum audit involves a whole school reappraisal of the purpose of homework and how it can be used to support the learning in terms of: length of time, its place in the learning sequence, the feedback given to pupils and parents and also the ways in which staff use the information to plan future lessons.

The audit necessitates thinking about homework in relation to the objectives of learning tasks for a particular class or year group across the curriculum. Some of the key questions teachers will need to address are these:

- Do the tasks set for completion in the home create situations for pupils to think about and evaluate their own learning?

- What opportunities arise in the homework task that invite parental participation?

- How can we amend homework activities to promote dialogue between the pupil and a co-learner?

A curriculum audit is a useful mechanism since it can provide the school with baseline information about how each department or faculty plan for parental involvement in the work sent home.

Example of Secondary Mathematics Homework Project

In 1998, the IMPACT team ran a project aimed at enhancing parental involvement in mathematics homework in a few interested secondary schools, with a follow-up in 1999. Given that homework is the mode of intersection between parents, child, and school-based learning activities, we wanted to provide support to parents helping their child. We were able to work within a variety of school settings and contexts in terms of geography and the socio-economic background of the pupil intake. One of the schools was a North London co-educational comprehensive. We had strong support from the headteacher and year head, and from the class teacher for mathematics. The Year 7 class taking part was of mixed ability.

We met with the teachers of the school to agree the support that would be offered to parents, a timetable of meetings for the term of the project and to hear the type of homework that would be set. The teachers involved in the action research thought that there were some pupils who would benefit from a supportive structure to help them to organise their own learning. We felt that parents would benefit from general guidance on how they could help their children, for example by asking the children to explain the homework to them. Parents needed to be aware that children do not always work best in a quiet place, but might prefer to be close to the rest of the family, and we wanted to build in activities that would be shared with other members of the family. So it was decided to produce a generic help sheet for parents at each school. This was discussed with both the class teacher and the head of year, who both decided what needed to be included in this help sheet.

Some of the schools had different schemes of work, so it was important that the homework related to the mathematics curriculum of the school (rather than as an add-on). We asked the teachers to indicate quite clearly the sort of homework that would be appropriate. These were then developed and produced by the IMPACT team. Dialogue was crucial in the homework tasks, so they needed to be interactive with the possibility of negotiating meaning. All the homework activities began with a starter activity that invited pupils to explain their understanding of the mathematical concepts and/or to discuss aspects of the tasks with a parent (or co-learner).

Example of pupil homework on scatter diagrams

The teachers gave out the homework on Fridays (which meant there was a weekend available for them to be completed in) and collected them in the middle of the following week. As has been stated, each homework activity directly related to work done in the classroom. The teachers marked the work and gave feedback to the pupils as usual. Communication was central to this project, so after each homework activity it was requested that both parent and child should complete a feedback sheet. The teachers also collected in all the feedback sheets and passed these to the IMPACT team.

Parents can easily feel that they cannot cope with the mathematics their children are doing. We found that this was for a variety of reasons. Parents can lack confidence in their mathematical knowledge and ability, the language that the work is couched in is often not very accessible, or they do not know how it relates to other work their children are doing. In addition to the generic help sheet, we decided to produce a Parent's Help sheet for each homework task. The language of the help sheets needed to be considered. The topic would have been already introduced to the children but we needed to consider in what ways the mathematical language was introduced and how it could be explained to parents. The Parent's Help sheets were designed to interpret mathematical terms that were likely to be unfamiliar to parents, to put the homework in an appropriate context, and to develop the underlying mathematical arguments so that they were in language that was understandable to parents. The format for all the help sheets included use of open rather than closed questions, explanation of terms, worked examples and answers to some of the questions.

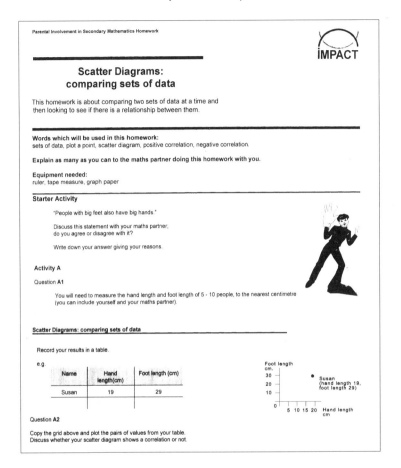

Parental Involvement in Secondary Mathematics Homework

IMPACT

Scatter Diagrams:
comparing sets of data

This homework is about comparing two sets of data at a time and then looking to see if there is a relationship between them.

Words which will be used in this homework:
sets of data, plot a point, scatter diagram, positive correlation, negative correlation.

Explain as many as you can to the maths partner doing this homework with you.

Equipment needed:
ruler, tape measure, graph paper

Starter Activity

"People with big feet also have big hands."

Discuss this statement with your maths partner; do you agree or disagree with it?

Write down your answer giving your reasons.

Activity A

Question A1

You will need to measure the hand length and foot length of 5 - 10 people, to the nearest centimetre (you can include yourself and your maths partner).

Scatter Diagrams: comparing sets of data

Record your results in a table.

e.g.

Name	Hand length(cm)	Foot length (cm)
Susan	19	29

Question A2

Copy the grid above and plot the pairs of values from your table.
Discuss whether your scatter diagram shows a correlation or not.

Parent's Help sheet

A letter announcing the project had been sent home via the pupils, and also pupils had been reminded in year assemblies, the school newsletter and by the class teacher involved. The project was launched at the first parents' meeting of Year 7. The parents were given the date of future meetings and the start time was negotiated and agreed upon. There were then two subsequent meetings organised by the school, at which the project was discussed in more detail with parents.

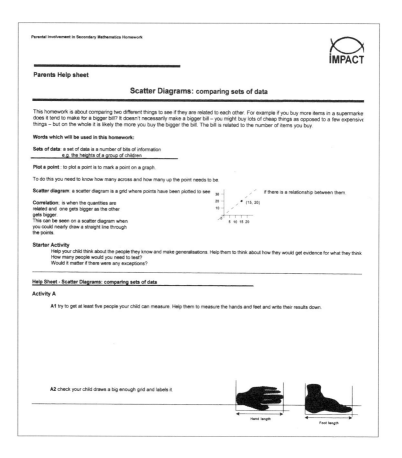

We wanted parents to agree to a regular allocation of quality time with their child on the mathematics activities. We wanted to be honest about the time required and to reassure parents that a 'cut-off' time (e.g. 30 minutes) would be acceptable. Parents would be expected to listen to their child explaining their work and should expect to be asked questions by their child. The parents were given information about the next three topics to be covered in class together with the help sheets and were asked to make comments.

These first meetings were seen as crucially important. Parents can very easily feel threatened by their children's school. It was essential to make the parents feel welcome. Food was organised, and the time of the meeting, the surroundings, and how the parents were addressed were all carefully considered. In most of the schools a crèche was made available, also part of the meetings were given over to the parents where the pupils were not included.

It was important for us that the parents could express their feelings and be supported. Contrary to commonly held views by teachers, parents are interested in their child's education; many parents genuinely try to help their child at home but experience frustration due to lack of information about what their child is expected to do.

The discussions during all the meetings revealed rich information among the parents about their own thinking and attitudes concerning homework generally and mathematics. Parents wanted to know about the changes to the mathematics curriculum (such as the Numeracy Hour), and how they could help their child in the home. Other views expressed and exchanged concerned: parents' anxieties about learning mathematics and how they had been taught; learning strategies (for themselves and with their child) that they had found useful; the impact of homework on the family time and the management of that time. We found that despite parents' positive or negative attitudes to mathematics, these did not affect their desire to support their child in mathematics. The final meeting with parents was after all the homeworks had been completed (12 weeks) and was an opportunity to discuss the project as a whole. There were individual interviews with the teachers and parents concerned.

There was a variety of positive outcomes from the project. The teacher reported an increased rate of handing in homework. Most parents and the teacher reported an increased motivational effect of the study. One parent commented: 'Usually she would come home, on with the telly and do the homework at the weekend whenever she gets time. But with this one, straightaway when she comes home, ... TV afterwards, she would do her homework first.'

The teacher reported increased confidence in the children taking part in the study. For example: 'They were keener to ask questions ... they were bursting to ask questions whereas before they were perhaps thinking "Don't ask me, don't ask me." The confidence has come through them. They actually believe in themselves.'

The attitudes of the parents showed a more varied picture. All the parents wanted to help their children as they felt it would help them in their future careers. The parents had very different mathematical backgrounds; some felt very confident mathematically, most felt apprehensive and some felt very unconfident. Some of the parents were still anxious about helping their children and concerned about the time it took: 'I felt very stretched just doing that.' However a majority reported more positive attitudes during and after the project: 'I enjoyed every bit of it. I don't want it to stop.'

Most of the children had very positive attitudes to sharing homework with their parents. Most had said they wanted their parents to help before the project started and enjoyed the experience of sharing homework. Most parents in the study reported that there was improved communication between themselves and their children concerning school. Most children also stated that communication about school had increased with their parents. One parent commented: 'He was telling me what he had learnt. It did open up communication between us. Otherwise I don't know what he is doing. You don't get much feedback from him. I enjoyed this.'

The children sometimes reported that general communication with their parents had increased: 'Me and my mum got closer because we spent time together. Before mother used to be downstairs and I was upstairs doing the homework and then going to sleep.' Most parents reported better communication with the school, and both teachers reported better communication with the parents taking part: 'The project helped to promote contact. (It was) the first time mum felt she had to contact the school.'

In the short time devoted to the project, there was unlikely to be a noticeable change in the mathematical attainment of the children. However, an improvement in their mathematical understanding was reported by the teacher. Most parents were also aware of increased understanding: 'Before she used to skip the understanding of concepts explained by the teacher. Now she doesn't want to miss a single word.'

Sometimes the need to explain the mathematics to parents reinforced the pupils' own understanding: 'Sometimes I corrected my mum. Sometimes my mum did not understand the mathematical language. I helped her with it. She did not understand algebra.' Most parents appreciated the support given by the study. The workshops were important in helping the parents not to feel isolated. 'I was very nervous at the first meeting. I listened to other parents and relaxed.' 'Meeting other parents, sharing with them, made me feel comfortable.'

The help sheets were also seen by most parents as an essential part of helping their children: 'I needed help every minute of the time I was helping my son.' 'The examples were very easy. They were highlighted and shaded. I understood every bit. If I did not have the examples, it would have been impossible for me to help my daughter.' 'Thank God for the help sheets. Without them I wouldn't have a clue what the volume of anything was.' 'Without the help sheet I wouldn't have been able to start.'

From the feedback sheets, it was clear that different families approached the homeworks in different ways. Some did it very much together. Sometimes the parents found it harder than the children and the children helped the parents. Sometimes the parent just checked through what the child did or asked the child to explain it at the end.

In the school, it became apparent that there were some children who could not obtain parental involvement for a variety of reasons. Various ways round this were found: specialist teachers for bilingual children struggling with English and curriculum support teachers were sometimes asked to take the parent's role. The support teachers, not being mathematics teachers, found the help sheets very useful. Homework clubs were also used and even here the help sheets were very useful because they were not Maths Clubs, where the children could have received specialised maths support. In these sessions it appears that the children were not looking for the help of a teacher but someone who could act as the parent.

After this initial project, we did some more work the following year with a Year 8 class. Since then the school has developed a homework scheme based on the IMPACT project which aims to be accessible to the parents, and they are now developing sheets to be used in the children's exercise books to continue dialogue and develop parental involvement.

Although it is difficult to isolate attainment indicators with sufficient rigour, parental involvement as a contributory factor can no longer be ignored. The issue facing educators concerns the circumstances under which homework can be beneficial to pupils and parents. School learning presents a unique set of learning resources that cannot be reproduced at home. In the classroom, pupils can draw on peer learning, artefacts, other pupils and the teacher as sources of knowledge to support their understanding of the task. In our teaching we strive to create environments 'conducive to learning'.

Likewise the home itself is a unique situation for learning, very different from the classroom. When planning homework, it is important to keep in mind what the home has to offer in terms of learning. Research does not support the idea that homework develops independent study.

It is our suggestion that the home environment can be a place to review learning and to develop concepts introduced in class, particularly if these activities are suitably supported by parents or carers. This also has the benefit of helping the parents/carers to feel more in touch with their children's schooling.

This project encouraged parents to come into the school to discuss the project, despite their fears. It can complement tutor group or class meetings with parents, reinforcing personal contact and using the project as a vehicle for developing relations with a small number of parents. The benefit will be felt beyond the project term, but due to the time necessary for an increased level of communication with these parents and the development of the help sheets, it will probably only be practical once per year.

In the next example, parents were not invited into the school and a greater number of parents could be involved at any one time. The PATCH experience in Manchester suggests the majority of parents welcomed their approach. It effectively acknowledged the distant nature of secondary home–school relations and focused the parents' attention on the interaction with their child, with few worries about their ability to complete the tasks set.

▓▓▓ PATCH interactive homework project

The Manchester School Improvement Service piloted an interactive homework project from 1998 to 1999 consisting of six English homework activities to be completed by Year 7 children with their parents. The main aim was to engage parents in the homework process, forging an early commitment to homework and therefore attainment, and helping parents to learn more about the curriculum and assessment requirements in a partnership between the school, pupil and parent.

The Partnership with Parents team writes:

'Parents were introduced to the project by letter and given simple instructions for each homework. The parents and children marked some homeworks themselves with answer sheets provided. Certificates of completion were awarded and letters of thanks sent to parents. The project was devised to give parents a clear, strategic way to help with homework. It was also designed to allow them greater insight into the English National Curriculum. Parents and children completed a final evaluation sheet.'

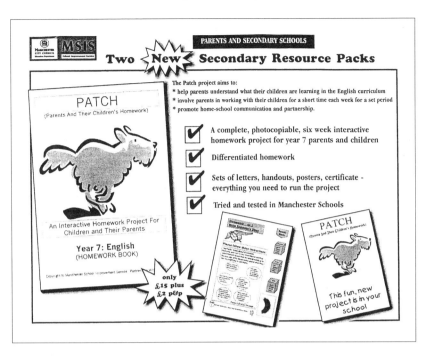

The evaluations demonstrated that parents and children enjoyed working together, the parents reported that they found the experience worthwhile and 90% requested interactive homework projects in other subjects. This encouraged the Manchester team to initiate a subsequent science homework project along the same lines.

Interestingly, when asked if parents would have preferred to meet with the English teacher rather than receiving a letter to launch the project, 27% on average would have welcomed a meeting, with the proportion varying between 12% to 44% in different schools. The value given to personal communication about the project varied according to factors including parents' own educational backgrounds, their work commitments and the ability of the pupils to explain the tasks themselves.

The success of the project was clear from the project evaluation report. Parents had found the work interesting and children had felt encouraged and motivated to do their homework by talking about it at home. Comments by parents and children confirmed that the project aims had been met. Further suggestions included setting these activities at weekends and extending activities, for example by visiting libraries to research homework together. If tasks are not set for completion at weekends, as parents who work are often not home early enough to participate during the week, it is important to clarify if other carers or family members can be involved instead of parents.

Homework resources

Departmental homework activities will provide for the majority of pupils and can be differentiated while planning lessons. Time is the necessary investment here. The only resources available that secondary teachers can use 'off the shelf' have been produced by small local projects as educational publishers appear to produce materials for primary schools but not secondary. The development of curriculum resources is evidently costly and consequently any resources that do exist have to be bought. Both the homework projects with active parental involvement described in this chapter were accompanied by the production of inexpensive activity packs that can be bought by schools.

IMPACT games and activities pack

The IMPACT pack consists of eight games and four card games to develop numeracy at Key Stage 3 with a parent or friend outside school. The pupil testing them for this book particularly recommended four: What's left, How heavy is your dog, Target 200 and Four in a Row.

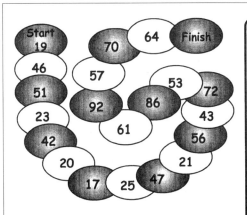

"We think this game was good as it challenges your
mathmatical ability as well as being a race to the finish"

What's left

Game for 2 or more players.

You will need a counter for each
player and a dice.

- Take it in turns to throw the
  dice.
- You then divide the number on
  the dice into the number on the
  square you are on and then move
  the number that is the
  remainder (e.g. if you first
  throw a six, 6 divides into 19
  three times (18) remainder 1 -
  you move 1 space to the 46. If
  you threw a five, 5 divides into
  19 three times (15) remainder 4
  - you move 4 spaces to the 42
  space.)
- The winner is the first player to
  get to, or past the finish.

(If this game is too easy for you
just add a '0' to each board number,
so you start by dividing into 190.)

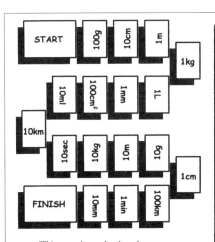

"This game is good as it makes you
think about how big things really are"

How heavy is your dog?

Game for 2 or more players.
You will need a counter for each player and a
dice.

- Each person places their counter in the start
  box.
- You then take it in turns to throw the dice
  and move that number of squares on the
  board.
- You then multiply the amount on the square
  by the number on your dice and state
  something that would measure that amount
  (you can check you answers by using the
  reference sheet included in the pack).
- If you are right you remain on the square, if
  you are not you return to the square you
  came from (e.g. if you throw a '4' at the
  start you move to 1kg - multiply it by 4 gives
  4kg - My dog is approximately 4kg).

★ You will need to agree how approximate your
  answers can be. Check your answers by
  looking in the grocery cupboard and using
  measuring devices such as bathroom scales,
  ruler, watch etc. There is also a reference
  sheet

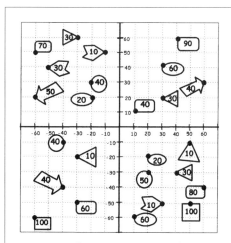

Target 200

A game for 2 players.

You need 2 dice.

- Take turns to throw both dice. Multiply each of the dice numbers by ten. You each start at the origin (where the two axes cross).

- The spotty dice is the distance you move across or back (i.e. along the x axis) and the numbered dice is the distance you move up or down(i.e. along the y axis). So if I throw a 3 spotty and numbered 2 I could move 30 across and 20 up or 30 back and 20 down or 30 across and 20 down, etc.). It is sensible to go 30 across and 20 up as this lands on 30 and you score 30 points.

- At each turn you add your score for that go (if you manage to score) to your total score (i.e. keep a running score).

- The winner is the first person to collect 200 points or more.

"This game is quite fun and it helps you think in four quadrants"

48	16	20	32	96	192	40
4	80	8	24	8	48	16
10	24	64	48	4	128	64
12	6	32	16	8	48	10
40	32	12	32	16	24	96
192	48	20	80	8	12	80

"This game is good for strategic thinking"

Four in a Row

Game for 2 players.

You will each need a dice and counters.

- Take it in turns to throw the dice.

- If you throw a one you lose your go.

- If you score any other number double the score on your dice.

- Keep doubling until you can make only one of the numbers on the grid. If you can make a number cover it with one of your counters.

- The first person to have 4 counters in a row: vertically, diagonally, or horizontally wins.

▰▰▰ PATCH English and Science packs

Two packs of materials for Year 7 pupils have been piloted and evaluated in a number of Manchester secondary schools. The English pack is available from the Partnership with Parents team. The Science pack is in production following its pilot phase.

▰▰▰ Textbooks

It is remarkable that the minimum of props for children's learning, such as key textbooks and basic texts for coursework, are so restricted in state secondary schools. In private schools, many more books are lent to the pupils, whereas keeping a book for a term or a year is unheard of in most state schools. The practice of lending textbooks has been discontinued for so long in some schools that pupils no longer even have lockers or adequate storage space for textbooks for all their subjects. The complications of providing the necessary books and resources to stimulate children's learning and independent study deserve a much higher profile. Of course, a newspaper or magazine may well be the most common resource at home, and quite appropriate for the occasional homework task. But lending textbooks to pupils for a term or more will provide invaluable homework resources, helping them to remember the lesson taught, illustrating the task set and setting individual homework activities into a curricular context. Providing textbooks for a lesson and then retrieving them at the end can remove the possibility of pupils recalling the lesson when it comes to completing homework. Exact lesson content will only be remembered by a few pupils, and this will depend on their type of memory more than on their intelligence or abilities. As subjects become more specialised, both informing parents about the curriculum and direct parental involvement will become difficult, unless detailed background information is provided, such as that ordinarily found in textbooks.

Book lists will help most parents to support their children. Some schools are concerned that poorer parents will feel pressurised to buy books and, as a result, decide not to share the information with any parents. It may appear fairer if all children suffer rather than a few. This prevents committed poorer parents from prioritising education. Many parents would be willing to help if they knew how, and many prefer to buy key books themselves to compensate for under-resourcing in the school, rather than see children suffer. The awful reality that a school, a centre of learning, does not have enough books for pupils can create guilt and shame amongst teachers, leading to a 'we must just get on with it' feeling. They may not want to admit to parents that such a basic item is not available, especially those who wish to uphold the school's reputation or keep it somehow above the murky reality of constantly cutting costs.

Reasons for the lack of resources for textbooks in comprehensive schools include problems in school and local authority financial planning, but may also reflect a devaluing of children's capacity to learn for themselves. Schools where pupils cannot be trusted to look after their books need to address this fundamental problem. They may find that parents can be engaged in the task of monitoring the pupil's use of books. Another answer to the problem of lost or defaced books is to introduce a scheme whereby parents buy the basic texts at the start of the year and sell them back to the school when that textbook is no longer needed. This will ensure greater responsibility amongst the users of the books, and if book vouchers can be made available to less well-off families, they could be reimbursed in the same form. The value of keeping certain books for reference and homework is obvious; if parents are in agreement, the cost of administering the scheme and book subsidies may be appropriately met by the small fund-raising efforts of a Parents' Association such as those described in Chapter 10. It is important to make the terms of the scheme clear, such as restricting the return of books to clean copies with no pen markings. Cleaning and repairing books can be a valid task for pupils to undertake as community service. School libraries should hold books that cannot be sold for loan to those who forget theirs.

It is hard to believe that in some schools pupils have to carry all of their daily possessions with them. Storing each pupil's books in the school is an issue that will arise now that the old flap-top school desk has entered its demise. Unless pupils have a base in the school where they can keep their belongings safely, a book loan scheme will be impractical, dissuading pupils from bringing loaned books back to school, and creating additional difficulties for those who travel between the homes of different parents and carers after school. They would have to carry around too many books for their lessons all day. Not having a base in school, or anywhere private to keep their possessions, is bound to have at least a psychological impact on the pupil's sense of responsibility for their work.

There may be little space, equipment or resources at home for homework and older children may have time-consuming responsibilities. They and their parents need to know how much homework to expect each week so that they can plan accordingly. The growth of homework clubs on site has been another response to this issue. However, the school libraries or learning resource centres where these clubs take place rarely have enough textbooks for a whole class to use for their homework and opening hours do not often extend long enough for the amount of homework the school sets for older pupils. Schools may also need to organise canteen facilities, perhaps in partnership with a local youth group, if pupils will be on site for several hours after school. Limited opening hours discriminate against children who do not have many books or an encyclopaedia at home.

Cultural sensitivity

In diverse schools, home often becomes the main site for specific cultural education and parent-led reinforcement activities. These can enrich the taught curriculum, primarily by children making links between school work and their experience outside school. Homework initiatives involving parents will help teachers to learn about the culture of pupils in a class, because homework will need to be sensitive to their backgrounds. Projects for active parental involvement should be designed taking into account parents' social and cultural backgrounds, and their experience of education. Children will tell teachers, if asked, how practical tasks would be done at home, and teachers will learn about normal family customs and activities from them, for example, the sort of foodstuffs that are plentiful and in everyday use at home, or the family members who are present when they do their homework. It is important to be honest about a lack of knowledge of home cultures, and to be open to learning. Other staff who know about different cultures will also be able to advise. Mainstream teaching practice can inevitably seek to minimise differences within the classroom, unable to recognise in lesson time the particular cultural and familial ties that contribute to an individual child's sense of self and achievement.

▨ Specialist resources

If a pupil has basic deficits in reading or writing, parents, carers or older siblings may need to be involved in a daily programme of support through homework. In these particular cases, a policy needs to be adopted that recognised that some children require much more reinforcement than school alone can provide, and only constant encouragement will bring results. In comparison with the private education sector where parental involvement in the development of basic skills is a prerequisite, state schools are not confident and, in hesitating to admit their limits, children lose out. It is, however, important to consider whether parents of children with special needs are best placed to provide this daily homework support, and if not, the child may be able to participate in a mentoring or learning support scheme using the published resources available. Specialist resources for serious literacy deficits amongst secondary pupils are rare but do exist. One is the *Toe by Toe* structured reading manual (K. and H. Cowling, 1993). Resources such as these can supplement the range of homework materials developed by school staff.

Interest and support by parents for their child's work will be tested and challenged by daily involvement in homework. The activities will have to become part of a family routine if they are going to be necessary every night. Otherwise, homework will become an imposition by the school on the child's, and occasionally the whole family's, free time. Parents are key educators from the appropriate position of the home but they cannot be expected to teach in a prescribed, professional way for a sustained period of time. If a secondary teacher feels the method they employ to help with basic skills such as reading needs to complement the school's approach, then it is their responsibility to train parents in the desired method. The projects described above require only short-term involvement in the school curriculum by parents, which is appropriate given their contribution to home learning is usually made without a school-led methodology.

Homework presents an opportunity for schools to keep parents in mind as partners in the educational process and to communicate regularly with them throughout the year about the curriculum and about their individual child's abilities and development. Regular communication using actual work, and channels for a dialogue in home–school diaries or planners, will generate the opportunity to revisit the purpose of discussions with parents in person. The school's task in these discussions is to focus parents' attention on specific issues in pupil progress.

Face-to-face talks about individual pupils are necessarily limited in number. The best possible use, therefore, needs to be made of them. One feels, on reading the transcripts in the next chapter, that in the occasional traditional meetings between parents and teachers that commonly exist, little is being said openly, but a mass of unresolved and unspoken obstacles to good communication are below the surface.

6 TALKING ABOUT PUPILS

'You sort of sit there – but you don't ask questions because, ... well, it might be a damn silly question.' (Parent)

'I always think you get a true story from Mrs Jones, but the others when they say to me 'He's getting on!' I think to myself, well you're telling lies, because I can see he's not, you know ...' (Parent)

'I would like to look at (her) work, and look at what she should be doing, but I don't necessarily think that needs to involve the teacher.' (Father)

(Teacher–Parent Interviews, 1983, pp.48–50)

A spirit of partnership in home–school communication becomes most evident when parents and teachers meet together face-to-face. Individual contact is the focal point for home–school relations, and most schools offer occasions for parents to meet teachers at least annually. Parents' evenings are regular events held for teachers and parents to meet to discuss pupil progress. Yet researchers who have analysed these encounters have found that historical problems in teacher–parent relations can still be seen in the dynamics under the surface of many conversations:

'The results of the research problematise policy 'buzz words' such as partnership and parental support. They suggest for instance that the relations of power and knowledge in these interactions are both highly complex and largely unrecognisable to the participants themselves while they are speaking.'

(MacLure and Walker, 1999, Internet p.13)

Even in schools that provide a range of ways for parents to contribute to the school and enjoy friendly relations with parents in general, age-old barriers seem to be present and unresolved. Records from the University of East Anglia research make uncomfortable reading, revealing inequalities and power struggles between the two parties that prevent constructive discussion about the pupil concerned.

This chapter explores some common problems that arise during these conversations with parents. The transcripts illustrate some typical tensions and uncertainties between the participants. From the teacher's point of view, a traditional 'interview' would probably be one in which the parent understands the basic message in the report and accepts the teacher's comments. But how do the interactions on such an occasion contribute to *progress* in terms of the benefit for that pupil? Written reports give as much information; verbal versions may give little more. Without questions or discussion there can be little reason to meet, yet even experienced teachers see the delivery of a report as an adequate achievement. In the first interview, the traditional format preserves an authoritarian style that is out-dated and prevents teachers and parents from talking on equal terms.

▰▰ Transcript 1: Example of a meeting beginning with a teacher 'diagnosis'

'T' = Teacher
'M' = Mother
'S' = Student
__ (underlining) = Two or more people speaking simultaneously

T Right, Very good. Mary, you are doing well. You're working hard and I'm thrilled to bits with your work, your notebook's good, and erm you ask good questions, you try to answer the questions, you've passed both tests. You got 66% for the first test, which was to do with the plant nutrition, you know, with all the ecology, all of that early work, yeah? And the respiration test you got 56%, you went down a bit, but it's a harder test, you know, the marks generally are harder on that, are lower on that one, because it's a harder test. Erm, I think that you're learning a lot of science. I'm happy with the way you're working. I think your notebook is good, and you do seem to understand what's going on, most of the time. I can only say you could improve on one thing and that is don't get sucked into the other group of too much gossip. Yeah? And I think I've done something about	**DIAGNOSIS** [T addresses diagnosis to S]

that, 'cause I've done some splitting up [M laughs] – all to help

M Good   [M replies]

T But you're a great girl and I'm very impressed –   [Summarizing: bringing diagnosis episode to a close]

M – Oh that's good, I'm really pleased,   [M acknowledging juncture]

---

well, erm ... the GCSEs with science [T: Yes], they obviously have to take science?   **DIALOGUE** [M 'opens up' the dialogue]

T Yeah

M So <u>that's not –</u>

S <u>– double science</u>

M Double science

S Is there double science?

T Double science, yes, that's what we would you would do, double GCSE science. So you get ten hours a fortnight next year, OK? That will be covering elements of physics, chemistry and biology, so you'd do double science, it would count as double. Two out of ten. <u>Is that all right?</u>

M <u>That's fine</u>, I'm very pleased

T Is there anything else you wanted to ask?   **CLOSINGS**

M No, not really, I'm quite happy

T Well you could double her pocket money on the basis of science

M [laughs] Well I won't tell her dad then! Well that's lovely, yes, thank you very much. I'm very pleased

T OK, we are, I am as well

M Oh good

T Mr Cheshire as well [other science teacher]

M Lovely

T Keep it up

M Thanks very much

T OK?

M   Thank you
T   Bye now, nice to meet you as well
M   Thank you
T   Bye Mary
S   Bye

(Maclure and Walker, 2000, p.25)

▓▓▓ Transcript 1: Commentary

Walker and Maclure denote the initial 'diagnosis' as a feature of 'institutional talk', with the direction and topics on the agenda of this meeting set at the start solely by the teacher. By the end of the 'diagnosis', the atmosphere has already become one of the end of a meeting, not the start of discussion. Teachers at a parents' evening that consists of five-minute slots usually assume the purpose of the meeting is purely to inform parents and so they settle too often for getting their message across. The value of *meeting* to do this rather than writing this message into a report is unclear. Few schools ask the parents' agenda for the meeting, and by creating a judgemental atmosphere akin to delivering a verdict on a child, it is extremely unlikely that a parent will try to find the less positive dimensions once the teacher has finished talking. In this example, the verdict is given with specific feedback on how the pupil is doing well. What is absent is any mention of how she could further improve her work.

In several transcripts in this chapter, the parent 'opens up' the dialogue even when they have been given a good report, because most parents do not expect to listen silently in a face-to-face situation. It is possible that a parent has been offered the promise of a *conversation* with a teacher, and feels the meeting is unfinished when presented with a brief *report* of this kind. Researchers have also proposed other reasons:

> 'Good news stories, especially if these lack detail about the student's work, may fail to convince parents that the teacher has given her full attention or consideration to their child.'

(MacLure andWalker, 2000, pp.12–13)

Some parents can see that little is achieved at such a meeting and find visiting several teachers merely to hear similar things is a waste of time:

> 'It seems, quite honestly, a bit pointless ... it seems a waste of a teacher's time just to go up there and ... say "Oh yes, this is fine, that's fine, the other's fine" and then go away.'

(Teacher–Parent Interviews, 1983, p.57)

The UEA research shows how often teachers are trying to bring these meetings to a close. Parental viewpoints recorded by the Community Education Working Party in Nottingham many years ago illustrate the impact of this – sensitive parents pick up the teachers' weariness, or even feel pushed out:

> *'F: Now that teacher's got to see maybe thirty or forty parents in a couple of hours*
> ...
>
> *M: We just go to say "Hello, good evening."*
>
> *F: We go because the thing is we've got to go round, they say "Oh, didn't see your parents last night", so we go. Because you've got the feeling that possibly they may be saying, "Oh, your parents aren't interested".'*

(Teacher–Parent Interviews, 1983, p.52)

Researchers have found that, in less effective secondary schools, lack of parental interest is often *blamed* for underachievement, whereas in more effective secondary schools with similar intakes, teachers have a more favourable perception of parents and enjoy better relations with them (Sammons, Hillman and Mortimore, 1997). If, in the staffroom, parents, or their lack of resources, are blamed for low standards, with comments like 'our parents are not able to support their children', or 'with parents like that, no wonder', scapegoating parents will gain legitimacy. If unchallenged, staff members will prejudge parents, making unbiased conversations with them difficult. It can translate into denial of parents' humanity, such as when teachers prepare to deliver a verbal report to parents, but have not anticipated the inevitable questions and challenges that follow.

The anxieties that prompted the conversation in the next transcript will be only too familiar to staff who have been given little support or guidance. They also, however, provide the motivation to try new approaches because enduring unsatisfactory meetings is tiring and unrewarding. Parents may see the occasion as the only time in the year when they might talk with someone in person about issues that are deeply important to them. This mismatch of expectations causes mutual reproach, and the resulting conversations can resonate with hidden accusations. Many of the encounters become a covert struggle between the adults involved. Educational research over two decades has confirmed that these formulaic and ritualised events are often painfully unsatisfactory (MacLure and Walker, 1999, 2000; Macbeth, 1989; Teacher–Parent Interviews, 1983). This type of meeting is bound to create insecurity and a distrust of parents' evenings, which, together with organisational constraints, hinder the development of a real dialogue between home and school.

Teachers still do claim that parents who do not attend are not interested in the education of their child. It is rare that teachers question the quality of the parents' experience when they interact with their school before making this judgement. They quickly give up on parents who stop attending, without analysing which parents are being put off. It may be that parents of children with bad reports find the experience too painful – their child being criticised hurts, even more so when it is heard again and again. Not seeing a way to object or fearing the consequences of strongly defending their child would turn most parents against a school. If it is mainly the parents of lower achievers who are being put off, a traditional parents' evening is acting as a channel for discriminatory practice, discouraging parents of struggling pupils from talking with teachers to resolve problems more than parents of bright pupils. There will always be exceptions because some parents are determined to defend their children, even if the experience is difficult for them. But broad patterns should be transparent by comparing parents' attendance records at these events with pupils' ability levels and reports.

Seeing more than three or four teachers on one evening might be overwhelming to a number of parents regardless of their class and education, especially when there is no tradition that parents will make notes to aid their memory after the event. Parents whose first language is not English and who do not already know different staff can find it particularly hard to enjoy the personal contact facilitated by the average marketplace-style evening.

▓▓ Transcript 2: Interview from ESRC report: Secondary School Parents' Evenings: A Qualitative Study

Anatomy of a blaming sequence

'T' = Teacher
'M' = Mother
__ (underlining) = Two people speaking simultaneously

T	... I'm, personally I think Josh is doing well and seems quite happy. Have you any problem, any questions you want to ask? ... You look like you have a question, yeah g–	[concluding his 'diagnosis']
M	[Hesitantly mutters] He's ... he has not understood on a couple of occasions the actual homework that he has been set to do.	problem statement/ accusation

He hasn't understood

T   Right, so he's been, what? In English, in particular?

M   Yeah, in particular about the Diary of the erm, the Witches' Diary thing. He, he was kind of quite upset that he didn't really understand what it was he was being asked to do –

T   – oh r–, he misinterpreted, <u>oh that's a sh</u>—   blameshift → student

M   – <u>no, he just</u> didn't really <u>understand</u> –   blameshift → teacher

T   – <u>follow it</u>

M   – what he was being asked to do, yeah, and   [personal he got a little bit upset about it, getting quite   information] stressed in actual fact, that he wasn't, he couldn't understand, well not he didn't understand, he just didn't understand what he was being asked to do, you know?

T   Right, er, it's a shame in a way if he hadn't,   blameshift → [stutters] you could have easily phoned up,   student/parent or asked him to ask me. I mean what they   blameshift – were doing was we'd read the play, the book   justification sorry, 'cause it was The Witches, wasn't it? [M: Yes] And we'd actually read the book,   [pedagogical The Witches, and what I'd said for them to   explanation] do, I said, 'Right, imagine you are the main character – [M: mm] – the lad that's in the story and choose the bits you enjoy, and imagine you just write a little diary of some of the main events in the story to show' –

)

M   – yeah, <u>well he</u> –

)

T   [loudly] <u>and that's</u> what they were, and it   ) was <u>like a, a</u>

M   <u>well he kind of</u>   ) [talking simultaneously]

T   <u>very easy way of</u>   )

)

M He kind of interpreted that to mean, erm, that he was expected to write a diary of every single event that happened in the book

)

T I did quite, and it was actually written on the book, quite clearly, it wasn't – one of the things I actually said [M: Yeah] was at the time, 'you are not expected to write the book'
    reassertion of problem/ accusation

M Yeah, I know   denial

T 'cause if that was the case

M yeah, no, that's what –

T – I'd have got, you'd have written the book –
    reassertion of problem/ accusation

M that's what, he, he seemed to, he seemed to think that's what he was meant

T oh, it was a misunderstanding
    blameshift → nominalisation ('no fault' version)

M – to be doing

T But no, that was, that's unfortunate

M Yeah

T In the case of that, if he misinterprets something, or he's unsure, by all means, contact me or tell him to come up and ask, you know
    blameshift → student/parent

M Yeah

T 'Cause quite often, I tell the whole class, there's thirty of them, you know,
    blameshift → 'neutral object'

M well, I –

T you assume that they've actually –

M [tries to interrupt] yes, so –

T – it's on the board and written, it doesn't always follow –

M – yes I know the problem [laughs]

T So, I mean if that's the case, then by all means make sure that you –

M – Yeah   agreement

T the next day he comes up, or if either one of

you contact me and say he's not sure, I'm
quite happy to re-explain it to him
M   Okay   acceptance of
                                                  responsibility

(MacLure and Walker, 1999, Internet pp.22–4)

The UEA researchers found in their discourse analysis that problems
are often created when the parent speaks up, because their questions or
comments can imply criticism of the teacher's professional judgement.
Parents may want to report a worry in the hope of finding a solution
together, but instead of focusing on the pupil, the conversation starts to
revolve around the fears of the adults present.

Teachers understandably feel sensitive if they see the parent's query
as about their own teaching instead of keeping the focus on the pupil's
learning. By virtue of their training, a professional is someone less likely
to make mistakes than amateurs, in a specialised area of work which
they are paid to do. However, teaching is also known as an art because
it is associated with flexible, wide-ranging and talented communication, as well as academic ease. It requires a teacher to use their personal
resources to such an extent that even inadvertently implying they are at
fault in the classroom or in their understanding of children provokes
strong reactions.

The most powerful dynamics develop in relation to the role played
by the teachers concerned, or how they perceive their role, so that even
teachers who are parents themselves may find that in this situation they
resist suggestions and challenges from parents. As Barbara Walker
writes in her paper entitled 'Meetings without Communication, a study
of parents' evenings in secondary schools',

> 'The parents' evening is a unique interactional event which creates a problematic
> interface between the power bases of home and school, ... Rules of engagement
> and the roles of participants are confused.'

(Walker, 1998, p.163)

Teachers occupy a different, less hierarchical position to that of a classroom teacher when they are with the children's carers but few authors
have defined the role they do play. 'Partnership' attempts to capture the
equal respect they should hold for each other. Perhaps 'collaborators' is
the closest term for their role, which requires trust and good communication; for teachers and parents to work together over a five-year period
there needs to be an ongoing dialogue in which a five-minute slot is
only an element in a sequence of communication. Meetings are an
opportunity for key elements of the relationship – respect, basic

familiarisation with each other and hearing information that is best discussed face-to-face.

Parents unwittingly carry an aura of accountability and have the power of knowledge of the child in question, but teachers can be intimidating to them in turn. Education is a hierarchical field in which assessment results rank people starkly. A fear of feeling stupid is common amongst adults outside academia, especially those deemed 'less intelligent' during their school careers, so parents can easily feel inadequate. Teachers are still professional public figures who represent learning and erudition. Parents are amateurs, whether experienced or not. Teachers can also make parents feel accountable and defensive because parents have 'made' their children behave in certain ways. Professionals, just like ordinary members of the general public, are indeed likely to judge parents as most responsible so that underlying the surface conversation is the expectation that parents, not the school, will do something first to improve the problem. Parents, in contrast, will expect the school to act because the problem is in the child's schoolwork. Responsibility for solving problems can be thrown like a ball between these two important figures of influence in a child's life. This avoids any real negotiation or discussion about suitable remedial action by the pupil and what sort of help either party can give.

There is a real difference of cultures between home and school, which needs to be bridged when representatives of each talk together. It is part of parenting to allow mistakes and to help children to accept themselves as they are. Their humanity with children, and constant capacity to forgive, helps the child to become secure, and sensitive to others. The rift between home and school is thus widened when parents perceive teachers as judgemental people who will not give them or their children the benefit of the doubt. In the second transcript, Josh's mother may be trying to explain things from her child's point of view, hoping that this will lead to a better understanding between her child and the teacher. She may be trying to protect her child's feelings in the future, such as would be the case when talking to another adult in the family. The teacher does not understand this 'emotional' agenda and concentrates on the professional one. This difference in their perspectives makes it difficult to talk. The parent may assume that the teacher shares their emotion about the child, making a pedagogical response sound impersonal or brusque. Empathy with the feelings of the parents concerned and an easy manner with them are valuable qualities in talking with parents.

Teachers reading the interview may recognise the point where the teacher takes refuge in the response 'He or she is not the only one you know' in defence against the parent's enquiries. The scolding manner that often accompanies this phrase is off-putting and should be avoided. It may reflect the unease, irritation or pressure experienced by a teacher in that moment rather than a thoughtful consideration of the problem presented. The pupil's confidence to ask when he does not understand is left unexplored until the last moment, and instead they seek to find hasty solutions or someone to criticise.

In terms of furthering the child's progress, a parent–teacher conversation like this one leads to an unsatisfactory result. The teacher suggests in the end that the parent takes responsibility for the solution by contacting the school – often presented as a realistic possibility but rarely realistic in practice. Getting through to a teacher on the telephone is extremely difficult and is best not suggested unless new systems are in place to guarantee a proper response to calls. The power imbalance has resulted in the teacher 'winning' the tussle with the parent, and effectively leaving all the impetus for change in the end to the parent, who can only operate through the pupil himself. What needs to be brought back into perspective here is the fact that better information is needed about what helps each pupil to learn well, perhaps by discussing some pieces of work brought to the meeting. Parents and teachers might then think together about formative support for the child at both home and school, to develop their interest or abilities.

Changing expectations

In today's anti-authoritarian society, parents' evenings can reflect a bygone era when the role of the parent was presumably to listen politely and think mutely about their child, perhaps feeling appeased by the fact that the teacher was in some sense acknowledging some form of accountability in the situation. The role of an adult citizen today is a more challenging one. It can be predicted that a parent will want some clear channel for negotiation if there is a problem with schoolwork, not just a series of critical reports accompanied by the expectation that they will not argue. Perhaps expectations need to change on both sides, so that teachers can see parents as jointly responsible for each pupil, and meetings with them an opportunity to communicate about their different but equally valuable perspectives.

Parents' evenings attempt to combine the aim of informing parents with the aim of discussing a pupil's progress whether past, present or future. One of the first steps for the improvement of these meetings is to clarify the purposes of their conversation and to predict how much this meeting can achieve. A letter posted in advance telling them the aim of the meeting and suggesting any content you can predict in advance is a minimum, so that both parties have time to prepare.

A conversation with a third party, outside the classroom, can be helpful if it is non-judgemental and encourages both pupils and teachers to think more deeply about their attitudes, or teaching/learning styles, or how to develop specific behaviours that would encourage progress. Teachers can create an atmosphere of shared interest by first listening to any query parents have, and then using most of the time to discuss at greater length the perspectives of the different adults on the same pupil. Give them the opportunity to share what they are thinking early on in the meeting. This will also provide an insight into the world they come from, if it is different to yours. Later on, you might give examples of what the pupil finds difficult, to help to describe their individual strengths and weaknesses. You might mention the range of steps that the school takes in this sort of situation. It is always helpful to summarise what action you have agreed to take in conclusion. If appointments are too short, they might air a problem, without time to agree what step should be taken next and who will be responsible for taking it forward. Planning how to respond at a later date to different types of suggestions and queries from parents will free you from the need to rush to a conclusion.

It should be made clear whom to talk to at a parents' evening if a problem, such as serious difficulties in a particular lesson, needs in-depth discussion. A department head or year head may need to talk with those involved to understand the situation in the classroom. Only the teachers and pupils themselves can act to change the attitudes they bring to each lesson so after parents and other staff have gathered more information, their role will be to support their in-class efforts from the outside.

It is rarely helpful if teachers use most of the time slot to justify a teaching method, complain about homework, or try to pacify the parent. Mrs Lesley Andrews, Assistant Headteacher at Llanrumney High School in Cardiff, states clearly, *'Parents should ask as well as teachers expressing their concerns or views. We need them, they need us and the kids need us both.'* Encouraging parents to attend meetings with some questions in mind will provide a better focus for a brief amount of time than a teacher's report. They could be given a leaflet or a questionnaire to complete with their child before they attend, which would help them to identify some questions. Staff may wish to discuss answers to the types of issues that parents bring, based on the experience of colleagues in the school, before the evening.

Improving parents' evenings

In many homes, it requires great energy to go into the school after the working day is over, with the accompanying childcare and transport arrangements. But unless parents are asked, they might not want to admit this, and once they have arrived, the demands placed on teachers by staying on late do not go unnoticed, so they may not want to complain. It is therefore worth finding out by direct questioning of both parents and teachers if existing arrangements are popular (see Chapter 2 for examples of consultations).

Teachers in many schools now ask parents to bring the term's report with them to a parents' evening, and questions, devised in advance with their child. Fifteen-minute appointments are increasingly used for meetings with parents of pupils of all ages. When the parent does not know anyone at the school, it can be bewildering to meet too many people. As a pupil grows older, too many short exchanges prevent a proper discussion when this might be what is needed.

Examples

- Llanrumney High School introduced meetings with form tutors for parents of Year 7 pupils in 1995 and saw a steady increase in attendance in the following two years.

- Philip Morant School offers 15-minute follow-up appointments after the Year 9 parents' evenings about options, to cater for cases where there are issues that need greater discussion. They are called consultation meetings rather than interviews.

Senior managers can help individual staff members both in person at the event and also from their position of seeing which issues are likely to be the greatest concerns to parents. Policies on relevant out-of-school activities, such as sports and homework, should be clearly displayed. In-school issues may also be prominent concerns, such as classroom behaviour. All teachers, especially those newest to the school, can benefit from guidance on how to reply to queries, for example by informing parents realistically about the child's range of options for coping with a problem, or explaining whole school strategies to standardise marking and homework. Teachers may otherwise find themselves taking responsibility for every problem personally or having to justify their approach without preparation. They should always be encouraged to get back to parents with an answer, not to try to deal with everything on the spot.

▬ Personal information

The next transcript includes reference to the social life of an adolescent, which is crucial to their development but is a subject more often raised by parents than teachers at secondary level. The open halls where these interviews are traditionally conducted are not suitable for private discussions, so the setting of the meetings could be failing to take into account the inevitably private nature of what the parent can say.

One difficulty in trying to respect the private content of these conversations is that the presence of other teachers can feel safer for staff. Teachers who do not feel at ease with the local community may fear that parents could be aggressive. The underlying reason for their unease may not be quite rational, as parents generally feel immense gratitude for good free education provided to their children. Teachers' fears may need to be resolved by looking at factors within the school, such as in schools where parents become angry because they have no channels for effective ongoing discussion with staff outside annual meetings. It is more difficult to trust each other if most occasions when parents visit the school are situations of crisis.

It should also be remembered that private information given by parents to teachers is deemed by the UEA researchers to be intrinsically challenging. Sharing information from home crosses the unspoken home–school barrier; this can feel uncomfortable when the teacher has their 'public figure' hat on, in what to them is a workplace. A parent's comments may sound inappropriate or conspiratorial, particularly if the teacher feels close to the child and not their parents, but in fact this sort of information is useful and should be interesting. There do need to be opportunities for a parent to inform teachers about their child's life outside school because this can influence their progress in school. Staff should be able to air their feelings about any difficulties in adjusting to this role, and be reassured by colleagues that personal information is relevant and acceptable, when it relates to the child's home life and its impact on them within school.

If parents introduce private information in such a meeting, pupils will want all the adults concerned to handle it with care. If the information divulged to teachers is sensitive, such as about a recent bereavement or an impending divorce, it should only be shared with colleagues with respect for the confidentiality a family needs. Ask the parent if the pupil will know you have been told. If not, specify to colleagues that it has been given in confidence, so that mention is not made of this information without consulting the parent first. Less sensitive information may none the less be personal, and should not be raised by a staff member with a pupil in a public place such as a corridor or classroom.

■■■ Improving interactions

Despite the fraught nature of these events, a number of parents do attend, and continue to attend every year. For parents of average and successful pupils, the experience may be one of the few times that they hear reassurance and praise from a number of sources. The parents' evening appears to be a ritual that captures an important part of the child's experience at school – the parent sees many different teachers in succession, some of whom have been mentioned at home. This is the only event at which the majority of parents can try to see most of their children's teachers, even in schools that have introduced other meetings for discussing progress, such as longer appointments with form tutors to discuss each pupil's reports properly. A range of parent–teacher contacts during the year should be developed so that one type of event is not overloaded. Together with new meetings with parents, you may therefore decide to keep short interactions once a year, with staff employing a different, consultative style.

Taking the cue from the parent can focus in on the issue they most want to discuss. The teacher in the third transcript asks an open question, that does not limit the parent's reply to a 'yes' or a 'no', at the start of the interview, allowing the parent to lead the direction of the talk. The father is then allowed to explore his worry with some reassurance from the subject teacher who feels confident enough to try to work out if his worry is justified and to contribute an opinion formulated by way of this brief discussion.

■■■ Transcript 3: Interviews with a subject teacher in the secondary school – Mr Walsh, father of Jean

'F' = Father
'T' = Teacher

F   Hello. My wife would have come tonight, but she has been ill. I'm Jean Walsh's father.

T   Hello, what would you like to know?

F   She seems to be doing very well?

T   I'm sure you hear this from everyone. I don't think it's only me that thinks this, but Jean is very studious and organised, a mature pupil really.

F   Yes, I wish she was a bit more outgoing with the other children really.

T   Do you mean she is being selfish?

F No, not selfish, but she's a bit nervous, not a very good mixer. She doesn't seem to ... er she doesn't seem to ...

T Usually girls like Jean are like that. They are so interested in their work, and getting on with that, they really haven't time for the other things girls of their age normally do. I think this is good, as long as later on they don't take it to extremes. In the case of Jean, I don't feel she is stepping outside her capabilities. Therefore, if she does go to University, and she should, I don't think she will be out of her depth.

F You don't?

T No.

F That's part of my reasoning, you tend to get some overpowering people there.

T Well, I think you will find when Jean gets there, and I sincerely hope she does as she is the kind of girl who ought to go to University ...

F Yes, that's what she wants to do.

T I think she will fit in easily. I don't think she feels she fits in here. A lot of the girls here are not interested in work.

F No, I know what you mean.

T Consequently, she is a bit of a loner. She hasn't found the other girls feel about work like she does, and that tends to isolate her.

F I know what you mean because I'm teased about being a loner at work. It's not that I am a loner, it's just that I don't particularly like doing what most of the others are doing, like going to the pub at lunchtime, and that sort of thing you know.

T I wouldn't say there was anything wrong with that.

F No, that's right, that's right.

T Well Jean's behaviour is also normal. I think she is an excellent girl. I always have. I was pleased when she did Biology because she is a marvellous girl to teach. It is true she doesn't mix with the other girls much, but I can't see anything wrong with that. As I said, she hasn't really found the kinds of personalities in her class to make friends with. If she gets to University, she will make friends easily, I'm sure.

F Well that's reassuring. We've not pushed her at home. She has done all this academic work off her own bat. We say, 'Do the best you can', and that's all. We've never pushed her, she seems to enjoy doing it you see.

T What is her English and Maths like?

F Er, well I've got the report here. Quite good. 51%. She was top.

T She wasn't top in Biology this year. I was glad. I thought she was surprised, I think she expected to be first. She was near though. I think it's better if she is not always first.

F This is what she says herself sometimes, like you say. The trouble is everybody expects it of her. I say, 'You don't have to be top. If you can be, without making yourself worry, alright.' I don't want her to make herself ill, I would be the last person to push her.

T Well, do you feel she is worrying?

F I don't think she is, but I sometimes wonder if she is doing too much, especially at weekends. Both of us say this.

T Well, what would you like to see her doing at weekends?

F I don't know, I suppose really we'd like to see her enjoying her-self more. She does go to discos on a Thursday evening, which is a break for her.

T Who is she friendly with?

F Sara, well ...

T Sara Lander?

F Sara Lander she is quite friendly with, and Maria she has been quite friendly with. They go to the disco together. To a certain extent, being with boys as well has done her a lot of good, because she was in a girls' school before she came here.

T That's a bit abnormal really.

F That's right, yes. It's better if they gradually adjust, rather than go from a girls' school, straight into the world, really.

T Yes, I taught in a girls' school, and I found the girls behaved well, on the whole, better than they do in a mixed school.

F That's right, they haven't got the boys to talk to, and get some of the things out of their system, they just take it out on another girl.

T Well, I think Jean is going in the right direction. She does her work; she is never any trouble in class; she is not antagonistic towards other girls; she seems to have friends.

F Yes.

T The rest of the girls don't resent her being better than they are. They expect her to be first in everything, they are surprised if she isn't. She certainly can speak up for herself if she needs to, and I can't see any problems with her mixing.

F No.

T I think Jean has got a strong personality, and when the time comes for her to mix with other people she will. She seems to be normal, well behaved, quiet and hardworking. I'm pleased to teach her.

F Well, thank you. Goodbye.

(Teacher–Parent Interviews, 1983, pp.25–7)

If the tradition of delivering the 'diagnosis' is removed, a wider talk becomes possible on more equal terms. The parent's interest in this interview revolves around the teacher's knowledge of Jean as a person, because he is worried about a personal quality that he shares with his daughter. It is the issue of social acceptance that bothers him. The teacher tries to understand what his worry is, thinking aloud to start with, which gets the conversation going. Once the father has expressed himself the teacher reassures him very successfully, presenting an image of another world, at university, in which the pupil will be more 'normal' and therefore probably less of a loner. Only the teacher and people who know Jean and the school well can judge if he or she is qualified to make this suggestion. It is perfectly possible that a subject teacher can build enough understanding of a pupil over time to discuss such a topic with their parents. However, some sort of system to check the accuracy of what is said is useful. For example, if a school often loses bright pupils to another local school there could be an incentive to teachers to elaborate on the truth somewhat, in an attempt to encourage them to stay.

Openly discussing advice that has been given to parents is useful to assess the consistency of a school's response to parents. The teacher's satisfaction with their chosen approach can be reviewed in a forum for training in this kind of interpersonal work, in which self-observation provides material for discussion. In this case, Jean's teacher was quite self-critical after reading the transcript:

> 'This father was obviously concerned with the amount of work his daughter did at the expense of enjoying her leisure in other ways. I, on the other hand, seem concerned only with telling him what a marvellous girl she is and how some miracle will happen when she gets to University. I do far too much talking, and not enough listening.' (Jean's Biology teacher.)

(Teacher–Parent Interviews, 1983, pp.30–1)

It is a valid observation that talking in these exchanges can become an obstacle to communication, but this teacher in fact listens more than in many of the interviews recorded by researchers. The teacher also replies honestly to his questions about Jean's work in her class and tries to encourage him to support her aspirations. The conversation appears perfectly satisfactory, so it is interesting that the teacher wanted a greater outcome. Perhaps this is because, by the end of the interview, she has enough information to observe the pupil from her father's point of view but not enough to weigh fully whether it would be beneficial to the pupil to encourage her in another direction. Both sides express themselves, but the teacher's view takes precedence over that of the parent.

The teacher's concern is valid – that she initially did not address the father's issue of Jean's behaviour as a loner, she tried to avoid it by presenting a brighter future several years ahead. But she returned to the issue, asking questions that test the reality of his worry and finding that Jean's loner behaviour is modest rather than extreme. She seeks to test if Jean is worrying overmuch about her work and sees that it is more a parental concern at this stage. Listening proves to be a vital first step to improving the discussion. She gives good, descriptive, specific feedback on Jean's behaviour and educational abilities (although in her enthusiasm to elevate Jean, she unnecessarily detracts from others in her class). She believes there is potential for Jean's loner position to change as the pupil grows up. And because the father's worry could affect an important educational choice Jean will make in the future, she is proved right to have explored it a little.

In some schools, particular staff members are nominated as responsible for an all-round picture of each pupil. Teachers can then signpost parents to these staff when they encounter a query that goes beyond their knowledge of the pupil. Form tutors, or mentors in a school with a mentoring system, might know a small number of children well and will have gained a more rounded understanding of the pupil than a subject teacher who only sees them once a week in a large class group.

There are limits to how responsive the school can be. If the father in Transcript 3 still felt that the issue needed attention after talking with several teachers, he would have to raise it with Jean herself, as there appears to be no educational reason to discourage her from working hard. If he went on to discourage her actively, against her best educational interests, it would become the school's responsibility to discuss it with him again. This would require good ongoing communication with the parents to make the link between the parents' evening conversation and Jean's behaviour in class. Another meeting would probably then be necessary. A deeper level of individual work with a child's carers requires more than five minutes and quite specialist interpersonal skills.

Teachers have to be careful not to overstep their limitations. A subject teacher may teach hundreds of children, and can only know them through the lens of their subject, even if they get to know a pupil well from this angle. Some subject teachers see children four or five times per week, for longer than their form tutor, whereas others teaching low-period subjects or who only see the child once in a double period lesson cannot get to know a individuals well. In the transcript that follows, the teacher appears confident that his understanding of the pupil is sufficiently adequate to comment. However, he introduces into the conversation an interpretation that proves subsequently to be mistaken. The emotional tenor of this interview proves more interesting than its factual content.

▬▬▬ Transcript 4: Interviews with a subject teacher in the secondary school – Mr Smart, Andrew's father

'F' = Father
'T' = Teacher

F I'll just put my cigarette out. How do you do, I'm Mr Smart, Andrew Smart's father.

T Oh yes.

F Yes. How are you? How is he doing?

T Well, actually, I've considered kidnapping him.

F Oh ah. [Laughs]

T I find him delightful, is that how you feel about him?

F Yes, we try to keep his feet on the floor, like, you know, but we are very pleased with his report, and I believe his Biology was an A or a B?

T B. I got the impression he is not too keen on the subject, actually.

F He has never said anything.

T He often asks me what use it is to his future. He has a straight way of putting things.

F Yes, very straight way of putting things.

T I doubt if he will continue with it when he reaches the third year. If he does drop it, I won't be too concerned because if he wants to do engineering, or something in that line, he will probably want to take computer science.

F I've had a good report from his History and Art teachers, and his English, very good, you know, all the teachers are enthusiastic, perhaps he might go in that direction. He has never said he doesn't like Biology.

T I wouldn't say he doesn't like it, what I mean is, I don't think he sees the relevance of it in his career later. We get on well together, and I like teaching him, he is like a breath of fresh air entering the room.

F Is he? Well that's good, very good. All the teachers have had something nice to say about him, you know, and his behaviour is obviously alright. We have no trouble at home with his behaviour. Does he get a bit forward sometimes?

T Yes, he is very straightforward in his approach, and he often makes comments which could be taken as cheeky, however, with Andrew, they are said in such a matter of fact way that they are acceptable.

F   Yes, very good. Oh ah, and I forget his mark again, it wasn't a bad mark, was it?

T   No, it wasn't a bad mark.

F   Do you think I should encourage him to keep this subject on?

T   I think you should let him make his own mind up. We can both encourage him, and I should hate to lose him next year, but when the time comes for him to choose options, if other subjects are more suitable for his career, perhaps he should choose them.

F   I see, well thank you, goodbye.

T   Goodbye.

The Pupil's Reactions

I think some of the comments were slightly wrong, for instance, 'and he likes Computer Science' was quite wrong as I simply hate that lesson. Also, where the teacher says that I wasn't keen on the lesson, well I am, and I am also most certainly going to take Biology in the 4th and 5th years. Too many questions were asked about my career, and this must have been most tedious for both sides of the conversation. More questions should have been asked about what I was like in Biology and how much I knew about it. Some of the comments were rather dramatic, such as, 'He is like a breath of fresh air coming into the room'! I thought this comment was a bit untrue. Comments like, 'yes, we try to keep his feet on the floor' which were made by my dad could have been avoided. Well, that's about all I can say about it. Otherwise, it was a pretty good talk, although it was a trifle too short. Perhaps my dad was being a bit big-headed about me in some of the remarks he made.

(Teacher–Parent Interviews, 1983, pp.19–21)

In this example, the teacher starts the conversation with a celebratory moment of sharing his appreciation of the pupil and his capabilities with the parent, which is a good way to set the tone of a trusting, open conversation. However, it can then be difficult to lead the conversation towards a more detailed and rounded picture of the pupil's strengths and weaknesses. The teacher in this example volunteers the hypothesis that the pupil dislikes the subject. The pupil's apparent ambivalence towards the subject is subsequently denied (in his comments above). The teacher's opinion must be based, as he says, on the fact that

Andrew often asks 'what use it is to his future'. The father's later point that Andrew is 'a bit forward' provides another possibility, that the boy's manner is generally not very respectful, although the teacher does not consider this seriously when it is raised. Perhaps these questions feel like a challenge to the teacher in class, especially as the boy is bright and most teachers would want such a pupil to stay with their subject.

There is bound to be an emotional impact on teachers of teaching bright pupils in a comprehensive school. Transcript 4 communicates this teacher's range of feelings well, from delight to defence against disappointment with a stoic resolve to be fair. Bright pupils can intimidate some teachers, especially those who were not the highest achievers at school themselves. Or the teacher can feel that a lesson is worthwhile when an intelligent questioner is in the audience – they can experience great pride in the pupil's results. The emotional subtext is influential in the classroom even if the teacher tries to distance him/herself. Teachers have to try to separate the shared enjoyment of a subject that reinforces the pleasure of teaching from their enjoyment of personalities. But perhaps as a consequence of this attempted distancing, the educational power of a pupil liking a teacher is often underestimated; in fact it is an extremely influential factor in subject choice.

In a mixed-ability group, it can be difficult to give the capable, likeable pupil the amount of praise and encouragement deserved, as teachers soon see the disappointment this creates for other pupils who are rarely top of the class in terms of marks or behaviour. However, where adequate direct praise is not possible in class, it is helpful to give the pupil's parents a strong picture of their child's strengths. The traditional parents' evening excels in filling this gap in a teacher's praise and rewards for brighter pupils, although the tendency even to praise pupils who are weak is considered disingenuous once results show their abilities on a national scale.

This teacher obviously greatly enjoys Andrew's presence in the class group (and Andrew's later comments imply the feeling is mutual). With his father, the teacher deflates his extremely good report as if to find a more realistic balance. This creates a different atmosphere to the previous comments and the parent is slightly mystified. It shows a feature of communication with parents which makes such conversations about a subject close to their hearts quite difficult – a small remark can have a memorable effect. He might be trying to make a distinction between the experience of the lesson and the worth of the subject for a career, which in many ways is a more mature distinction than the average Year 8 pupil would make. Perhaps the teacher pushes away the initial unconditional praise in order to counterbalance their less 'professional' nature.

The teacher's strategy proves to have a beneficial effect in a way, because after he is honest about his own feelings, he focuses more squarely on Andrew. Instead of simply sharing their appreciation of Andrew's qualities, they progress to talk about how the father might advise his son in his future choice of options. The father seems open-minded, allowing the possibility that his son could go for arts or sciences. But he asks the teacher how he should encourage the pupil to continue with the subject and the teacher has achieved a neutral position from which he can give good advice. In a year, he knows Andrew will be able to make his own mind up, without undue influence by his parents or teachers.

Although the outcome is good, the method of achieving it involves the teacher twice claiming facts that are subsequently disproved. His personal impression that the pupil is not keen, and the intellectual justification given for doubting the pupil will continue with the subject, appear to reduce his own anticipated disappointment if Andrew does not continue. Hypothesising in this way helps the teacher to communicate that the boy is likeable, capable and good to teach, but leaves the parent with the impression that the teacher is suggesting he does not have a particular affinity for the subject. In fact the teacher is trying to focus on what will benefit a good all-round achiever the best, i.e. whatever subjects are necessary for his chosen career. A further problem is that if all the other teachers are simply giving good reports, then this one will appear negative. Taking into account the combined force of their remarks is impossible unless teachers have discussed how they intend to talk with parents beforehand.

This transcript illustrates the complexity of the communication involved in these meetings and the sensitive and personal nature of both teachers' and parents' comments. The Year 8 pupil's comments draw attention to his youth and to the benefit of meeting with parents independently, as he does not understand the value of the longer-term view explored by the adults concerned. He does, however, make good points about the possible use of the time, drawing adults back to the present from their predictions and interpretations. His comments imply that the pleasure the teacher describes in the teaching and learning relationship is mutual, and he focuses much more clearly on this than his teacher.

Improving the dynamics

Records of exchanges between parents and teachers can easily be made in most secondary schools, revealing the dynamics in these face-to-face meetings. Looking at actual interactions with parents recorded by schools, however one-sided this may seem, can be a valid starting point. Research in this field tends to value subjectivity: personal impressions can help to identify areas for improvement with more relevant detail than generalised survey results. Recalling a brief conversation will illustrate quite clearly what has actually been achieved, and will allow a review of how well the meeting met its aims. Beyond this lies the task of a more detailed analysis of the subtextual dynamics of parent–teacher communication, to understand some of the nuances in the interviews conducted.

■ Producing material for discussion

Ask teachers during an INSET session to role-play being the parent and the teacher in pairs or threes, with an observer whose job is to record the sequence of interactions. Staff who are parents themselves will draw on their experience to make sense of a parent's reaction rather than defending against it. This process should enable questions to be asked about the meetings that go beyond the immediate experience of the event – such as, are the meetings contributing effectively to children's education?

■ Getting parents' evenings off to a good start

An INSET session attended by several schools can look at the design of the welcome made to parents. This sort of cluster or LEA-based training is likely to generate discussion about practical, organisational aspects as well as psychological considerations in encouraging parents to visit the school.

A parents' evening is an event that tends to focus staff attention on methods for improving home–school relations in general. Firstly, there are straightforwardly practical problems concerning the number of people involved. Keeping people waiting is unpopular in any public service. At a training day in the former South Glamorgan authority area, deputy and pastoral heads and education welfare officers based in a range of schools were asked to imagine a situation in which they went for an appointment with a professional who kept them waiting. They called to mind appointments with lawyers, a bank manager and a doctor. Most said they were fuming and described the frustration, dependency, anger and loss of control that they felt at the time.

'Welcoming Parents to Your School'

Trainer: Jacqui Stevenson, a former teacher and governor, and a parent herself.

Aims

1. To explore participants' own experiences of trying to be effective in an unfamiliar, potentially threatening situation by recognising emotions which may have been evoked in them.
2. To acknowledge the range of needs parents/carers have and the need to ensure they all have equal opportunity to access information and staff.
3. To identify flaws and positive features of present practice in their school and accept that improvement is possible and necessary.
4. To consider the skills of effective listening and attending behaviour and the importance of creating an environment for meeting which respects the parent/carer.
5. Actively to involve participants in agreeing a set of guidelines which would encourage and improve the quality of contact between parents and staff.

Training Programme

9.30am	Welcome
10.00am	Brainstorm: Why parents don't come in. Which can we begin to address?
10.30am	The visit
11.00am	First line – Phone, reception, who do they contact, messages, images, directions, access, time
	Meeting – Where, skills of staff, listened to, recorded, agreement, actions, interruptions
	Post-meeting – Feedback, follow-up, accountability, comeback

---

Those who attended the training day were surprised to make the link between their own feelings in other environments and how a parent might feel coming to see them. Working well with parents involves imagining how others see you. Only once a feared figure starts to treat you like a human being with respect can Chalkie, the unreasonable old-fashioned teacher from cartoon images, sink back into the imagination.

■ Equal opportunities

Generalisations about parents are more easily avoided with records of real conversations and accurate information to hand. Discussion should take into account the school's approaches and responses to parents as well as the history of the family. Information will be needed about home backgrounds to trace disparities between outcomes for different cohorts of children. Staff discussion after an event can also consider how parental views and expectations have been created before the event.

- Preparing parents before the event

You may wish to give parents some guidance in the form of a leaflet so that they can use the evenings in their existing format more effectively.

What can be achieved when you visit the school for a parents' evening?

How to get the best out of your parents' evening

... despite the good intentions they can sometimes be difficult experiences. This is nobody's fault. There are no rules of behaviour. No-one quite knows what to expect.

Parents want to show their concern and support without appearing pushy or over-anxious. Teachers want to demonstrate their professional competence, and to inform and engage parents.

For teachers it offers a chance to inform parents about their children's progress, and to ask for support if necessary. For many parents this is satisfactory. But for those who have information of their own, it can be a difficult pattern to break. Both parties can also be looking in different directions. In general teachers are happier to look back and report on past progress, while parents are keen to look ahead and discuss future possibilities.

Children can find the meetings a source of anxiety. If they do not attend, they know that powerful forces are discussing them, but if they do attend, they can find the experience difficult to handle.

- Talk to your child before you go.

Is there anything they would like you to mention or ask?

- Write down anything you want to say before the meeting.

Points and questions can be forgotten in the flow of conversation.

- Take a notebook.

Make a note of the teacher's main points.

▓ How well does the teacher know your child?

Be aware that the teacher may have spent relatively little time with your child's class, if this parents' evening is scheduled early in the school year.

▓ Do not attempt to make the interview deal with serious issues.

Parents' evenings are useful to gain a general impression, to put faces to names, to reassure ... But it is neither the time or the place to deal with serious problems. They will require another separate appointment. If you have become aware of a problem some time before, contact the school and get it sorted straight away. Do not wait.

▓ Is your child invited?

Try to include the child in the conversation as much as you can. They can find the meeting embarrassing and difficult.

▓ Ask for clarification.

Do not hesitate to ask if, for instance, a technical term is new to you, or percentage in a mark book means little to you.

▓ Ascertain the scale of the problem.

Sometimes teachers are surprised by the force with which parents react to what, to them, was a fairly minor problem. On the other hand, an important point can be overlooked.

▓ Ask what you can do to help your child.

▓ Follow things up.

If necessary, in due course remind the teacher (gently) and yourself. Notes can be helpful.

▓ Use the phone.

It can be difficult to contact individual teachers by phone at school, but do persist. Often a brief telephone conversation is enough to set minds at rest.

▓ Remember that teachers can feel intimidated by the meetings as well.

'Parent power' can intimidate teachers, especially the newly-qualified.

(Source: B. Walker, TES Learnfree website (now closed))

▨ Conclusion

Parents' evenings are likely to continue while they provide the only annual opportunity to give or receive information in person and individually. But few would describe the traditional encounter as a good meeting or a harmonious sharing of information. The teacher's initial diagnosis featured in 126 of 184 interviews in the UEA research. Both parties tend to present information to each other in the tone of 'a report' rather than negotiating ways to improve behaviour or schoolwork.

Traditional power imbalances are played out during these meetings. The teacher has most of the power, and the meeting is on their territory. One parent interviewed during the Norfolk research said, *'It's a teacher's evening!'* (Walker, 1998, p.172.) The parent carries a certain power in knowing the child well and acknowledging their satisfaction or otherwise. They can listen to the teacher but make the report on the child seem a report on that teacher too. If the teacher feels defensive, it is natural to try to shift perceived blame or responsibility elsewhere. The anxieties of the parents may be masked by polite deference because they sense the power with which the teacher can affect their child's happiness, and do not like to challenge them. Practical limitations of time or privacy exacerbate the interpersonal difficulties. A five-minute conversation with such pressures is likely to create a silent no-man's land of common ground in which a parent is forced to agree out of fear of a teacher's influence over their child. It is not surprising that many parents become disaffected with the whole event, especially parents of pupils who are not getting good reports. There is also immense pressure on teachers within the noisy, marketplace-style evening, in what Jennifer Nias describes as *'a cross between a social security office, a doctor's surgery and King's Cross station'* (Nias, 1981, p.92). New teachers and all parents need more guidance about what to expect.

If teachers allow more time for the discussions, with training on how to conduct the meeting to best effect, some of the inevitable difficulties can be worked through and a constructive, focused discussion will be easier. In my opinion, it is worth at least extending the time for the form tutor to meet with each parent, rather than repeating the dysfunctional communication that often takes place in five-minute slots. The extensive difficulties have led some schools to abandon the old-style parents' evening altogether.

IMPROVING DISCUSSIONS WITH PARENTS

In this chapter, two priorities for the effective management of discussions with parents are explored. Firstly, whole school strategies for working with parents in large schools need to be designed so that they will have the potential to involve a range of parents. Teachers are increasingly acknowledging that the organisation of large events can unwittingly discriminate against the parents of underachievers or ethnic minorities, and have developed approaches that respect differences between individuals more fully than traditional 'majority' events have allowed. Meetings *en masse* need to be planned and monitored to ensure they benefit a comprehensive majority of parents. The case study of Review Days offers a structured model for a type of meeting that involves fuller discussion about a pupil's progress.

The people chosen to talk with parents are also fundamental to the quality of home–school relations, whether during an organised occasion or an informal chat. Staff responsibilities need to be clearly defined to encourage communication with appropriate family members, and between the various staff involved. The second part of this chapter recommends greater definition of these responsibilities by articulating the tasks undertaken and the skills necessary to complete them well. The roles of teaching and non-teaching staff need to reflect their strengths in working with parents as well as recognising the opportunities for professional development that this work provides.

Parental support for pupil progress: review days

Schools that have focused on designing egalitarian approaches to improve access for all parents, not just the resilient or the brave, have created new meetings in which parents and teachers can talk in a less pressurised situation than the traditional parents' evening. One such meeting is the Annual Review, in which parents and teachers, and often pupils too, meet for a structured discussion about the strengths, the academic progress and the potential of the pupil. The meetings take place by appointment, often during the day, and are attended by a much higher proportion of parents in the schools that have introduced them. They respond to the parent's desire to discuss their child's progress in more detail and face-to-face. They make extra demands on parents, who have to organise work and childcare around the new arrangements once a year. They require school staff to prepare to hold a fuller discussion, 15–20 minutes on average, about individual pupils. Their apparent success indicates that the vast majority of parents and teachers think this extra effort is worthwhile.

A longer discussion will create the opportunity to describe the different influences on the individual child, focusing a parent's and tutor's mind on the school world through that pupil's eyes. If a pupil is working well or is a high achiever, their stresses may be expressed in their behaviour when they respond to peer pressure to try less hard. Tutors might mention strategies employed by different staff to encourage the pupil to keep trying during the year and discuss with parents how to reinforce these effectively. Pupils who feel very anxious near examination times may need help organising their time so that revision is not rushed, or may just need more attention from their parents who will need to be aware when the pressure will start. The parents will also be able to help them by hearing what sort of line different teachers will take at exam times.

A key element of general review meetings is considering a detail or pattern in the pupil's work brought by a form tutor, mentor or particular member of staff who knows the pupil well. Parents can then notice parallel qualities at home that otherwise would not appear connected with characteristics or patterns noticed at school. If there is a specific issue to be discussed, for example if a pupil has a tendency not to finish their maths homework, a parent might connect this with the child's tendency not to see things through in their life. Alternatively, the problem may be to do with skills or abilities such as numeracy, or a broader need to improve their concentration, especially if other teachers have noticed this. If their attitude towards the maths teacher seems the issue, only an adult who knows them well might understand why. Confidentiality and trust between teacher and parents should allow for a frank discussion about personality issues as well as the professional standards offered by the school.

Most parents have an understandably broad interest in their child's life at school, from their peer friendships to particular skills and talents, so if there is a focus in a review meeting, it should be named at the start. Willows High School shares pupil tracking and target setting information with parents at academic reviews as well as discussing the year's work with them and the pupil. Monitoring progress over time requires a consistent framework for assessment that can be shared with parents.

▬ Year 7 case study: Willows High School, Cardiff, Wales

Willows High School introduced Review Days following a staff training day on target setting organised by their Assessment Co-ordinator. The staff had been discussing the role of the form tutor within the school so when the opportunity arose to focus on action planning with individual pupils, it was decided form tutors would pilot the new approach. Baseline attainment levels of all Year 7 pupils in 1997 were obtained through reading age tests and core subject National Curriculum levels (Key Stage 2 results were sent from primary schools at the start of the autumn term). Target setting began with Year 7 as the school's major strategy to improve standards of achievement.

Year 7 form tutors were involved in additional training on interviewing skills. They were supported by a Working Party responsible for developing and implementing the initiative. The Working Party produced an interim report sheet, on which each subject teacher was asked to comment on each pupil. The pupils were asked for their own assessments and ideas about how they could improve. Their form tutor, stressing strengths and weaknesses and areas for improvement, then completed the reports and subsequently posted them home, with an invitation to parents both to comment and to attend a 15-minute interview with the form tutor and the pupil.

The aims of the interview were clear:

- ▪ To discuss the pupil's work individually with his/her form tutor.
- ▪ To highlight areas for improvement.
- ▪ To agree specific ways in which to improve in these areas.

Another innovation of the scheme was to allow all Year 7 pupils to work at home throughout the day of the interview, with work provided to be brought to school the next day. In this way tutors were available throughout the day, supply cover costs were minimised and parents were involved in making special arrangements in order to be involved in a special and important meeting. The same process and arrangements were made for data collection, reviewing and interviewing at the end of the year in July. The Review Days have been popular and well attended.

- The process of review has been incorporated into the half-hour tutor period so that every pupil has time with their tutor twice per term to reinforce the targets.

- Over a four-year period, staff skills in setting targets improved and the strategy was extended to the three subsequent year groups.

Willows High School: Timetable for Academic Review Day

Monday 14th June	Year 7 & 8 exams start Review sheets available in staffroom for gradings using criteria Attendance & punctuality from start of year up to 11th June Examination % can be added when available
Tuesday 22nd June	Examinations end
Friday 25th June	Review sheets completed → Form Tutor
Wednesday 30th June	Year team meetings (discuss setting appropriate 'smart' targets)
Friday 2nd July	Pupil comments & Tutor comments completed, sheets photocopied Letters sent to parents with review sheet, copy of grading criteria and appointment slip
Friday 9th July	All appointments complete
Tuesday 13th July	Review Day Year 7 → Learning Centre Year 8 → Resource Centre

Target sheets for review days

	pupil's name	year	grp	date set	to be completed by ⇒ by		TARGET MET
TARGETS 1							
2							
3						teacher _____	

Llanrumney High School in Cardiff has also introduced an Academic Review Day.

LLANRUMNEY HIGH SCHOOL
TARGETS SET ON REVIEW DAY (NOV 1999)

NAME [   ]   FORM [   ]

TARGETS		
TARGET	**DATE ACHIEVED**	**STUDENT COMMENTS**
1.	/ /	
2.	/ /	
3.	/ /	

SIGNED: [   ]   FORM TUTOR

SIGNED: [   ]   PARENT

SIGNED: [   ]   PUPIL

Target setting

Two important considerations need to be highlighted from the out-set:

Targets are **one-off activities concerned with improvement**; they represent an opportunity to get to grips with specific aspects of the overall job – they are not the job in itself.

Growth is incremental and begins where the individuals are **now**, not where the teacher hopes or believes they should be. **Developments must be planned in achievable stages.**

SPECIFIC   The target must be as definite as possible, thus avoiding ambiguity.

MEASURABLE The target will be expressed as an end result not as a process or activity, e.g. '... to produce a report' rather than '... to evaluate a scheme'.

ACHIEVABLE   The target lies within the ability and the author-ity of the appraisee. Sufficient thought must also be given to the time allowed for the activity.

RELEVANT   The target must focus on an essential/core part of the work and not on any peripheral activity.

TIME LINKED The target will have as an integral component the dates for completion. This will not only focus the mind and effort of an already busy person but will assist in ensuring that the target is achievable.

Key issues found by staff at Willows when setting 'smart' targets:

- Need to establish baseline assessment (as precise as possible)
- Important to put strengths and interests up front
- Need for clarity – what is the difference between curricular needs and learning objectives
- Targets should be precise, realistic and assessable
- Difficult to separate some needs into curricular and non-cur-ricular
- Timescales – need to identify length of time for targets – related to overall needs of pupils

> - Often easier to identify strategies and methods for achieving targets than the actual targets themselves (no problem if outcome is the same)
> - Need to clearly record who is responsible for what and when
> - Pupil involvement necessary at all stages
> - Acknowledge resourcing issues
>
> At the end of Key Stage 3 all pupils will receive a report containing their attainment in their Standard Tests together with comparative national and local data.

(Willows High School Staff Handbook, pp.87–8)

At this sort of meeting, parents have time to respond to the teachers' comments about how the pupil works and behaves in school, with reports and targets acting to give detailed information about the efforts of those who support that individual pupil. Teachers and parents can then share what needs to be done from their different perspectives and suggest what the pupil needs to do, as well as what sort of support they can each provide. To reach this outcome, both need to feel they can speak freely and honestly. The teacher's facilitation of the meeting determines the extent to which this will happen. Training can be provided to support the staff adopting this role.

Introducing this event will also have an impact on both curricular and pastoral decision-making across the school. If the staff involved have the scope to feed information from parents into policy development and discuss individual progress with relevant colleagues, they will start to occupy a pivotal place in school development strategies. They will develop an overview of the effectiveness of assessment and marking policies, and will learn what parents understand about homework, behaviour, discipline and academic progress. It is vital that this understanding and knowledge is discussed with colleagues and relayed to middle and senior managers, so that suggested areas for improvement can be monitored. The Review Day should not become an isolated annual event because of the many opportunities presented in these individual meetings for improved home–school dialogue throughout the year.

In the examples above, the work with parents is integrated with developing the younger pupil's awareness of their individual achievements. As pupils develop a greater awareness of their own capabilities, their contribution will become an increasingly important part of the meeting.

Year 10 case study: New Heys Community Comprehensive School, Liverpool

New Heys Community Comprehensive School introduced Year 10 Pupil Reviews in 1999 which have now been adopted for every year group.

Aims

- To provide the form tutor, pupil and/or parent with a realistic amount of time to engage in a purposeful overall review of their performance.
- To enhance the form tutor, pupil and/or parent relationship with respect to academic tracking.
- To allow for the identification and analysis of trends in performance across the curriculum.
- To set realistic targets for action to help the pupil make progress.

A Pilot Project

1. The Year 10 parents' evening will be replaced by a Review Day.
2. Year 10 will be working at home. A study pack will be provided.
3. Each pupil and parent will have an appointment to come into the school for 15 minutes to meet with their form tutor to discuss their progress.
4. The form tutor will follow guidelines to discuss how the pupil is coping with GCSE study, what the pupil does well and why, areas of concern, attendance/other areas, and an action plan with targets and deadlines.
5. The Head of Year will be available and supported by the Senior Management Team. A Senior Manager will telephone any pupil that misses an appointment immediately.
6. Pupils will still have their interview if the parent does not attend.
7. Pupils are expected to wear full school uniform.

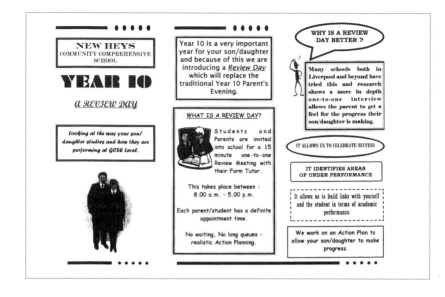

Evaluation – responses from tutors, parents and pupils

Form teachers

Strengths

- Attendance was much higher than previous parents' meetings – four forms out of seven attended 90% and higher, two forms 80–85%.
- Form teachers commented that the day proved successful.
- Fifteen minutes was just the right amount of time to give a meaningful summary of progress and engage in a discussion.
- It was more relaxing in that there was no rush or queue, although some staff found the nature of the work tiring.
- It gives the parents and teachers an opportunity to get to know one another.
- The action plan required pupils really to think about what they could do to improve their grades.
- Positive and constructive dialogue took place.
- Parents/pupils attended, and liked the privacy and one-to-one arrangement.
- Pupils were genuinely interested.

NEW HEYS
COMMUNITY COMPREHENSIVE

YEAR 10 GCSE REVIEW

**MY PERSONAL
GCSE ACTION
PLAN**

Name: _____

Form _____

**COMMENTS FROM
THE REVIEW WITH
MY FORM TUTOR**

This is the personal record of _____

Review Date _____

COMMENTS TO NOTE FROM MY REVIEW

MY PERSONAL ACTION PLAN

I need to _ _ _ _	By _ _ _ _
1	
2	
3	
4	

General comments or reminders

Areas to address

- More time is needed to prepare.
- Teachers can feel vulnerable and isolated.

Parents

- 'Good idea. I found out about my child's behaviour.'
- 'It is a change for form teacher and parent to meet. This is good.'
- 'Support from the teacher was excellent.'
- 'It encourages the child to do better.'
- 'I would like quarterly reviews to monitor performance.'
- 'This encourages a higher standard of work from problem pupils.'

Pupils

- They felt free to ask questions and to talk. They felt this was important at their age.
- They welcomed the revision pack.
- There was less waiting than in a normal parents' evening.
- They liked the action plan and would like it followed up.

The Review Day is a practical example of how teachers can share responsibility with parents while maintaining their respective relations and roles. On an affective level, it vividly confirms to the pupil that the two worlds of school and home are co-operating in order to further their development. Like a conversation between parents who live apart, it captures the strength of the bond and shows them that regardless of differences, disagreements or conflict, both parties care enough to take an active interest. The pupils belong to both worlds, and are not being asked to take sides.

The staff members who are responsible for talking with parents at Review Days will develop their practice, skills and understanding in sharing information and negotiating with parents within a very structured meeting. Their ability to use their experience in other types of individual meetings with parents will depend on how staffing for work with parents is organised, and the skills of the staff who are responsible for the work. The next part of this chapter explores the roles, responsibilities and abilities of staff who work with parents.

Where responsibility resides

Talking with parents at an early stage will help teachers to understand the family, their culture, and the resources available in the home environment to support their child at school. At primary level, it is recognised good practice to talk with parents when a teacher notices a child's sudden mood change or out of character behaviour. Day-to-day contact with parents is practically easier, and primary teachers can also talk in more familiar terms, as they build personal understanding of pupils quite quickly. In secondary schools, parents rarely meet teaching staff and may themselves be working or unavailable during the day. General discussions with parents are just as important if a member of staff notices a child is unhappy at school or in a particular lesson, but it is rarely clear whose responsibility this is. The staff who do get to know parents may depend on their role in the school and the needs or behaviour of the different children (dealing with lunch money, uniform, or medication, marking late arrivals, interpreting or supporting special needs). An adequate system for communicating between staff as they get to know pupils is important. Records or notes can be passed from non-teaching to teaching staff, and subject teachers need to share with the responsible person how the individual pupil engages in different lessons, to create a foundation for the work necessary if a pupil needs more support. Form tutors sometimes have a clear remit to make contact with parents when necessary.

Communication with parents is inevitably part of every teacher's job, in that all teachers deal with homework, assessing progress which is reported to parents, behaviour, and systems of rewards that can be especially powerful when parents are informed, such as through praise cards sent home. Non-teaching assistants are increasingly taking responsibility for early stage conversations with parents. Communication about welfare issues and behaviour is often conducted by form tutors, but if a non-teaching assistant already has good relations with a family, it may be more effective to delegate the initial conversations to them. The head of year's role is often to co-ordinate different types of communication, so that parents do not receive a praise card one day and a disciplinary letter on the next. A record form kept in the child's file summarising all contact with the family will be useful. Pastoral specialists may well see work with parents as an integral part of their jobs, in which case the responsibilities of other staff will need to be clarified so that they know what is expected of them. It might be agreed, for example, that communication with parents about subject progress, including homework, can be initiated directly by subject teachers with an agreement to pass the matter on to the tutor if talking with the parents does not result in improvement.

The form tutor's role is a difficult one because they are responsible for understanding and integrating the personal, social and intellectual qualities of a child, whereas subject teachers are not: *'A tutor is a teacher whose subject is the pupil herself'* (Marland, 1997). In order to maintain an overview of individual pupil behaviour, aptitude and progress, they need to be regularly informed by subject teachers and assistants. The pupil's style of engagement with work, teachers and their peers provide information about their coping mechanisms and personality. The tutor's ability to guide their pupils will be shaped within tutorial time, in which their relationship with the same pupils is reinforced day-in, day-out. This time provides a gateway between home and school life, even if the size of the form group makes individual time difficult. The larger the group, the more tutors will depend on their colleagues for individual information about every child. They also need to be informed about *ad hoc* conversations held with any form member's parents by their colleagues. If they co-ordinate curricular and pastoral aspects of school life for individual children in this way, they may want to handle all face-to-face meetings with parents. The system chosen needs to prepare those staff who are responsible for communication with parents to discuss individual pupils' whole personal development.

The opportunities organised on a whole year basis to meet secondary parents face-to-face should be carefully allocated to staff in accordance with their role, as they are infrequent and command limited resources. There are few occasions that cannot be delegated to form tutors, provided these same staff will maintain the relations with parents and get to know families over a sustained period of time. If this is not possible, key meetings such as individual Home–School Agreement meetings with new parents will need to be conducted by more senior staff, who are likely to remain in that role for several years. It helps if form tutors and heads of year do not change frequently, so many schools arrange for children to stay with the same form tutor and head of year, at least for the first three years of secondary school, if not the whole five years. In some schools, it is felt that the changes during adolescence are so extreme that a 'step-change' between Years 9 and 10 helps pupils to make the transition into Upper School more easily. Schools with a sixth form often change pastoral staffing at the end of Year 11. Much will depend on the behaviour of children at the school, as coping with a change of tutor requires a personal effort and can be disruptive. A handover and clear documentation in individual files are essential if tutors change. The new tutor will have to meet parents afresh, and can combine these meetings with an age-appropriate induction of pupils and families into the demands of the year ahead. These meetings are necessary even if the tutor remains the same, so the decision may depend on how many staff wish to take on the form tutor role and how many existing tutors have built up family relations that will be valuable during the demanding older years.

Those who are primarily responsible for ongoing discussions with particular parents will need to arrange other occasions, apart from annual reviews, whether structured or informal, to build and maintain good relations before a problem arises. Small meetings with all parents of a tutor group can be held once a term, for example. If a problem arises, it is unlikely it will be resolved from one brief discussion, so the teaching timetables of those responsible for talking with parents need to be examined to ensure that appropriate time is available.

By differentiating between first and second stage communication with parents, it may be possible to define the roles and responsibilities of staff who undertake different aspects of the work as part of a wider staff team effort.

First stage: Parent's Contact Person

A member of staff should be named *Parent's Contact Person* and it should be spelt out that this is the person with whom a parent or carer can communicate at any time during the year, with the pupil's agreement. This is usually, but need not always be, the form tutor. Many schools leave parents to work out for themselves that the form tutor is in fact the person they should contact. If the child has a special needs assistant who is in regular contact with parents, it could be more appropriate to name them as the contact person. If the child is from a minority ethnic family where languages will create communication barriers, it might be best to ask a teacher who speaks their community language to be the family contact. Non-teaching staff will need the list of PCPs. As day-to-day communications with parents (about sickness, medication, lunch or missing equipment) are usually shared between office staff and the teacher concerned, a record of these types of contact should be given to the Parent's Contact Person too. Responsibilities of the Parent's Contact include passing on information to other relevant staff, within agreed confidentiality guidelines.

Second stage: more focused discussions

Ensure a member of staff with a substantive post takes formal responsibility for sustaining good relations with the school, even if there are problems that require the involvement of other staff or outside agencies. A basic trusting relationship with the parents throughout a pupil's school life is essential for their well-being and progress.

Form tutors are best placed to co-ordinate discussions between different subject teachers and support staff who work with a child. If a child is not coping with schoolwork or friends and the Parent's Contact cannot shed light on the situation, or if there is an issue with a particular colleague, the form tutor may need to make a request for the involvement of the head of year. The history of attempts to intervene and the tutor's analysis of the problem help the head of year to decided whether to get involved directly, or to support the Parent's Contact or tutor behind the scenes by discussing their approach separately. Teachers' own notes on discussions held so far will help at this stage.

It is appropriate for year heads to get involved with a family if tutors fear the pupil may otherwise quickly reach the final sanctions available to them, such as suspension or exclusion. In schools where the work with parents to improve pupil behaviour at an early stage results in fewer crises, there is less need to involve senior staff. Special Educational Needs departments have greatly improved their relations with parents in many schools, and staff within them can offer insights on working with parents.

▆▆▆ The involvement of support assistants

A school community where learning is encouraged not just by the teachers but by a range of staff with different qualifications enables non-teaching staff who are parents themselves to keep this experience in mind and see they have relevant skills. Their support might be especially valued at a time when teachers are being encouraged to focus in on the specialist cognitive framework of teaching rather than on pastoral work, in keeping with the trend towards increasing specialisation within staff roles. Their perspective, given a different career experience to the majority of professional teachers, can bring a greater acknowledgement that 'pastoral' work with families is specialist and requires specific skills. However, many teachers welcome a mixture of pastoral and curricular responsibilities and may perceive the involvement of assistants as a threat. Opportunities for teachers and non-teachers to discuss the work are crucial, to prevent an artificial split emerging between 'personal' work with individual children/parents and 'professional' work with class groups. Clear line management of support assistants can provide a structure for communication about their work as well as increasing opportunities for delegating initial work with parents. For the continuity of school relations with families, it may not be possible to give support staff responsibility for more than first stage communication with parents, as many assistant posts are sessional and hours can vary from year to year.

Many assistants who support behaviour or learning without professional qualifications are in a suitable position to talk with both parents and teachers about an individual pupil. Their stated motivation to enrol for the Open University course is frequently to help their own children by gaining access to professional knowledge.

> *'Most, it seems, are working in schools because they are parents. Work in school enables them to work when their children are at school and to be available as mothers when they are not.'*

(Hancock and Cable, 2000, p.4)

They are then put into a role that requires them to support the delivery of the curriculum, by understanding what the teacher wants. The two main areas of the job of a Learning Support Assistant are improving behaviour and enhancing individual pupil learning skills through work with individual pupils and small groups on and out of the classroom. They are frequently directed by teachers to achieve specific tasks, just as pupils are. The position they occupy helps them to see school life through the eyes of the uninitiated children more easily than the leading professionals. Subsequent descriptions of their experience in the teaching assistance role convey their increased confidence, in addition to identification with the pupils, and their sense of belonging within the school community also increases over time. As a result, they have a range of appropriate knowledge and many will have the ability to translate the inner workings of the school and current education policies into ordinary language.

Given the tendency for teachers and parents to encounter difficulty in making meetings effective and informal, the parenting experience of mature assistants can ease the communication problems quite substantially. They are likely to have an appropriate level of identification with parents. They might explain emerging problems tactfully to parents, with a high level of empathy and sensitivity. They are likely to be interested in child and adolescent development, even if their own children are younger. Of the 364 who started training with the Open University on their Specialist Teacher Assistant Certificate course for primary helpers in the year 2000, 362 were women and a great majority were parents themselves. Most were paid rather than volunteer school helpers. The average age was 38. The Open University course includes study of their role, how children learn, working with teachers, working with groups, working with individuals and home–school relationships. All are topics equally relevant to the secondary environment.

From information given by participants over the four years it has been running, it is possible to predict the range of interests, skills, and experience of the majority at the start of their employment:

> *'Family life has helped my skills in terms of patience, tolerance and understanding. It has also developed my skills at motivating children and being a good listener – skills I use daily in classrooms. I believe that children have to believe in themselves before they can learn to the best of their ability. Having my own family has given me insights into the stages of child development. I know that children develop physically, mentally and emotionally, although not always at the same rate as each other. Maturity can be dependent on a lot of factors and experiences – the birth of a baby or an upset at home can considerably affect a child's learning at school. From my experience, play and conversation are excellent educational tools and are often not used enough in schools. Promoting independence in children is a main aim for me as a parent and as a Classroom Assistant.'*

(Hancock and Cable, 2000, pp.3–4)

They can occupy a position on both sides of the home–school divide, holding the role of a neutral third party or advocate for pupils and families. This is often uncomfortable, as they have reported that some teachers see them as 'attached' to a particular child rather than helping the adult teacher, and so do not talk to them. Furthermore, Dr Roger Hancock, Lecturer in Education at the Open University, comments that teachers sometimes dissuade relations between parents and assistants, despite the experience and appropriate social skills of assistants. In a sense, these workers bring the divisions and the difficulties of a multi-class, diverse environment into a formerly homogenous staff team where one profession has dominated.

Assistants could aid creative solutions to problems in home–school relations in three ways:

- Classroom support requires a different approach to teaching. Adults who circulate in the classroom become very aware of an individual's off-task behaviour – and thus can provide important information at parents' evenings and in other discussions about pupils.

- Assistants might forge stable relationships with families so that behaviour problems can be resolved with less anguish on both sides.

- They can also hold an important role as a third party in teacher-initiated meetings with individual parents.

The case studies in Chapters 4 and 9 of administrative and project work at Deptford Green School demonstrate that home–school differences can be moderated by recognising the talents of third party workers who are familiar in the school but free of the expert status of teachers. Yet little has been written about the detail of their work or the communication skills that they evidently employ on a daily basis. The interviews with Roz Ryan and other support workers (in Chapter 9) illustrate the kind of role that can be played with both parents and teachers.

In Langdon School, nineteen of the twenty-two Learning Support Assistants are parents themselves. Their responsibilities for supporting home–school dialogue include helping children who have special needs with living skills and travelling independently back and forth between home and school. They have become specialists in dealing with individual children, in contrast with the large group management skills of the teachers. In cases of severe relationship difficulties, it has been observed that Learning Support Assistants could benefit from further training in order, for example, to prevent the child becoming dependent on a particular assistant in a way which replicates their communication difficulties. Appropriate training courses might increase their capacity to bring special knowledge from a wider pool of experience than their own, while holding onto the value of their own life experience. Existing courses in the fields of counselling and child development offer skills and theory to increase the conceptualisation and understanding of the dynamics in learning support work, and tend to include guidance on the use of one's own life experience in an interpersonal working relationship.

There will certainly be an increase in the numbers of paraprofessionals working in secondary schools in the near future and they may be usefully directed to work at the home–school interface to prevent problems developing at school.

The responsibility of senior managers

If a meeting with a parent is the last resort in a crisis, the task of contacting them often falls to a senior manager. Although meeting with senior staff can help parents to feel they are being taken seriously, it can also escalate a problem prematurely. The tendency for cases where parental involvement is needed to go higher in the staff structure than is really necessary can, for example, lead to children reaching exclusion point without a school taking all the necessary measures to prevent a downward spiral in behaviour. Headteachers and senior teachers may still conduct the bulk of meetings with parents simply because they became accustomed to doing so during industrial action by other teachers in the late 1980s. It may also be because teachers over the age of 41 feel more confident to deal with parents, as expressed in a recent survey of teachers' attitudes (ATL, 2000, p.27). As older staff members have more experience of adolescents in their school careers, dealing with parents of adolescent children may feel less threatening. But interestingly, respondents refer to life experience, not the teaching role or existing teacher training, as most helpful to this work. It is important not to lose sight of the value for the pupil concerned of talking to their parents, because those most comfortable with the parents may not be best placed to work directly with individual pupils. Fine communication skills do not accompany age in all cases by any means, so it should not be assumed that older staff handle meetings with the best results.

The ATL survey shows that younger staff urgently need to feel more confident to maintain their responsibility for work with parents. They will then be less likely to refer problems upward in the hierarchy as discussions progress. Face-to-face meetings with parents may become difficult, but involving any new person midway can be counter-productive. If the staff member holds a powerful position, they will need detailed information to take over from someone else, otherwise they may purely be in a position to deliver a stricter message rather than working to solve the problem. If they are too busy to deal with the issue properly, parents can feel suddenly obliged or pressurised to agree with them, or make unrealistic promises. Guidance from more senior colleagues or a line manager outside the actual meetings with the parents can be more appropriate and helpful. Clear whole school policies can also support the staff member with first line responsibility to sustain discussions with parents.

In Deptford Green School, Lewisham, 'job descriptions' have been produced to reflect the key tasks involved in responsibility at every level. These help to prioritise responsibilities listed in Teachers' National Terms and Conditions, reinforcing the particular values and ethos of the school. Work with parents is given a high priority.

Deptford Green School Staff Handbook

HEAD OF YEAR

The Job

Year Heads have a responsibility for the overall progress, social and academic of the pupils in their year. They lead a team of tutors who work together to implement school policies and to ensure a consistency of approach to the situations that arise.

In order that the Head of Year builds up a complete and ongoing record of each child in all aspects of its development throughout its school career, the Head of Year and the team of tutors will move up the school with his/her form from Years 7–11.

The team of Year Heads is co-ordinated by a Deputy Head to ensure that there is a common approach across the school and that similar standards are expected from all year teams.

At the heart of the job there must be a commitment to raise the achievements of all pupils through organising the best efforts of a team of tutors.

The job of Head of Year demands considerable knowledge of the pupils in the year, negotiating skills, patience and stamina among many other qualities.

ACTIVITIES AND RESPONSIBILITIES

Curriculum

To be central to the school's drive to raise achievement through:

Listening to comments from pupils and parents about learning experiences and feeding them into staff discussion as appropriate.

Liaising closely with Heads of Department and making themselves familiar with departmental expectations.

Ensuring pupils understand the implications of choosing subjects in Year 9.

To enable staff to understand and develop the potential of all pupils by making them aware of all the information on a pupil's ability and performance and by working with them to set targets.

To monitor the setting of appropriate homework for the year across departments, in accordance with school policy and the homework timetable and to act upon information gained appropriately.

Management and administration

To ensure suitable records are kept of all aspects of the team's work with pupils and parents.

To record and monitor attendance figures and to ensure tutors maintain full, completed registers each day, follow up on unauthorised absence and complete weekly percentages. To work with the tutor team to maintain a high level of attendance.

Staff management, support and development

To lead a team of tutors developing their pastoral and tutorial skills and building a sense of team spirit and co-operation.

To devise pastoral and tutorial activities appropriate and specific to the year group that fit within the pastoral aims of the school and dovetail with the work of the other years.

To ensure that through inset and the observation of good practice the year team experiences professional development.

To liaise with and to support colleagues in the classroom through discussion of strategies and clearly defined procedures for dealing with behaviour problems of individuals or groups of pupils.

To be available to staff both before and after school.

Assessment, recording and reporting

To ensure that through the reporting and monitoring systems individual pupils' progress across subjects is closely monitored and appropriate action taken to enhance and support that progress.

To organise the tutor team to liaise with subject teachers, learning support staff and teachers of statemented pupils to monitor the progress of pupils of all abilities.

To ensure effective communication with parents and to ensure they are kept informed of pupils' progress, including the organisation of parents' meetings.

Staff skills and abilities

The aim of almost all discussions with parents, whether formal or not, is to identify how the child could progress in school with encouragement from home. Parents can only help if they understand what their child faces in that environment, and it is a skill to help adults to learn without making them feel patronised. A member of staff who inadvertently puts them in the place of a pupil will impair their freedom to ask questions.

The success of meetings often depends on the talents of the staff involved. While many staff already talk constructively with parents, it is rare that these are articulated in the form of the range of skills and abilities employed.

Preventing problems with pupil behaviour and progress

Skills

- Conveying respect to adults – parents, carers, visitors and other staff
- Using clear non-educational language
- A non-patronising manner which communicates equality of personal status with parents and all non-professionals in the school
- Not making assumptions on the basis of class, culture or individual ability
- Arranging appointments with realistic timing
- Conducting meetings with clear aims, within the agreed time
- Observing details in conversations and unspoken communication

Abilities

- Noticing strengths in parenting
- Self-awareness
- Communicating informally but efficiently
- Showing empathy for parents
- Listening and creating space for the other to talk
- Naming the important issues
- Combining emotional and rational understanding
- Detachment when appropriate from the classroom role

Experience/Understanding

- Personal experience of parenting children and adolescents
- Stages of child and adolescent development
- Possibilities within families and individuals to effect change
- Role with parents as a school representative
- Boundaries in relations with parents

- Degrees of confidentiality of pupil information
- Own manner and style of communication

This list has very different features to the equivalent specification for a classroom teacher. It is not surprising that newly-qualified staff express such a need for support and training, and even experienced staff find talking with parents challenging. If a school has not already decided on staff responsibilities for work with parents, one way forward may be to assess who is most suitable for the work within the current school staff. All staff can be asked to assess their own level of confidence in these areas on an annual basis, through in-house questionnaires. Senior managers can then develop a strategy to ensure those most suitable are given the required responsibilities, or such an exercise can help to decide which staff to move into vacant pastoral positions as they emerge.

In-school support for staff

In brief telephone conversations, the emotions of a parent may dominate the first few minutes of the conversation. Usually, it will have taken a lot of deliberation and some nerve to pick up the telephone; it is not done lightly. In reaction to the parent's stress levels, the coping strategies of a teacher are uppermost and can detract from a constructive conversation, creating an impression that they want to leave the conversation by reassuring the parent too hastily. The teacher at that time may not be in a frame of mind to listen to more than the basic facts and may push feelings about the query aside. After listening to the problem or query, arranging another time to talk or an actual meeting may be a better way for both parties to think calmly.

Support from others will help a member of staff to reflect on the experience after they have dealt with parents. If there is a clear line manager or mentor who can provide this support, their guidance may be sufficient and developmental. Other methods may also be suitable.

Observation

If a teacher is willing to share their experience with colleagues, it is interesting to arrange for another staff member to sit in on a meeting as an observer. Space to think about one-to-one conversations with parents helps the teacher to become more effective. Observation is one common exercise where it is difficult to think on one's own about a problem; it aims too to develop a teacher's self-awareness. An observer helps to reflect on and develop understanding about how the conversation is likely to accomplish its stated aims. During the meeting they need say little or nothing, but after the meeting they can feed back what they heard so that the teacher can gain from another point of view without feeling judged. This may become standard practice so that parents and pupils expect to meet more than one person; if not, it will be necessary to check that there are no objections to the new arrangement, and to ensure that very confidential information will go no further. As Grace Marriott writes,

> 'It is important that the observer is not someone to whom the pupil might feel hostile.'

> (Marriott, 2001, p.41)

The observer's role needs to be neutral, and the conversation with the teacher afterwards should include reference to what both parties appeared to want to achieve in the meeting. Both practical and psychological factors are relevant:

> 'As an observer you will be looking at the effectiveness of the interviewer in establishing a positive atmosphere where parents and pupil are confident that they will be dealt with fairly. Has the teacher prepared properly for the meeting and let the parents have all the relevant information in sufficient time? If an interpreter is needed, is it someone in whom the family will have confidence? Do the layout of the room and the seating arrangements help to establish the right sort of atmosphere? ... Are there opportunities for the parents or pupil to ask questions and put their point of view? ... The interviewer might be particularly good at putting people at their ease or summing up the decisions which have been made. You should be able to explain how this is achieved, for example the ability to focus on the issues and not the personality ... If an interview has not gone particularly well then it should be possible to work out why. If the parents did not understand the issue, did the teacher try to restate it in different ways? Was it suggested that a brief break to allow someone to calm down or get over being upset might be helpful?'

> (Ibid., pp.41–2)

Further professional training courses often recommend using video to observe. It is a more private means of being objective about a subjective experience. Detachment can be important because many obstacles in joint working are due to powerful fears and feelings, on both sides, that are too intense to observe in oneself. Teachers will develop the confidence to think during the meeting about the issues at stake and how the child will best benefit, instead of reacting automatically and defensively to apparent criticism or complaints against the school.

▄▄▄ Teacher support teams

Teacher support teams were originally developed for team support in work with pupils with Special Educational Needs, akin to a confidential problem-solving case conference. Their suitability for work with parents comes from the vehicle they provide to acknowledge a teacher's individual frustration and normal feelings, allowing discussion of an emotional dimension which becomes a valid subject for study. Many professionals that find the personal world of the pupil is otherwise somewhat taboo, even when the nature of their work with parents relies on emotionally-charged and personal interactions. In a pressurised secondary environment, it is essential that a teacher develops the ability to recognise stress and finds *'open and collaborative organisational structures'* (Daniels, Creese and Norwich, 1998, p.120) to support the most difficult work. Teacher support teams offer a structured method to receive confidential support from colleagues and practical ideas for improvement in work with particular children and families. They aim to improve listening, convey new strategies or interventions with pupils and their parents, and encourage teachers significantly through collaboration that reduces the inevitable isolation of the lone secondary practitioner. They will also contribute to professional development, which requires an under-recognised ability to assess oneself privately and honestly in order to improve one's skills.

The teacher support team model consists of an established team of three peer teachers, which is convened by any teacher to discuss for half an hour, at least once, the issues surrounding a particular case, whether a pupil, their parent or a group. The motivating factor is usually a difficult problem in a particular case so more than one meeting may be necessary. The facilitator needs to ensure the group listens to a full history of the problem and the work so far, without interruption, and private notes are kept of advice given in order to review its effectiveness.

Teachers can experience difficulties when parents are powerful or lose their self-control. It can be frightening, particularly if a teacher is young, to have to deal with emotional situations with parents when one is experienced only in working with children. The force of an adult's anger can be upsetting. Allowing the parent to be heard and maintaining the strength to contain their feelings while thinking how to achieve a constructive outcome are quite advanced skills. In many cases, the parents who are most worried for their children are the most caring, so a teacher needs to listen and convey respect for their feelings, before asking for the same respect in return. Teachers have to develop their skills in these difficult areas from week to week and examples of real conversations rarely have a forum for discussion which is confidential or properly attentive. Through this sort of peer support, teachers can learn from each other in a systematic way.

Academic discussions

It is important to create a forum for discussion, such as an after-school seminar, in which a range of perspectives on home–school work can be discussed. Discussions may help the development of awareness about the starting point for encouraging parental involvement, or increase clarity about the different roles played by staff. Including non-teaching staff in seminars is important.

It is sometimes hard to remember that both teachers and parents acquire expertise in child development, albeit from different perspectives. A parent knows an enormous amount about their child that would be inappropriate to share with the secondary school, so they need to judge carefully what to say in every conversation with a teacher. The task of improving communication with parents will be seen to have a concrete outcome when they can voice their personal understanding of their child in a way that is useful to the child's progress at school. Teachers need the skills to facilitate the parent's contribution as well as informing them about how they and their child can contribute and participate in the school community. Some staff members evidently possess the skills to do this, but few staff teams discuss systematically why meetings are successful, or disseminate good practice in working with parents.

Opportunities for professional development

Good practice in meetings with parents goes beyond both classroom and pastoral work. The teacher's manner differs from that employed in the classroom because the teacher is talking with an adult, and often about individual human issues, rather that discussing academic topics with adolescents. In addition, affective and psychological sensitivities when discussing a child's character and behaviour with the people responsible for bringing them up cannot be underestimated. The communication skills and abilities deployed can be seen as professional skills, but are mainly named as such in professions other than teaching, such as counselling, psychology and marketing. In schools, they prove essential in more senior posts so access to these responsibilities should not be limited to other workers or non-teaching professionals who come in to work within the school setting. Once a teacher has decided they would like to aim at middle or senior management positions, work with parents can help to bridge the leap up into the supervision or management of colleagues.

▩ Other links

Serious problems that interfere with a child's attendance, homework or ability to concentrate may be due to a housing problem in the family, or a mental health need of a carer. Once such a problem has been discovered, the teacher responsible will need access to other staff colleagues with special experience or links with services in the local community. All the children's services outside school need to be linked in with the school without requiring unrealistic levels of staffing. A letter from the headteacher will then prove useful. Listing the special links of each staff member in the staff handbook, along with any community languages they speak, will be useful in work with parents. The responsibilities of the link person are simply to get to know key staff in that department, such as housing, social services or health, and keeping in touch with them, referring particular families to them as the need arises.

Once a regular cycle of events and meetings with parents have been developed, and staff responsibilities clarified, further professional development in face-to-face work will be possible. The next chapter explores the dynamics of this type of work more fully.

8 SKILLS AND THEORY FOR ONE-TO-ONE MEETINGS

Face-to-face discussions become landmarks in home–school communication because parents of secondary-age children develop an understanding of the school at a distance. Most information about the staff and pupils comes gradually from listening to and observing their children. Written information specifically for parents is usually brief. The only contact they have with schoolwork is that created actively by teachers, in the form of reading, projects or homework appearing regularly. What they hear and see will vividly convey the specialist nature of the work, the range of subjects and the number of different teachers involved with their child. The differences between their child's experience and their own memories of school are likely to make them feel remote.

Individual meetings become unique, rare opportunities as they give information from an adult perspective about several dimensions of school life at once. They enable parents to forge a human link with a fairly closed world so those who attend (and feel the effort was worthwhile) tend to value one-to-one meetings extremely highly. They often wait long periods of time before speaking about a problem, firstly to see if it improves without them and then waiting for a 'good' moment to arise which may be the next event at the school perhaps in several months' time. If the personal contact is unsatisfactory, the memory lasts a disproportionately long time. If the meeting goes well, discussions in person can reduce time-consuming problems at school.

Unfortunately, new or young staff members can dread meetings with parents, and try to limit them. Even experienced teachers can find it difficult to make time for one-to-one meetings. Some teachers do not feel comfortable prioritising those who have the confidence to ask to see them. Others find it daunting to face the issues in the lives of the parents who appear in the most difficulty. Speaking a professional language can be a problem, necessitating 'translation' for the general public before the matter can properly be discussed. Schools are generally organised for large meetings, making it difficult to devote time with individual parents. Ensuring that parents' queries will be heard properly rather than dismissed or quickly explained away, in the middle of a busy day in the midst of a busy school, is an art.

Developing one-to-one meeting skills requires an interest in the detail of interactions and human psychology. As there is little debate about these sorts of conversations during teacher training, it will become important to create a forum for the discussion of good practice and relevant theory between staff in the school who see work with parents as part of their professional development. In the preparation, conduct and evaluation of one-to-one meetings, staff will benefit from wide-ranging further training to enhance and develop their skills.

Pre-meeting considerations

The first priority is to make parents feel they can trust the school representative. Without trust, it can seem too difficult to be honest with each other. The success of initial personal contact will be determined by preparation before the meeting. This will involve thinking in advance how to keep to agreed times, reminding oneself to carry out agreed action and promises, and planning to get to know each other so that the conversation is not just one way.

Social, cultural and class differences make mutual trust more difficult. The comprehensive environment is a general leveller amongst the pupils, but exerts less influence when talking one-to-one with adults. Personal differences reassert themselves and in some ways counterbalance the anonymity of group culture in a mainstream school. Hearing an individual parent's thoughts and feelings will help the listener to get beyond apparent barriers of background and education. Accents, eccentricities and unconventional behaviour can otherwise seem out of place in the school setting, and unusual mannerisms or habits of speech create embarrassment or affront. Parents who do not observe normal courtesies, such as knocking on doors or shaking hands, can cause discomfort, especially if the teacher is not familiar with their culture. If teachers see these individual factors as interesting, they will initiate rich conversations about the personality and culture of pupils. First-hand information from parents will help teachers to understand how resourcefully they support their children, whatever their economic situation. Home life can also be the main site for a child's cultural education, which teachers may otherwise never hear about. Private conversations can build a foundation from which both parties feel comfortable to ask questions about each other's environment. The benefits can influence policy-making and the whole school ethos. For instance, learning about actual home lives in individual meetings can prevent teachers from making class-related assumptions.

Teachers might be able to bridge differences by remembering examples of when they have themselves been in a similar situation to the child who will be discussed. This can help parents to feel less formal and awkward. Similarly, if the teacher understands during the meeting how the parent is feeling, they should say so.

Parents who have not visited the school before, or have never met a particular member of staff, are likely to be feeling rather nervous. Attention to interpersonal details in the meeting will help to allay their fears.

Names

Using the correct name or style of address (in some cultures using first names is inappropriate) may make an enormous difference. But pressures in the school environment result, on embarrassing occasions, in forgetting names or getting a parent confused with another. If necessary, ask a member of office staff to telephone in advance of a meeting or before sending a letter to get the names right. Check you are speaking about the same child, and make sure the parent knows who you are at the start of the meeting. Do you feel comfortable with them knowing your first name? If you do, you will have to make it clear that the pupils call you 'Miss' or 'Ms' or 'Mr', not by your first name. Respect for the original culture of the individual can put a discussion onto a more personal footing, if you are comfortable trying the form of address that a person of a different culture would be most likely to use. If this is not possible, share the school convention with them and ask if you can similarly call them by their family name (surname) too.

Official names and 'Known as'

Ensure staff ask parents for official names, e.g. 'As we will be entering your child in examinations, we need to know which names are on the birth certificate or passport.' The form that records basic information about each child on their entry to the school needs to have space for several names and parents who remarry should be encouraged to inform the school of any change of name.

Multi-cultural considerations: Naming systems

('Welcoming Parents to Your School' pack, produced by INCLUDE,
adapted from resources developed by Leeds City Council department)

RECORDED INFORMATION			
Surname:		Forename(s):	
Chosen name:		Known as:	
Gender:		Date of birth:	

(Langdon School format)

The meeting itself

The intense dynamics in work with parents demand skills, abilities and understanding in a new framework for the training of teachers and non-teaching staff. Existing teacher training courses do not acknowledge that staff will need to meet and talk with parents, and may not articulate the unique interpersonal dimensions of one-to-one meetings. Furthermore, expertise in this area is rarely documented, because it is intrinsically hard to generalise about the complexity of individuals and their relationships. Adam Phillips argues that one needs to revise one's notion of 'a professional self' in a counselling role, and similarly professionals in schools will find it difficult to hold broad and honest conversations with parents if they try to retain a formal style. Competence when with parents can only come from resisting one's expert status and using skills hardly ever taught to teachers.

Improving individual meetings at the school

- Hold individual meetings in an appropriate environment that suits the nature and confidentiality of the information that both parties might need to introduce.
- Talk with a range of other teachers before the meeting and gather specific examples of how the pupil behaves and manages in class.
- If there is a problem, think how to phrase an open question rather than a complaint about why their child might be behaving or working in this way.
- Prepare yourself for an extra dimension to your role in a meeting with a parent – as well as being a teacher, you are an adult who shares joint responsibility for their child.

▓▓▓▓ Psychological perspectives

The psychological effects that accompany visiting a school or talking with a teacher help to identify the skills and understanding needed to work with parents. The mother interviewed here brings her experience as a professional in the field of psychology to analyse the dynamics of difficult one-to-one meetings.

> Schools provoke profoundly conflictual feelings in parents. Teachers need to be aware of the extent that parents regress on entering the school or encountering a teacher. Memories of their own schooldays, their current dependence on their child's teachers and identification with their own child, all combine to make parents feel like children themselves.

> But even while feeling so peculiarly powerless, they are painfully aware of their responsibility for their children and toward their children. Hence they approach interviews with teachers feeling needy, guilty and anticipating a ticking off rather than a mutually beneficial exchange of views. Fearing blame they easily become defensively blaming.

> Parents are inevitably reluctant to contact the school. And when they do they might sound hesitant, apologetic, or aggressive. They worry that any approach they make to staff might rebound badly on their child. Imagine an interview with the police – they might protect or prosecute you. A parent might beg for help from the teacher but also wish to protect their child from the teacher.

> The teacher can feel an equal reluctance to encourage a parent to approach the school. But they do need to give the parent permission to talk. The permission has to be specific to what the school needs to know. If the teacher on a first meeting tries to get to know the child via their parents, with a phrase such as "so tell me about your child", the parent feels at a loss – it's too open. They do not know what the teacher needs to know.

> The teacher, consciously or unconsciously in touch with parental expectations and aware of their own limitations, can feel as nervous as the parent. When a parent voices a fear about their child, the fear can't be

heard because of the teacher's levels of anxiety. The teacher identifies as a parent figure – as part of the school power structure – yet like a child they feel accountable to the actual parents.

Both parent and teacher feel inadequate – both are likely to have very high expectations of the other, unrealistically high expectations that provoke idealisation and defensive denigration. Both suffer from guilt. Mutual distrust and defensiveness ensue. Opposition impedes co-operation, although a sort of pseudo-cooperation can be achieved by banding together against the child rather than in the interests of the child.

Co-operation only develops when each manages to hold onto their fears, making it possible for the other to have their say. For example, if the parent voices a concern, rather than dismissing it – or pouncing on it – the teacher can avoid an anxious or defensive response and encourage the parent to elaborate their worries. Both can contribute to the child's well-being if they can put aside guilt and an 'it's your fault or my fault' frame of mind.

Parents are hungry for honest appraisals of their child's strengths and weaknesses. A pooling of information focused on specific behaviours of the child is important, whether in connection with work or relations within school. Parents need to be given enough information for them to ask questions. Simple written information prevents parents from feeling excluded and disempowered and enables them to support their children.

(Rozsika Parker, psychotherapist and parent of two children
at secondary school)

The feeling of being a child that a parent experiences (and other adult visitors to schools comment on it too) makes them afraid of being intrusive or excessively demanding. Influences can be working on an unconscious level – determining thoughts, words and behaviour without either party being aware of the underlying dynamics of the conversation or situation. This makes it very hard to deal with. The feeling might register consciously but momentarily as a parent physically approaches a school building or a headteacher's office. It can also be recreated in a parent's mind as soon as they think of a school, not just when they actually visit, which is why their reluctance to talk with staff extends to times when they might consider contacting the school and hastily dismiss the idea. After the feeling has surfaced, the familiar coping strategies of that adult when they are put in this sort of situation reassert themselves. It is these coping strategies that a teacher will encounter, and will need to handle with a sensitivity based on what the parent is (was) feeling but with the aim of finding non-threatening ways to discuss a solution.

The setting of the meeting, on school grounds, and the feelings of the parent when they arrive, make it likely that the teacher will carry more power than the parent, at least initially. The starting point is not equal and one task for the teacher is making it feel more balanced, so that the parent can contribute and speak up. To redress the imbalance of power, invite them to contribute to the discussion as an adult, rather than confirming their position as a childlike one of ignorance or lack of understanding. Create an atmosphere of equality by describing the problem as specific to the child at this moment in time, rather than a label for life, and asking, 'So what can we do about it?'

Interpersonal 'transactions'

The psychodynamic school of Transactional Analysis can be used to consider interactions between parents and teachers to show why difficulties arise. Three parts in the human mind that can be simply represented as Adult, Parent and Child were described by Eric Berne in the 1960s.

In Brown and Pedder's outline of psychodynamic principles and practice, the help-seeker relation to the help-giver is explored. This bears direct relevance to the situation of a meeting in school between adults about a child's progress.

> Let us ... consider various situations where any person seeking help (on the left) may consult any help-giver (on the right). Parent, Adult, and Child parts of each are represented by P, A, and C (*Figure 2*).

Figure 2

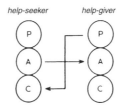

If, for example, we take our car to the garage for a service, this should remain an emotionally neutral, and therefore purely Adult–Adult, transaction or working alliance (A ↔ A, *Figure 3*). However if, for example, we go to our bank manager to ask permission for an overdraft, we might think we have perfectly good grounds and that this will be a purely Adult–Adult transaction (A → A) and then be taken aback to find the bank manager behaving like a heavy handed and lecturing parent, as if we were a demanding child (C ← P, *Figure 4a*). On the other hand, we might go along feeling like a guilty child asking for more pocket money and expecting a stern parental refusal (C → P); we may then be pleasantly surprised to find that the request is granted as a perfectly reasonable one and that the manager treats us straightforwardly as another adult (A ← A) (*Figure 4b*).

Figure 3

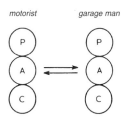

Figure 4a   *Figure 4b*

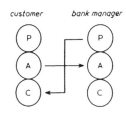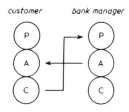

If we consult a doctor about a fairly trivial and emotionally neutral problem (for example, an in-growing toenail), this should remain a straightforward Adult–Adult transaction (*Figure 5a*). But when we are more anxious about ourselves, or when acutely ill, we tend to regress to more childlike levels of functioning and invest doctors or nurses with whatever good or ill we may have felt towards parental figures in the past (*Figure 5b*). As we have already said, this matters little in acute illness as it is readily reversible. How, indeed, could a patient requiring emergency surgery permit a stranger to cut into his flesh unless the child part of him were capable of considerable basic trust and of investing the surgeon with goodwill as a benevolent parent figure?

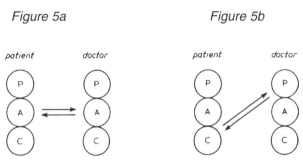

Figure 5a   *Figure 5b*

However, the same regressive phenomena may cause problems in less acute medicine and not be so easily reversible. For example, in the past the admission of patients to remote mental hospitals for long periods robbed them of their adult responsibilities for feeding, clothing, and supporting themselves. Treating them as children, and thereby infantilizing them, exposed patients to the risks of institutionalization and added to whatever underlying disease process there may have been.

(Brown and Pedder, 1989, pp.59–61)

Professionals in role, in a position of power, will almost certainly be used to starting the conversation in meetings. This may be appropriate if they have called the meeting and inappropriate if the parent has requested the meeting. With polite parents as listeners, an initial introduction by the teacher can extend to several minutes or even lead to the teacher talking for most of the time available. Teachers can also find that from talking, the other person is silenced. If they speak for more than a few minutes at a time, the parent may rapidly find themselves listening silently as if they were back at school. If one finds this has happened automatically, it can be changed by being aware of the need to take conversation onto an adult–adult footing. The teacher could, for example, express a concrete difference between their role in the classroom and their role in this meeting. The atmosphere created will then be one of dialogue and partnership. Slowing down and analysing every moment of a meeting in which a parent was mainly silent can develop a teacher's self-observation skills.

'We <u>transfer</u> feelings and attitudes developed in earlier similar experiences, espe-cially where there are no particular clues available as to how we should react.'

(Brown and Pedder, 1989, p.58)

It is important to give the right 'clues' to the parent as early in the meet-ing as possible. Agreeing the aims and structure of the meeting with them at the start can help to situate the parent as a participant instead of a recipient. Sharing the teacher's own experience of parenting or car-ing for children might create a bond of understanding. Stating explicitly that the teacher is learning about their child makes it clear why they are listening closely to the parent. Indeed, by understanding and seeing the parenting influences to which a child is subject, teachers can develop more effective strategies for behaviour and learning.

During the meeting

- It is paramount to create an adult atmosphere which invites a parent to speak up. Even if you have called the meeting, wait for the parent to volunteer information after a short introduc-tion. A brief explanation of the purpose of the meeting should be sufficient, making it clear that both parties will speak and lis-ten to each other.
- Expect to ask questions and to listen rather than talking at length about the school's perspective.
- Set the scene by including reference to your respect for a par-ent's role. Counterbalance any feelings of vulnerability if these emerge. Acknowledge their role in the education of their child – the invisible army providing clothes, food, shelter and moral support to the best of their abilities so that children can make it to school in a reasonable frame of mind.
- Try not to seek to gain the upper hand or be right.

NITS – Neurotic Interlocking Triggers

Imagine a scenario in which a young female teacher, who prides herself on performing well, confidently gives a good report to a bright suc-cessful pupil's (older) parent and seeks reassurance that the parent is pleased. The teacher feels the need on a personal as well as a profes-sional level to obtain the parent's approval. The parent's response will depend on how they can relate to a young teacher, and in the moment of communication, what memories or feelings her first words created. If they had a daughter who did not tell them much about school, but sought their approval out of insecurity, they might feel suspicious (or irritated, fobbed off, anxious, nervous). The teacher's praise and attempt to curtail the meeting to a brief report might then elicit closer questioning, such as about a detail of the pupil's behaviour, or whether she could be given harder homework, making the teacher feel deflated, or disappointed. The teacher might react defensively; even if she managed to respond professionally, she might feel inhibited to give the parent what they wanted, not just because this could set a precedent for other requests, but because their questions make her feel undermined, like a pupil herself instead of a teacher!

Most 'normal' people have their own neuroses, which help to make them into the unique people they all are. Our psychological make-up enters into our choice of career and professional identity, as well as our style of parenting. Margot Sunderland at the Institute for Arts in Therapy and Education describes situations in which a couple's 'NITS' contribute to the downfall of their relationship. Neurotic behaviour and reactions are provoked (triggered) for personal reasons, sometimes reasons in the past that the other person may not understand. They come into play in an exchange that sustains or embodies a current relationship. They appear as an area of sensitivity, and if the person we are with then feels provoked for *their* own reasons, an impasse can result. Real contact or relatedness is prevented by repeated incidents in which these sensitivities are expressed but not understood. Separation and, in the context of a marriage, divorce can result.

When the relationship is between people who work together, their work is bound to suffer and may be untenable. When the relationship is between a parent and teacher, they can either avoid each other, or the separation can result in an educational 'divorce', if the parent takes their child away from the school or the school excludes the pupil. In a school where home-school relations are dysfunctional, teachers are very isolated. If parents are able to take matters into their own hands, teachers can feel emotionally attacked, because they cannot avoid parents who come in to see them. So schools with a high proportion of professional or middle-class parents are likely to do the most work to keep relations good, in response to parental demands; other schools may find middle-class parents drifting towards these schools.

In the scenario above, the teacher wanted to create an impression of the pupil that represented her work fairly. A major difficulty is that the teacher would be expected to take the lead, and would need the skills to facilitate the discussion whatever the parent's response. A start might be to find an area where they agree that the pupil could improve their effort or understanding, and discuss what both could do to support the child's development in that area. Either party might get stuck in one position, such as the 'child' position of seeking reassurance, or the 'parent' position of 'are you good enough?', and not be able to move freely between ego states as would be helpful and healthy. They would then find it difficult to resolve the miscommunication.

In *Games People Play* (1966), Berne characterised interactions as gentle or violent games, naming stages that can be progressive – from first-degree games to second- and third-degree games. Most exchanges in schools are first-degree games and will not end up in court. But situations can go that far, particularly if the child's exclusion or their access to special resources is at stake. Teachers can usually spot a worsening situation. In conversation,

- One person can spot the game and move from parent to adult or child to adult.

- When the person complaining feels powerless to change the situation, the other person gives an empathetic response which shows their feelings are being heard and understood. For example, when a professional is suggesting many solutions and keeps getting 'Yes but ...', they can stop suggesting and say instead with empathy, 'It must be hard to feel as if your child is out of control', which can help the parent to move from a passive role.

How to create productive synergy, rather than retreat or conflict

- The power held by teachers may command respect or fear, so it has to be handled with care. Listen for how the parent perceives you before assuming or expecting that they will treat you as an equal partner immediately.
- Ensure your remarks will form the basis for a dialogue, in which power is experienced alongside and together with a parent as a person of equal stature, rather than over another or from another. Maintain the aim of creating adult–adult dialogue (Berne). If the parent seems either deferential or overbearing, try to ask questions that invite an equal adult response.
- Remember the importance of negotiation and partnership: 'We can', 'Let's do this'.
- Try to observe pupils through their parent's eyes so that you can identify the pupil's emerging abilities to cope with independence. A parent can see the positive in the child, which is a resource. From there, it may be possible to see why they struggle.

▰ Skills and abilities

The skills, abilities and understanding necessary to conduct effective meetings with parents need to be articulated for the professional development of teachers responsible for home–school relations.

▰ Conveying respect and equality of status

Every parent or carer has already shown the strength to bring up a child over many years and it is therefore well within their capabilities to support their child's education. The ability to think positively is important, even if the strains on them deserve sympathy. One can be sympathetic without losing sight of the point of the meeting. Reassuring underconfident parents that their situation is not unique is crucial at moments when they feel worried about how to work out a difficulty. The more questions that a parent can ask about education, the more they are likely to believe the school is inclusive and open. Questions, however odd they seem to a teacher, may reveal that parent's background or ignorance and require sensitive handling. They provide an opportunity to learn what parents think and know. The way in which we reply will reflect our own needs for authority and status.

▰ Self-awareness

Once a staff member has started to be aware of the psychological and emotional dynamics inherent in this work, they will hopefully become more interested in their own reactions to parents. Self-awareness is a challenging, fundamental and enduring feature of professional development. It increases the choices we have in how we relate to people, in both our professional and personal lives. Professional development that can help individual staff should emphasise self-awareness in emotional conversations. Local counselling centres may have qualified staff with training experience who could run an INSET session to develop the self-awareness of staff who meet with parents regularly. Teacher's skills and confidence in relating to parents relies on their ability to use their emotional selves in their work as well as their capacity for rational thinking.

Imagine a parent sees a phrase about providing school equipment in a home–school agreement and asks what this would be and how much it will cost. A teacher who can respond neutrally, aware of the various possible reasons for the question but not assuming the question comes from an inability to afford the equipment, is likely to be able to state the school's position clearly. A teacher who feels prompted to reply apologetically or defensively out of embarrassment may be unintentionally misunderstanding the reason for the question and inadvertently patronising the individual in front of them. Their guilt or sudden subtextual alarm may be, for example, because of their knowledge that in the area of the school families are poor. An apologetic manner introduces into the atmosphere their subconscious or even unconscious thought about the parent as one of an 'other' group, making a bond of understanding with the individual parent more difficult. Once they have got to know the parent better, it may be appropriate to convey sympathy with the parent's feelings about the matter. But until the response is based on genuinely knowing this individual's feelings and thoughts, it will only be an expression of the teacher's own concerns.

An attitude of 'It is not my fault if the parents do not make themselves heard' can reflect weariness on the part of the teacher. This may not just be a result of their levels of tiredness, it could also have been created in the atmosphere of a meeting if the parent is feeling worn out. Being in touch with what one feels before a meeting helps to separate one's own issues from that of the parent.

Avoiding an emotional cue, such as a note of hesitation in the parent's voice, or an arched eyebrow, can lead to misunderstanding. Unless cues are picked up, the parent may assume that you agree with them, whatever they are thinking. Or you may both pretend it is a minor issue. It is a mistake to think a problem will go away – it will simply appear elsewhere, such as on the day when the sports equipment is first needed. The objective of the meeting must be to sort out any possible difficulties, not to delay them appearing. Facing difficulties and making it clear that the parent is not alone in sorting out such things will mean you can both get on with the task of arranging how to overcome any possible obstacles to the new pupil being an accepted member of the school community.

The importance of being oneself

A genuinely anxiety-free response to tension expressed by the parent will make private matters easier to talk about. False reassurance is unlikely to lead to good results. Either the parent will sense it is false, harming the development of a trusting relationship, or the teacher may find they do not do what they promised because they were not genuine in their intentions. It may seem moralistic or simply obvious, but honesty is extremely important.

If teachers make mistakes, parents will see they are honest and human from the way they discuss their own error, rather than covering it up. If there is a disagreement, the important thing is to stay in touch and tolerate the conflict rather than avoid each other. Many adults will be able to work on the problem sensibly.

Empathy

The quality of empathy is enormously helpful in discussions with parents, but by definition it cannot be learnt or applied like a technique. In *On Becoming A Person*, Carl Rogers describes empathic understanding of a client by a therapist:

> '[When he is] sensing the feelings and personal meanings which the client is experiencing in each moment, when he can perceive these from 'inside' as they seem to the client, and when he can successfully communicate something of that understanding to his client.'

(Rogers, 1967)

Empathy is a communication in dialogue, understanding what things mean to the other on the basis of hearing them express themselves, and letting them know that you have understood, whether through word or deed.

Listening

Listening is not just hearing the words, but hearing and digesting the words and the context of them, and hearing the feelings behind them. The art of listening has been developed further within and beyond the humanistic field since Rogers was writing in the 1960s. It requires a separation between what one is feeling because of the other's feelings and what is there because of one's own feelings. Simply expecting one's intuition to be right can lead to dreadful assumptions about what another person is thinking or feeling.

The quality of the teacher's listening is important, because only by putting together information gathered from the parent with what they need to know from the school can the teacher find a direction for the conversation. Listening does not mean agreeing with the parent or saying nothing in response. It does mean making space for the other to express themselves and to communicate their thoughts or feelings. It is fundamental to conveying respect of the other, in the sense that it allows them to 'be' instead of occupying the entire space in the meeting oneself. Partnership, still an ideal more than reality in home–school relations, can only begin to emerge from mutual respect and an atmosphere of working together rather than lecturing each other. When people are not used to listening, they may not notice how much of the meeting time has been taken up with them talking. They would not then be in a position to know whether the other has decided to support their point of view or not.

▓▓▓▓ Space to talk

The skills and manner of the staff member and their presence in the room will create space for the parent to speak honestly. What happens if a question mark in the parent's mind is hanging in the air during a meeting? If the parent does not directly voice a concern, how will the teacher find out what this unspoken question is about? A way must be found to help the parent to voice their thought – by guessing or asking directly if they have a question or if they are worried about anything. Direct questions have the disadvantage of putting people on the spot so that even if they would like to be open and honest, they end up avoiding the question because they feel too uncomfortable to answer straight away. Informal conversation about a relevant matter might be helpful. A calm and patient look without any words might be all that is required to give the parent the signal that their feeling has been noticed. If providing the space for them to talk does not help, or silence persists for too long, an indirect reference to questions or worries may help. From my observations of teachers in small meetings with parents, it is common for silence that would have been helpful *for the parent* to prove too uncomfortable *for the teacher*. A teacher is used to working in lessons and large meetings where they or other adults are talking whenever people are interacting at all. Waiting for another to speak without feeling impatient (such dynamics can be sensed by the other which makes them feel rushed) is a skill that in many schools is not learnt through talking with the pupils. A rule of thumb to keep in mind is not to be afraid of silence.

Sometimes giving parents space to talk may result in more than is bargained for. Perhaps the parent's hesitation in the example above about PE equipment is actually to do with practical domestic arrangements in the wake of a difficult divorce. Children often stay in more than one home in such situations, and both parents might need a copy of the agreement, or at least good information from the school, to organise kit for different days. Perhaps behind the question is a worry about the mixed gender environment and where their child will be changing. If your child was going on an adventure holiday with a local youth group in the first week of your moving to that neighbourhood, you may have similar questions in your mind. Schools sometimes assume that, because they are government-regulated, parents should automatically trust them. This is much easier when you work inside a school, and see the care that goes into planning, safety and staffing. Parents may have no such inside information and those from other countries may not be able to imagine all the arrangements made in the education system here to protect their children.

▬ Ask open questions

'Open' questions to parents are more useful than closed questions which merely require a 'yes' or 'no' answer. Open questions are those that start with a 'what', 'how', 'why', etc., requiring a fuller answer. Explore an issue before commenting on it. The research on parents' evenings interactions by MacLure and Walker (1999) shows how often teachers try to close down conversations and remain in control of them. In general, they would benefit from enabling the parent to make more of an active contribution than traditional reports allow.

▬ Naming important issues

Resolving doubts in the parents' minds is a stage further from listening well. It may be necessary to summon up the courage and skill to name difficult issues. The language you choose here should communicate that you are describing the action, not the child. Parents may be helped to understand a bad report by clarifying that the teacher concerned is not commenting on their child's whole character, merely their behaviour or progress in a specific area. Plan with them how to overcome a problem rather than delivering a diagnosis that implies their child is fundamentally flawed. Observations should reflect the teacher's understanding of the problem rather than purely criticising – it is better to explain: 'My worry is that Peter will not learn to concentrate if he does not learn some self-discipline now.', or 'How can we help Kim to get on better with her classmates?' than purely 'Jo keeps interrupting me in class and bothers other children too.' Roger Ellis, former Master of Marlborough College, has commented that in his experience parents are frequently shocked at the different behaviour of their children at school compared to home. It can be useful to describe the whole situation in which the behaviour arose so that the parent can recognise aspects of their child's behaviour, instead of assuming they will believe your word over their child's.

▬ Confidentiality

Pupils can feel betrayed if teachers do not respect the privacy of certain conversations. Sometimes just knowing, without mentioning that you know, is enough. It may be necessary to agree with a parent that they will tell their child whom they have told about a home issue, in case the pupil needs to talk with someone who will understand.

Understanding

Child development

Studying how children develop in terms of personality and behaviour as well as academic ability can be a rich form of further training for pastoral staff and non-teaching staff with pastoral responsibilities. It can help to create a language for how maturity develops and thus can help staff to find a common language with parents about pupils.

Theorists and practitioners have increased our ability to conceptualise and describe the development of children. Child development researchers and child psychologists have advanced professional understanding in health and social services of how children grow and thrive. Those who work with disturbed or troubled children outside schools have, during the twentieth century, articulated what nurturing entails, from infant development through to adulthood. Nurturing is a skill that involves holding the child in mind and helping them to deal with relationships as well as attending to their physical needs. In the psychoanalytic world, writers have focused on the mental influence of early relationships and Melanie Klein emphasised the mother–infant bond in particular. The child psychiatrist, D. W. Winnicott, said *'there is no such thing as a baby'*, a radical statement to emphasise the infant's emerging sense of self in the context of others as he later explained:

> *'I once risked the remark, "There is no such thing as a baby" – meaning that if you set out to describe a baby, you will find that you are describing a baby and someone. A baby cannot exist alone, but is essentially part of a relationship.'*

> (Winnicott, 1962, p.137)

His contribution to contemporary thought includes a memorable description of the process by which an ordinary devoted mother 'thinks her child into being' – *primary maternal preoccupation* or *a maternal reverie*, which allows imagination to play a valid part in child rearing. Self-immersion into what is real to the baby gradually weans them off illusion and helps them to understand and accept what is real outside themselves, in the world. Birth mothers have held the child in their body, which gives their feelings a particular intensity and they very gradually over time achieve the physical separation necessary to send them to school. Any main carer who holds the child in mind is performing a crucial developmental task – she (or he) nurtures the child's presence of mind, ego strength and ability to think, which continues throughout childhood, alongside the teachers who share this responsibility. It is natural for a parent to devote intense thought to their child's well-being and developmental potential.

Attachment theory

John Bowlby deepened our understanding of how caring helps a child to become secure from infancy. His ideas, and further work by child specialists after him, articulated how security of attachment promotes a young child's ability to grow into an independent member of society and to learn.

> *'Evidence shows that the toddler who knows his mother is reliably available when he needs her can use her as a secure base from which to venture to explore his environment. He can concentrate well and play independently because he feels safe ... Attachment to mother may become less secure when mother goes out to work, gives birth to another sibling, is depressed or bereaved. However, as the child grows older his attachment pattern becomes increasingly a property of himself, and is less responsive to changes in parenting.'*

(Hopkins, 1990, p.16)

Infant and personality development provide fascinating insights into how an internal sense of security leads to independent thought and behaviour throughout life. Just as these child psychologists used their understanding of normative development to work with disturbed children, pastoral staff may find theories of development useful in grounding their approaches to dealing with pupils with problems. They may themselves be performing some of the functions of a parent, noticing when an individual child is about to lose self-control or needs to increase their self-esteem in order to do well at school. Coping strategies that adolescents use often hark back to how they learnt to cope when much younger. So by noticing when a teenager feels insecure, a teacher can present this sort of situation to a parent for a discussion about how both parents and teachers can help the teenager to learn to cope better when these feelings are experienced.

Schools also need to take on board what other carers can tell them. Another family member may have become a key figure teaching children how they can look after themselves and cope away from home. Fathers and grandparents, and figures outside the family, from friends to childminders and teachers, are all providing formative relationships within which children learn and grow. But although caring may be divided between them, and particular teachers may offer similar qualities and skills as carers, the relationship to mother is still special and to some extent completely unique. A mother may not publicly value her own contribution, but her sense of how a child will cope at secondary school could provide an important perspective for teachers whose responsibility it is to stimulate the child's thinking skills. Mothers deserve special respect, however self-effacing they appear.

A mother's worries about their child and possible solutions to problems at school are often irritating to the teacher, either contrasting or competing with their own style of emotional attachment to the children in their care. Kindness in dealing with parents who are anxious should reflect a perception of their abilities, not make them feel that they are 'not good enough'. Although the majority of teachers are women and many are parents, very few in their role as a teacher exercise an understanding of how mothering engenders self-esteem. The professional education environment seems to de-gender many of the interactions that take place and to monopolise the culture of meetings, even between women. The secondary environment is even less forgiving of the kind of thinking a parent has to do to work out constructive solutions with their children in mind.

A parent's nurturing differs crucially from a teacher's influence in the development of the child. A parent who strives to be better, or the best, and is not confident with their parenting or satisfied with their child as they are can foster personal insecurity and harm the child's self-esteem. Winnicott invented the term 'a good-enough mother' to help to describe the humanity necessary in parenting rather than mechanical perfection. Bettelheim (1987) extended Winnicott's term to embrace all in a parenting role, coining the phrase 'the good-enough parent'.

Being judgemental when presented with descriptions of behaviour management at home that we do not identify with needs to be carefully checked, and put aside until we understand the family interactions, unless, of course, there appears to be a perverse element or risk of danger to the child. Our judgement of what a good-enough parent will do may be culturally-specific and need to be adjusted in certain communities. For example, in some cultures, separation is not regulated at the same pace as in western societies, so security may be created over a longer period of time by a larger number of people. These differences will then be reflected in different habits, which sound odd to those brought up in this society, such as sleeping arrangements in South American families where families normally share space at night and find privacy in the day (Morelli et al., 1992). Assuming the mother is over-protective because she still allows the child to sleep with her may be missing a consideration of her background. Nor should the options open to her be judged as limited by her origins – she may find it helpful to be presented with other choices that arise from the family's move to the UK.

Systemic thinking

The sense of self of the child determines how they respond to control and authority over them by adults, and this sense of self is formed by the interactions they have with adults and peers throughout childhood. Consistent and reliable adult figures in a child's life sustain communication with a child or adolescent that deepens their relationship over time, with meaning attributed increasingly independently by the child. Systemic views place the child at the centre of their individual network of relationships, including all the adults and peers who have an influence on their attitudes and behaviour. The saying that it takes a village to raise a child has thus been given a frame of theoretical reference. By focusing on the importance of relationships in the process of development and change, solutions could involve anyone significant to that child. No figure, whether parent, aunt or grandparent, can be excluded from the system of influence. Several parties might be involved in bringing about change, such as when pressure in one relationship is alleviated by someone else in the child's network.

Experienced teachers will also know how children behave badly at school when they might feel compelled to behave well at home, for example when they are trying to preserve peace between their parents or having to shoulder adult responsibilities outside school. Difficulties in one environment can be processed emotionally in the other, and have an immediate effect on a child's ability to learn. Communication between the adults concerned can be the only way to piece the different parts of a child's life together. One of the points of influence in a child's sense of security is at the interface between the different adult figures.

Children integrate their learning from both home and school environments. The exact significance to each child is a matter of individual complexity. For example, when a child uses different accents with different audiences, they may not believe it is safe to be 'themselves'. Other children in their class can help the odd one out if they accept everyone is different, or at least try to understand how someone is different instead of simply feeling they are strange, and avoiding or teasing them.

Another instance of predictable difficulty in an individual pupil's endeavour to integrate home and school worlds is where they find a lesson does not make sense to them, because at home they do not have the same codes, values or customs. Learning about the cultural backgrounds of children in the school will help to avoid misunderstandings with both pupils and their parents.

Theories of self-esteem

If a child develops self-esteem, confidence and ease of communication with others, learning can become a pleasure rather than an ordeal. A child with appropriate self-esteem is more able to make use of critical feedback, whereas a child with low self-esteem may be too fragile to do so. The care-giving environment at home is the main place for the development of the self and all consistent relationships have the power to make a difference. In the modern-day field of personal development, the power of relationships has been studied and detailed interactions are analysed, using affective language (*affect* is emotion associated with an idea or set of ideas). Affective terms acknowledge that feelings are integrated with rational thought. In a false dichotomy easily made between thinking and feeling, emotional development can be relegated to the parent's role instead of acknowledging its part in the interventions made by all adults who care about a child. Emotional development is not confined to the home and relates fundamentally to a child's ability to learn. Teachers can raise or lower a child's self-esteem over a period of time.

The impact of a child's experience of school on their self-esteem is seldom studied, but common sense and seeing school life through an individual pupil's eyes, as form tutors or mentors do, help teachers to monitor how each pupil is developing overall. If a parent makes an emotional appeal, where for example bullying, racism or another distressing personal or social problem is reported, teachers often respond quickly, showing an understanding of the urgency of the issue. If a child is severely distressed, their feelings are often easily understood and accommodated by both individual teachers and school systems; for example, some teachers can put on their comforting parent's hat – 'to come when they cry for help' – or a system may be used that sends the child to a sick room or home. But where a situation appears less urgent, few teachers have time or patience to respond. When a parent tries to talk with them before there is a serious or obvious problem, it appears too difficult to make time for a conversation about the general development of their child. This is short-term thinking given the parent's privileged view of their child's overall security and happiness at secondary school. Parents can also be unduly alarmed on the rare occasion when a teacher does talk with them, because they have not been given enough information about their child's behaviour or friendships at school to make a judgement about the seriousness of the reported problem.

▒▒▒▒ Adolescent development

An off-putting factor in encouraging meetings with parents is noticing how little adolescent pupils seem to want contact between the two groups of adults. Yet unless teachers and parents find ways of communicating that survive independently of the children, pupils are in a better position to control the amount of contact parents and teachers have. The child who does not want adult supervision may be purely acting on a natural instinct during adolescence – to assume their power as individuals with a voice. Because they need space for their own development, they cannot necessarily facilitate the inclusion of adults in their life at either home or school. Thinking in even more rigidly divided terms than adults, they rarely relate the involvement of their parents to their learning at school. They often perceive their parents' right to know about school as part of their home relationship with them, not as part of their school lives. They can also prove their emerging adult power by dividing parents and teacher in order to try to control information that could make their lives more difficult in the short term, such as not passing on letters or not informing parents that they have a detention. If no one is home after school anyway, why tell parents that the lateness is for this reason rather than blaming it on a delayed bus? It is a parent's job to assess whether a child is right to keep adults at bay or is in fact restricting their own development by separating influential figures in their lives. When communication proves worthwhile and appropriate, pupils welcome it.

During the early years of secondary school, challenges for individual children include coping with a large number of teachers who know a lot about the subject and little about them, competing with other children, and developing personal aspirations. Parents who notice that an eleven-year-old has difficulty using reference books out of school time, and offer encouragement by extending searches for information, will be helping at moments when the child is most interested in learning. At this stage, puberty may be approaching, with all the accompanying anxieties and embarrassments, and sharing the school's sex education policy with parents is crucial so that they know what their children will find out and where the gaps might be from their perspective. Physical maturity increases in parallel with a young person's power and desire to manage on their own. The transitions experienced are rarely smooth. Independence, self-interest and surprising moments of childishness are all familiar in mid-adolescence. Wherever a child sits in their increasing maturity, throughout secondary school their parents or main adult carers will still feel ultimately responsible. By this stage, teachers will have adjusted to the growing independence of pupils and may need standard procedures to ensure the school involves parents as well as pupils, not solely one or the other group.

Both physically and psychologically, children seem to mature earlier than they used to and surprise us with their worldly wisdom. Research in the mid-nineties, described in *Transitions into Adulthood*, suggested that different aspects of growing up have become dislocated from each other (Morrow and Richards, 1996). Children feel older sooner, yet live at home longer, and often do not have one main home. They are pulled in different directions by the resulting psychological conflicts. They share emotional and physical growing pains with their peers, but teachers and parents may not understand them as easily as when they were younger. Parents often struggle with the strain of trying to maintain some influence in their teenagers' lives. Despite the image of maturity given by young adult films and towering sixteen-year-olds, and the real maturity heard in young people's voices, parental figures have to find a way to 'parent' young people for longer and longer.

Both parents and teachers today are facing the need to move on from a relationship with a child into a functioning relationship with a young adult in which they become friends as well as responsible adults. Teachers and parents both have to talk with adolescents in an adult way and also to treat them sometimes as if they are young. Opportunities to share their tactics and strategies are helpful and voicing the feelings commonly provoked by pupils will reinforce the alliance between home and school. Parents may not have any experience of other children of the same age or at the same stage of development whereas teachers do. Some parents may try to maintain control over their child's life rather than living with the young person's independent choices. Others may have few worries about their loss of authority and could provide examples for teachers of what they have learnt works well at home. Parents who are having trouble may find it useful to see what is possible when a teacher at school provides a model of how another adult can talk to a teenager. If there is a stark difference between what is expected of them in the two places, pupils might need help to cope better with this difference. Involving the pupil in a meeting with parents can therefore be very effective. Discussing a task or plan of action which will focus some of the pupil's interest in themselves, whether in terms of behaviour or academic work, can also provide a valid way in for the attention of their parents.

It is important to recognise the school's relationship with parents as distinct from relations with the pupils, even if pupils are involved in many of the meetings with their parents. This can be achieved by talking directly to the parent in the meeting so that the pupil can witness the adult communication. The parent's view must be requested, and a working alliance created with them as well as with the pupil. Some direct communication with the parents may need to continue even to sixth form level. At the end of their school career, recognition of the contribution they can make in the wider world may be shared with parents as part of the departure of both pupil and parents from the school. Parents and the pupil will appreciate a personal letter of recommendation to the admissions tutor at colleges or universities as a complement to the formal reports.

Understanding each other's role

Being helpful is defined by Carl Rogers as 'a warm interest', 'wanting to understand' and 'a strong and growing mutual liking and respect' (Rogers, 1967, p.44) – lessons from other professional helping relationships such as therapy can be translated to help teachers who work with parents in schools. Cultivating an interest on both sides seems a challenge. A warm interest requires both parties to care about the child being discussed and also about each other. Wanting to understand is communicated by attention to the detail of listening to each other's needs and thoughts, and a determination to persevere in making the links between the adult's words and the child's situation.

Principles upon which helpfulness is based must be thought through in order to keep discussions appropriate to the goals of the school and parameters of the relationship. Talking with parents cannot be restricted to 'educational' subjects, as 'social' matters may be equally appropriate – drug or alcohol abuse at home, for example, may interfere severely with a teenager's capacity to learn. Keeping the individual pupil's education in mind is important, as is knowing the limits of one's own role. The context of the work with the parents or family can also provide a boundary. At its widest, work within the Special Educational Needs department might embrace a holistic plan for improvement, involving parents in behaviour management, basic skills support and work with a therapeutic family agency, with both teaching and non-teaching staff meeting with parents, co-ordinated by the SENCO. If, in contrast, there is an eruption of bad behaviour by a pupil whose parents have never been contacted before, the teacher whose lesson was disrupted may contact the parents to start with, enquiring about both subject-specific and personal issues on that day. If the picture does not become clear, the pupil's form tutor might have to pursue the task of researching possible causes, and talk with both pupil and parents about it before getting back to the subject teacher. The aim of the school's home–school work should be to help children to develop so that they can learn. It is for this reason that it is quite correct that discussions are initiated with other agencies, such as housing and social services departments. They reflect the part the school may occasionally have to play in supporting the least able parents to provide the basics necessary for the child. The school representative is still contributing to the core learning objectives of every member of the school community.

The parenting role

Parenting attracts assumptions by those who are not parents, which are heard in the ease with which the general public comments on the qualities of a 'good parent' without knowing much about the personalities involved. There are similarities with the idealised role of a teacher, summarised in equivalent generalisations about 'a good teacher ...' that are far from the everyday reality of the task.

A parent's task is famously thankless and their influence is gradual. Teachers who can appreciate strengths in a parent will not just be those who are parents themselves. They are likely to be the most observant and understanding of what individual children need. Parents become interpreters of their child's needs, and during adolescence the wisdom they have gained in earlier years helps them to predict how a child will respond in different situations. Boundary issues may repeat challenges that feel familiar from toddlerhood, and with the advance of years come modern-day challenges like mobile phones and the computer age. The negotiation that allows the teenager to grow up, with a mixture of reluctance and flexibility, is hard work. As the parent takes responsibility for a pupil until they leave home, they will need to understand what the school can do in response to the demands of adolescence, and make parallel adjustments in their management of behaviour, homework or leisure activities. If communication with teachers is difficult, this becomes impossible.

In meetings with parents, secondary teachers need to acknowledge that the parenting role is uppermost in the parent's mind when talking with a teacher, regardless of how they would behave in other roles in life. A parent operates in an intimate domain and feels exposed when talking with a professional about their child. Their vulnerability is compounded when their child is criticised. Teachers who are parents themselves describe meetings with their child's teachers that leave them shaking with hidden emotion, be it anger, fear or joy. It hurts to hear your child criticised, however mildly, by someone you do not know yourself.

The teacher's role

One of the reasons for a school's attempt to contain and control activities at school without the involvement of parents appears to be the teachers' perceptions of the limitless nature of their responsibilities. Teachers feel emotionally committed to children with a depth of feeling that belies their purely professional role. This brings emotional conflict when they have to face another committed carer, a conflict which has a territorial feel. Both teachers and parents tend to keep home and school worlds too separate if they are afraid of the clash of overlapping responsibilities when they meet. The physical distance can imply that all responsibilities are somehow transferred from parents to teachers in the morning and handed back at the end of the school day. There are in fact major differences between the time-bound responsibility for the physical safety of a child on the school site, and the complex responsibility for their mental and emotional development, which is not bound by temporal or geographical limits. Sharing the responsibility for a child is crucial.

It is hard to limit the sense of responsibility because of the evident interaction between what is learnt in life as a whole and what is taught at school. We know that children learn in other environments and not just at school, and teachers do forge special intellectual or personal connections with pupils. These connections can feel particularly sacred when a pupil's home life does not appear to offer them much, but this judgement in itself usually fails to acknowledge how children learn. It is imperative to try to build on a pupil's whole situation instead of isolating their home and school lives, as their overall development will result from how they integrate both.

Even when a child is physically at school, their mind is still not purely subject to the influence of their teachers. But observers have posited the powerful construct of education at school, creating a space and a world to which the child belongs where their thoughts can travel and grow, regardless of the pressures and demands of their lives. In keeping with this idea, teachers hope that external pressures will be kept at bay. Even more poignantly, children themselves try to compartmentalise their lives and cope with school differently from if they were always mindful of outside difficulties. They have a sense of a school self, and a home self. When home 'interferes' invisibly with learning or working, it probably will not be recognised as already being part of that child's mind. Difficulties at school can equally distract a child from thinking and learning. The boundaries around clear thinking space or a pupil's ability to concentrate are confused with the boundaries around school. Home is an 'outside' influence. It is 'guilty' for detracting from the ability to learn. School is the centre of their social networks and support systems, so the idea that home worries are being kept out of lessons is wishful thinking. In fact, the child is relating to new knowledge in the context of existing relations to the world and other people.

Sharing responsibility

A newly-qualified teacher described a difficult situation of inviting a parent to the school who did not speak much English. The teacher said she felt uncomfortable when the parent and pupil were talking to each other in their mother tongue about the issue she had just presented. Her question was 'what is my role in this situation?' It was suggested that she had no active role at such a moment, as she had facilitated a conversation between the appropriate parties and could simply wait for them to finish their discussion, asking for a summary in English of what had been agreed at the end of their talk. The teacher's role was to provide the information and to hold the meeting, creating a shared space with the parent as a partner equally responsible for solving the problem. To say nothing can be a crucial step in itself because it illustrates the trust placed with the parent so that they can assume their own role. The pupil in the room can thus experience the respect that each holds for the other, and see that they will support each other to find a solution without competing for pride of place. Teachers need to share their ownership and habitual control of the school space in meetings with parents to ensure the child benefits from both influences.

Yaacov Katz restates the boundaries within shared responsibility:

> *'There is interaction between these environments but the family is responsible for development in the home, and the school is responsible for formal educational progress.'*

(Katz, 1997, p.14)

Emotional and personal factors evidently impact on formal progress, and therefore have to be acknowledged in the school environment through the systems of pastoral care and communication with the significant players in the child's circle of influence. It is the school's responsibility to help parents and pupils to trust them so that they share this sort of relevant information. Schoolwork done at home or outside school becomes a shared responsibility, shared by parents, teachers and of course the pupils themselves. Progress in schoolwork is dependent on teacher assessment and expertise, and parents are reliant on full information in order for them to contribute and support as necessary. Home influences if they impact on learning – such as a pupil's ability to hear praise or criticism – are issues for teachers as much as parents or carers. We have moved on from an era in which *in loco parentis* was taken at face value.

A modern-day challenge is thus to allow differences and boundaries between home and school without splitting responsibility down the middle too. In a young person's life, division in parental influence can be developmentally unhelpful. Where pupils perceive a split between parental authority figures, whether these be divorced parents or parents and teachers, they find an opportunity to avoid being parented. A feature of adolescence is to try to evade authority, as they assert their independence in the process of growing up. Parents and teachers both experience the importance of thinking through the challenge they are being given. Where the challenge is warranted ('Sir, can we do our homework over the weekend? It needs more time.', or 'Mum, why can't I use the telephone? Sophie does?') and the parent figure decides they need to adjust to the adolescent's forthcoming ability to make adult decisions, they rightly allow them to win. The parent figure is still determining the degree of their freedom, and will increase the teenager's responsibility as they mature and can look after themselves more carefully. Aspects of their development into an adult are being allowed to grow in an appropriate way. Where the adult does not give a thoughtful response, or gives a standard or inflexible response and cannot hear the complexity of the teenager's question, the teenager's development is not being furthered. Luckily in any relationship, there are many second chances and a 'good-enough' parent or a 'good-enough' teacher will learn to handle the challenges as the child learns over time too.

Other approaches

Many teachers comment that they cannot focus on these individual developmental dynamics within their existing jobs. Some manage to incorporate their interest in development and the accompanying meetings with parents into their jobs. When this is not possible, or the need to work with parents to benefit particular children imposes too great a strain on resources, secondary schools have created other projects and services which specialise in working individually with parents and pupils. Staff in these projects tend to have different training backgrounds from teachers, but they need to work within the school's ethos and contribute to an integrated home–school relations plan. Existing school staff will then learn from their work, which will nourish discussions and skill development within the school. The next chapter examines this more specialist work within mainstream schools.

9 SPECIAL INTERVENTIONS

There is a wealth of experience throughout the UK, within secondary schools but on the margins of mainstream educational activities, in special interventions to benefit a small number of targeted pupils and parents. This partly reflects the more acute needs of the pupils who need extra support at any one time, often requiring a holistic response from both home and school to make any impact. Special provision has also arisen in home–school work because of the lack of resources for much work with parents and carers, forcing senior managers in school to look elsewhere for funds. They have creatively built partnerships with charitable foundations and other funding bodies that support the interests of pupils who are particularly disadvantaged. The non-statutory remit of such work with children and families has resulted in projects with broad but essential goals, such as increasing children's self-esteem so that they can cope with school or raising attendance of those likely to drop out of education.

Targeting resources

These in-school projects and activities have addressed home, school and environmental factors from a multidisciplinary perspective, acknowledging that indirect barriers to basic educational attainment need to be tackled with immediacy rather than referring children to external agencies. As this type of support is resource-intensive, involving a higher level of individual attention than class teaching, it needs to be focused on pupils and families who are identified by indicators such as school attendance, cognitive ability test scores, reading ability or behaviour problems. Indicators such as these clarify that referral to a project is non-discriminatory and based on an objective need for extra support.

Staff responsible for the special interventions described in this chapter have encouraged hard-to-reach parents to contact schools more confidently. They have promoted better relations between parents, non-teaching staff and Special Educational Needs departments and improved pupil progress and behaviour. However, the marginal nature of these types of projects also means they have a precarious existence, especially as their funding tends to be less secure or shorter-term than mainstream funds.

The interventions described have helped to target scarce resources for work with pupils and families who would otherwise present needs for which the school cannot cater. They overcome socio-economic and cultural barriers, redressing social inequalities by prioritising the school's response to individuals with particular needs and to those who belong to minority groups. The work tends to require the skills and understanding described in the last two chapters, so the presence of such projects on site can make a major contribution to the work of pastoral staff. They fulfil the need in many schools to complement whole school and year group strategies with more targeted work. Parents of pupils who are not coping well at school or who are underachieving become more aware that the school is sensitive to their child's needs and is giving them extra support.

Targeting for literacy – Parent School Partnership at New Heys

New Heys Community Comprehensive School in Liverpool worked with a local Parent School Partnership (PSP) scheme to target parents and carers for an additional boost to their literacy and IT skills. They piloted a Family Literacy Project course for parents for seven weeks, one day per week, and the relevant pupils joined their parents on the course after school for an hour and a half. The PSP scheme also runs courses for ten weeks in other schools in Liverpool and is open to all parents, although schools tend to focus the promotion on the parents of underachievers where there are known difficulties.

In the pilot year, the school identified families by prioritising children whose verbal reasoning test scores (NFER) were three or four years below their chronological age. The deputy head and head of English then talked with the parents, asking them how they felt their children had settled in and if there was anything they were worried about. They often said reading and writing, and if so, they were offered the free course. The course was run during the day, which did not prove problematic. Grandparents and other adults responsible for the pupil were also welcome.

The course was promoted to primary school parents who attended the school's Open Evening and secondary staff also mentioned it when they visited primaries. The pupils concerned were loaned notebooks (a part of the course involved working with their parents on computers) which helped them to overcome their initial suspicion. Liz Heydon of the PSP scheme writes:

'It is notoriously difficult to involve the children and the parents at secondary school level and the gains are often more obvious for the parents. They then offer the children quite a different role model if they go on to further education. The original target groups for all of our courses were parents with basic skills needs although that emphasis seems to be shifting slightly with the funding coming more through the Standards Fund.'

(May 2001)

Course Outline

Session 1	Introduction: Learning begins at home. Learning is fun: How children learn through everyday activities.
Session 2	Reading is fun: Print is everywhere.
Session 3	Sharing books: What makes a good book? Asking questions and talking with children.
Session 4	Teaching reading: Find out how reading is taught at school. How can you help at home? What to do if there is a problem.
Session 5	Writing/Spelling: How can you encourage children? How much should you help? How can you help?
Session 6	The National Curriculum: What does it all mean?
Session 7	End of course party with the children's work on display. Parents who completed the course were given a 'Parents as Educators' Open College Certificate and a 'Communication Skills' certificate.

Grouping pupils into a 'special project' can be stigmatising if the children involved feel they are attracting a bad name from being offered a different opportunity to everyone else. From a pupil's point of view, normality is the best position to be in – fitting in, not sticking out. On the other hand, they can see that they are not all the same and they rely on teachers to differentiate between their needs. Teachers can reduce rivalry for special attention by pointing out the differences between individuals, without returning to the old-fashioned language of remedial education. They need to make it clear that all members of a school deserve respect for their particular abilities, so that they do not reinforce stark judgements made by children about their inferiority or superiority. If minority ethnic pupils are not fluent in English, it is everyone's responsibility to help them while they are in class, instead of isolating them further by teasing or laughing at them. When individual support is essential, other pupils need to learn that helping one child to cope in the classroom will benefit the whole class. When withdrawal from some lessons is necessary, teachers need to cater for their predictable needs when they try to catch up for missed lessons, instead of ignoring their previous absence or resenting it.

It is best to be open about the method of selecting the target group with both parents and pupils, explaining for example that pupils have been chosen by calculating the difference between Cognitive Ability Test (CAT) verbal and non-verbal scores to try to see who has potential that is not yet realised. Teachers need to broadcast the message that everyone can achieve more by participating in extra-curricular projects or cultivating special skills according to their abilities. Drama clubs and music lessons are other types of (less targeted) provision that communicate the value of diversity.

Targeting attendance at Llanedeyrn High

A First Day Response scheme was piloted by a committed Education Welfare Officer based in Llanedeyrn High School, Cardiff, who identified target groups of pupils in each year group who would benefit from intervention at an earlier stage to discuss problems with school, using their attendance as the main indicator for referral to the project. He rang any pupil on the same day they were late or absent, to prevent problems escalating. After the pilot, Deputy Head, David Jordan, developed a joint bid with a local community charity for extra funds to resource the work. They were successful after a year and an attendance project at the school staffed by workers in training to work with children and adolescents started in September 1999. The charity was well known to the school and already worked with several other schools in the region, running extra-curricular activities, play schemes, youth groups and residential trips. The first project worker was based in the school and took referrals from teaching staff of individual children and families who needed to tackle attendance problems.

All parents were requested to ring the school early in the morning if they knew their child was not able to attend that day for any reason. If any child had not arrived by 9.30am, the project workers rang home or the next emergency contact number given. Their caseload consisted of cases where there may be an issue behind the surface of the attendance problem, and cases referred from each year group by pastoral managers and year co-ordinators. They also attended a weekly care meeting with year co-ordinators, pupil support services and the Education Welfare Officer. When a parent came to the school, they were asked to join them, as the telephone calls had made a personal link. Trust developed easily between the young project workers and the pupils, who could then turn to the project workers when things went wrong.

▓ Home-school workers

Home–school workers have, over a decade, observed problems between home and school and many committed workers have acted as intermediaries between parents and teachers, with good results. When appointed to make a special intervention with a target group of pupils, relevant skills and training are important. It may be necessary to recruit the worker with the help of a community group or local voluntary agency operating locally, in a relevant field.

Isolation needs to be minimised when asking a pioneering worker to run a special project on the school site. Terms and conditions of employment also need to be devised to suit the nature of the work, which is quite different to teaching.

'In Instep we are all project workers with conditions similar to community education workers. We work running clubs and transition groups during the

holidays and may also have to do evening work such as After School Clubs or visit parents who work during the day. We all do child protection training and take part in school meetings along with other support staff. We can also participate in in-service and can take advantage of courses offered through the Education Department.'

(Jenny Suttie, Co-ordinator, Craigmillar Instep Project)

If home–school workers are appointed to work in the school, a clear brief from the school will prevent the different cultures of services clashing with school culture. Youth workers, for example, have to value education and not see themselves in opposition to it. They will need to decide whether to allow pupils to use their first names or not when they run extra-curricular activities, and if so, how to maintain respect when they meet pupils on the school site. Informal ways of working developed outside schools are certainly helpful, but project specification needs to include aims and desired outcomes, so that both home–school workers and in-school teachers recognise the results they achieve.

Connections with school staff should be maximised by inviting the workers to attend ordinary weekly updates and all whole staff meetings. Their line manager in the school can help by ensuring they know about other opportunities to discuss the casework. The staffroom should not be a 'teachers-only' zone. Internal staff lists should always include their names, and invitations to 'staff' activities and school events put in their pigeonholes alongside everyone else's. This responsibility for internal communication should be clearly stated in relevant staff job descriptions.

Improving attendance – Deptford Truancy Challenge, Deptford Green School

Roz Ryan works with children at Deptford Green School who have low or irregular attendance. Year 7 referrals are identified by the children's primary schools during the term before their arrival and staff within the school refer pupils whose attendance drops below 90%. About sixty children had been referred from two years (7 and 8) at the time of the interview.

As the project does not hold statutory responsibilities for ensuring good attendance, contact with families can be supportive and non-threatening. Roz writes to each parent concerned, inviting them to meet her with the head or deputy head of year.

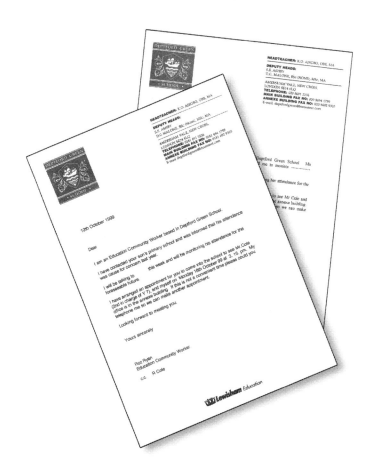

If they do not attend, she visits them at home. She gets
to know the pupils and families quite quickly and sustains informal contact with them. In work with the child,
she finds out what they think about particular subjects
they find difficult and, as she builds trust with them and
their parent, uncovers some of the hidden difficulties
they experience with school.

Interview with Roz Ryan, Education Community Worker

Roz attributed the good relations she establishes with
families to the fact that she shares the local culture – 'I

talk like 'em,' she said frankly, in her South London accent. She becomes an informal port of call for parents in crisis or at a chaotic point in their lives. This can be in a literal way as a link between parent and child, 'Can you tell Maria I'm going to her gran's ...' or it can be more fundamentally in the role she plays with a pupil.

One mother had a drink problem which involved neglecting her responsibilities at certain times. Her son, Alex, was in Year 8 when he was referred to Roz. The head of year had noticed he tended to miss school on Mondays, during a term in which swimming was on Mondays. She described her role with him as 'being on his case a lot', including going to get him when he stayed away. She used an exercise with him that involved colouring in his timetable with three coloured pencils to identify his best and worst lessons which led her to discuss with him the lessons he did not like and why. She could see he was shy in swimming because he was skinny and didn't like taking his clothes off. At first he was a defensive boy with an answer for everything. He was adamant he wasn't going to go to swimming. He didn't see the point of modern languages. He would use his home situation to claim he could not come in, because 'his uniform wasn't ready'. Roz got to know him well enough to be able to pop over to his house on a particularly difficult day.

She talked more with Alex about the subjects he did not like. She explained why he should go to school and what would happen if he didn't, in terms he could understand. She talked about why exams are needed. She encouraged him, using smiley stickers in his homework diary, to record his attendance at the end of every week. Her role with teaching staff was to work out what they would see as an improvement, and then help him in that area. They felt he could organise himself better, and he did. She negotiated extended time for some pieces of work, and asked them to explain the work again to him so he could have another try. They used her as a resource to know when things were bad at home and told her when he was doing well so that she could include these comments in her sessions with Alex.

After about a year, his mother started contacting Roz herself. She phoned Roz when the family moved to give her the new number and kept in touch from then on despite the difficulties. She was reported to Social Services several times in the course of the three years Roz knew her, and Roz occasionally attended case conferences with her and Alex. She denied she had a drink problem and used to complain about her son. At times when his mother was not able to cope, Roz found his uncle was an alternative carer who could bring the two secondary age children to school. She tended to see Alex the most at these times, on a daily basis for a few weeks followed by four quieter weeks. She could see that he got stressed doing his schoolwork and this understanding came from the time she spent with him. He knew that she knew what was happening at home which contributed to their trust. The main achievement Roz named in his case was preventing him from dropping out of school. He stayed in school and got some GCSE qualifications in Year 11. His mother now has a new partner and a new baby. But Roz was adamant there are no magic cures in this sort of work. Alex's sister was still in the project when Alex left. She had been babysitting for a friend of her mother who also misused alcohol.

Background to the post

Roz Ryan did her placement at the school while on a two-year Turning Point Diploma of Higher Education in Community Work. This is delivered through field-based Apprenticeships in the community. The course is mainly funded by Lewisham Council and Goldsmiths College (University of London) and is in its tenth year. The mature pupils on the course tend to have few academic qualifications but their participation increases their access to a professional training. Turning Point has received reports from graduates of an astonishing 100% success rate in gaining employment within six months of completing the course.

In the event of a difficulty with one of the pupils in their caseload, home–school workers are well placed to attend joint meetings with parents and teachers. Roz Ryan described an instance of the mother who trusted her asking what she needed to know when the child was recommended for alternative education in Year 10. Roz then lent her moral support during a daunting meeting in which the parent needed to ask questions of a senior member of staff, about what the proposal would mean to her child's future.

▇▇▇ Culturally-sensitive services

Home–school workers from minority ethnic groups are an extra resource to staff where the culture of pupil communities is under-represented on the teaching staff team. Through their understanding of particular cultures, value systems and home lives, they facilitate good parent–school relations and increase diverse cultural activities within the school.

Cultural difference can otherwise make working with parents difficult and ineffective. There are reasons to expect pupils to learn the local way of doing things in this country and, however different their home culture is, they need to observe the school rules. But when meeting with their parents, it can be both imperialistic and unrealistic to imagine that they will understand how the school environment operates, what is expected of pupils, and how to help their children at home, especially when their English is still rudimentary. Their experience of racism or exclusion in society at large can make it even harder to overcome barriers between parents and teachers.

At North Westminster Community School in London, minority parents have commented on their feeling that the headteacher has allowed an understanding to grow within the school of the particular problems facing their community. Bangladeshi and Moroccan home–school workers have helped the school to welcome families from these minorities, increasing their sense of belonging in the school, while acknowledging the stresses of immigrant life in the world outside school. There are also numerous cultural events held at the school, reflecting the diversity of its pupils. The school is very large, and stretches over three sites (called 'campuses'), yet the personal relations by nominated workers have created the sense of a school community amongst the families involved.

▇▇▇ Bangladeshi and Moroccan Family-Liaison Workers at North Westminster Community School

Job description for both posts

I   THE ROLE

I 1   The role is to contribute to the success of pupils of Bangladeshi or Moroccan background by enabling their families to make best use of the school for the education of their children and to best prepare and support their children.

I.2 The Family-Liaison Workers should also assist the staff to work as closely as possible with those families.

I.3 As nearly 30% of the school's pupils are of Bangladeshi background and 10% of Moroccan and their GCSE results have been worryingly low, these are very important posts.

I.4 The Moroccan post-holder will divide the time between the three communities in proportions to be agreed based on the population of the pupils of Moroccan origin in each. Each of the three Bangladeshi workers is campus based.

I.5 On each campus the Family-Liaison Workers will be responsible to the Director of Campus, who will be responsible overall for co-ordination and support. The Director will establish working arrangements for the Family-Liaison Workers with the key people responsible for the pupils: House Year Heads (and in Upper School the Deputy Directors of Upper School) and Head of English as an Additional Language on that campus.

II THE TASKS

II.1 The overall role will be largely carried out through the following tasks, though the post-holders will be expected to suggest any additions or variations which she or he consider necessary. The list of specific tasks required to implement this substantial ambition is variable, could differ in balance between campuses under the leadership of the Director of that campus, and should be seen as the minimum.

II.2 **Consultation**

(a) Assist with the applications for places from Bangladeshi or Moroccan families, liaising with home and other schools as necessary;

(b Take referrals from House Year Heads and Directors of Campuses on all three campuses to contact Sylheti- or Maghrebi-speaking parents of pupils;

(c) Make contact by phone and be able to discuss issues with the families as agreed by the House Year Heads or Directors of Campuses;

(d) Give oral and written reports back on the outcome of the phone calls; liaise regularly with House Year Heads and Educational Welfare Officers;

(e) When required, consult with the Director of Campus or Special Educational Needs Co-ordinator to help with assessment of Bangladeshi or Moroccan pupils thought to have special needs, and to explain the procedures to parents;

(f) It might be desirable to have specified times when available for the parents to contact over any concerns regarding school or their children.

II.3 **Parents' Consultation Meetings and Reception Interviews**

(a) Contact parents (e.g. phoning them) prior to Parents' Consultation Meetings in order to try to increase the number attending parents' meetings;

(b) Be available for interpretation at Parents' Consultation Meetings;

(c) Attend reception and other interviews and parents' meetings to act as an interpreter for the families.

II.4 **Information to Parents**

(a) Plan ways of informing parents how the school works and its requirements;

(b) Concentrate especially on homework assignments and schedules for handing in work, including course work for GCSE and GNVQ in Upper School.

II.5 **Written Translations**

(a) Translate letters to be sent home, and letters received from home;

(b) Translate standard letters and invitations.

II.6 **Records**

Monitor registers for Bangladeshi or Moroccan pupil absences, update 'on-off roll' records, take details of pupils to go on the waiting list, and deal with travel cards, free dinners, and pupil records for the Bangladeshi or Moroccan communities within the school.

II.7 **Community Liaison**

Support the school's working relationships with appropriate community groups.

Person specification for the Bangladeshi worker

QUALITIES AND SKILLS SOUGHT

We are seeking someone with initiative, interest in the achievement of young people, energy, and commitment, who has the following specific skills, knowledge, and experience:

I   Knowledge of:

I.1 the Bangladeshi community in North West London;

I.2 the current secondary-school system, its methods of working, and requirements of pupils.

II   Skills:

The candidate appointed should:

II.1 be a fluent speaker, reader and writer of standard English and Bengali;

II.2 be a good communicator in Sylheti;

II.3 be able to translate accurately orally and in writing from Sylheti or Bengali to and from English;

II.4 have good inter-personal communication with parents and fellow professionals;

II.5 be able to word-process, copy edit, and proof-read in Bengali;

II.6 be effective at making presentations in writing and orally on appropriate aspects of the needs of Bangladeshi pupils to appropriate groups in the school, e.g. SMT, pastoral teams, site staff meetings or governors;

II.7 be a competent keeper of records;

II.8 be able to plan well the use of time.

III   Experience:

The skills and knowledge are the key requirements, and the sources in which these have been gained are considerably less important. Nevertheless, it would be an advantage if the candidate had any of the following work experience: child care, journalism, office work, publishing, public relations, reception, school support staff, social work, teaching, translating.

IV General:

The post-holder will both need to be independent and use initiative as well as be able to work flexibly as a member of a team.

For simple statistics and records a reasonable level of numeracy is required.

It would be an advantage if the post-holder were to have a first-aid certificate or be willing to undertake training.

Finally, a knowledge of and commitment to equal opportunities is essential.

Home–school workers from minority ethnic groups are an extra resource to staff where their culture is under-represented on the teaching staff team. They facilitate cultural relations between teachers, parents and community groups, increasing diverse cultural activities in the school. Teachers learn more easily about local family cultures and imagine what pupils can realistically be encouraged to bring to enhance the mainstream curriculum from other environments.

▨ Refugee project – North Westminster Community School

In the same school, a specialist worker for refugees works in a secondary school to meet the unique needs presented by refugee families. Before the refugee support service started, the characteristically high mobility of the refugee population took its toll in the classroom, and pupils suffered in isolation.

Interview with Wafa Hussein, Refugee Welfare Liaison Worker

Pupils who are bewildered by the new world they are in can be reassured by someone speaking their own language, who helps them to feel less strange, and more able to ask questions. Wafa emphasised the importance in her work of understanding the particular background of each family, as their original socio-economic status, education and culture or religion, layered with the trauma of witnessing abuse and violence, will influence how they cope with the host community. Multiple trauma in the past can lead to appalling behaviour in the present, triggered by apparently small events. She can pass on contextual information where appropriate to help teaching staff manage difficult behaviour, such as when a refugee child is bereaved. She can see families in a private room and discuss confidential information. She is well placed to make referrals to agencies outside the school when necessary, and works with the SEN department on individual plans.

Wafa described the nature of her casework and some of the systems she has evolved to meet the needs of pupils and their families who are referred to her. Refugee status is recorded on the school admissions form. Wafa circulates to staff lists of countries of origin and trigger points for referrals. Pupils suffer from bullying, racial harassment, and from the inevitable language barriers. They are humiliated by others who laugh at their accents. Their frustration can boil over, so staff sensitivity is necessary to look into the circumstances of the aggression and to prevent refugee pupils being labelled in the longer term.

Wafa's role also includes helping families to get their statutory entitlements (from free school meals to social benefits) and has found her work encompasses advocacy and interpreting with a range of departments, particularly housing. There are frequent legislative changes, new systems and new provision for refugees. She makes sure she is well informed by local and national advisory agencies.

Somali Community After-school Club at Hampstead School

The Head of Information and Communication Technology (ICT) at Hampstead School has forged a partnership with a local Cultural Centre in Camden, North London, which serves the Somali community. The Centre already ran a homework club for children of all ages on a Thursday and Friday after school. In order to attract parents of Somali pupils into the school, a new after-school club has started within the school, in the Learning Centre which houses the library and recently improved computer facilities.

The school had been awarded funds that were conditional on sharing their facilities with other schools and community partners, and the headteacher had noticed a lack of communication with the parents of the approximately one hundred Somali children in the school. The teacher in charge, Phil Taylor, explained that he had taken the advice of the Somali co-ordinator in making the new arrangements for parents. The development process required sensitivity in his manner and approach so that they did not feel the school was trying to take over a community facility, with the overtones of white imperialism that would have carried. Mr Taylor's task was to develop the project using ICT, but he stressed the importance of a down-to-earth approach that took into account the starting point of the community group. They needed books to help with literacy and numeracy, and funds for their running costs, so he helped by bidding for an extra grant to meet some of these needs. He worked with them to find a practical way to start new activities that would not detract from their existing work. A crucial part of his work was sustaining good relations with the Somali club co-ordinator, who he saw most weeks in term-time.

They encountered transport difficulties when they initially tried to move the Thursday club to the school, which highlighted the number of younger children being cared for by the mothers who were helping their older children at the same time. This experience helped them to cater for younger siblings when a new Wednesday club started in January 2000. The parents at the Wednesday after-school club in the Learning Centre talked about the basic skills that they felt their children needed to improve. They sat with their children, and the tutor circulated between them, explaining the work to both parent and child. One mother had attended the secondary school herself and felt she understood what her children would need to succeed later in life. I was struck by the similarities between the concerns of these minority parents, who were in full Islamic dress, and those of all the parents I had spoken to in the course of my research for this book. The specific cultural sensitivity of this provision undoubtedly encouraged their attendance and involvement in the homework club, but the issues addressed within in were fairly universal.

The Headteacher, Tamsyn Imison, reported that the work with this group had resulted in two of the Somali parents attending one of her Year Forum sessions (described in Chapter 10), which she felt was a direct result of feeling more interested in the school.

Home visiting

Visiting homes briefly and informally might be the best way forward if meeting parents at the school is unlikely to be successful. Meeting a parent at home often leads the family, including the pupil, to be more open and less anxious, providing a greater understanding of the family and a space to convey the school's approaches more clearly. Staff who conduct home visits used to be limited to non-teaching staff and exceptional individuals who were determined to understand the children in their tutor group or primary classroom. Projects such as Instep have made it possible to focus home visits where they will have the most impact, in particular situations and at times when they will make a great difference. With this understanding, a wider number of school staff and home–school workers may choose to use home visits when necessary.

The Craigmillar Instep Project at Castlebrae Community High

The Craigmillar Instep Project was launched through Urban Aid funding in Scotland in 1992 as a major new school improvement initiative focused on working with existing and future parents of Castlebrae Community High School in Edinburgh. A team of home–school workers has engaged families with school activities, initially reaching out to parents of prospective pupils by surveying their views on the school. Home visits were fundamental to their approach, when they visited parents at home several times before the first year of school and ran after-school, summer and Easter activities, for targeted priority groups.

Their experience has been that home visits definitely help to improve relations with a secondary school when trust amongst local parents is guarded or non-existent.

Visiting all parents formed a crucial part of the early groundwork in the first few years of the project, after which time it could be scaled down in the light of more precise understanding of its benefits and effectiveness. They now focus on using visits to inform and engage parents at key points in a child's education.

Jenny Suttie, Co-ordinator at the Instep Project explains, 'These key points for the secondary school pupil are: choosing a secondary school; the transition from primary to secondary; subject choice on second year; Standard Grade Exams; leaving school or staying on; the world of work, college or university.' She reports that home visits are concentrated around these points to achieve the greatest impact 'in terms of attending parents' evenings, keeping appointments at the school and understanding the relevance of the Standard Grade Exams, the Home School Contract, post-school opportunities and supports.' Jenny also comments that all parents, even the minority of parents who are not able to sustain their interest in school success as much as others, 'can be engaged around the subject of school leaver opportunities and supports.' Their experience suggests that it is important to communicate with parents at these vital transition points, even if parents cannot visit the school.

Assessing risk

Home visits when parents are disaffected can sound frightening, particularly to new teachers who are not familiar with the local area and local families, or who come from a very different background to the majority of families at the school. It is important that they are able to assess risk in any given situation and that they feel adequately supported. Carrying a mobile phone is standard, as staff can rarely visit in pairs.

Instep Project experience of home visiting

'To double up and visit two by two is possibly intimidating for the parent and makes what could be an efficient piece of work unwieldy and heavy on manpower. We have a mobile phone which can be taken along on a visit and before setting out on a visit we can log where we are going and when we expect to be back. However, with new families there is an element of assessing the risk as you go along. Carry out your visit on the doorstep if you are at all uncertain.

Skills Useful in Home Visiting

Good active listening skills
Integrity and honesty
Non-judgmental approach
Having a realistic mindset about what you can do and what you can offer

In the early days of the project where it was particularly important to build trust and credibility with the parents, team members needed to develop a counselling-style approach with good active listening skills and an ability to communicate effectively with a wide range of people. It was also important, where possible, to have a balance of male and female team members.

Boundaries/Confidentiality

If a parent is telling you something sensitive you always ask whether it is in confidence or 'Do you want me to pass this on to someone?' They may be telling you the information precisely so that it will be passed on or just wanting someone to listen but the information to go no further.'

(Jenny Suttie, Co-ordinator, Instep Project)

Health visitors, youth workers, and education welfare officers in services where home visiting is normal practice may be willing to introduce a new teacher or home–school worker to their patch. Once initial barriers or stereotypes have been broken down, staff generally find the insights gained from meeting parents at home are of immense educational value.

The Cambridgeshire Secondary Support Service

Bob Sproson, Head of the service, writes on his experience of home visits with parents of pupils at risk of exclusion:

'My current role involves me in negotiations between parents of extremely 'difficult to manage' young people and the providers of their children's education. Despite the widely held belief that such parents are often 'bad parents' or that 'it is the parents who are to blame', my own experience has been that this is not the case. I have met a significant number of people who are not able to parent appropriately either because their own lives are in such disarray that they have neither the emotional strength nor the self-esteem necessary to meet the needs of a 'demanding other' or because they have no concept of the appropriate relationship which needs to be formed ... they do not know how to offer love and to draw boundaries at the same time, but have rarely met any who actively choose to behave in a manner which is contrary to the best interests of their offspring.

I have found the first principle to be that I have to go and meet these parents on their territory. In their own home, they feel secure. Having made this decision I have to accept the mores of behaviour which exist in the home. I have a right to state my own 'standards' if I feel myself to be threatened verbally or physically, but not to impinge upon the accepted behaviours within the home. Thus, in these circumstances, I do not pick up on swearing. I often find that during initial visits parents need to be angry – they feel angry with the 'system', often feel that they, or their children, are being unfairly treated by an unsympathetic bureaucracy. In almost every instance I have found that it is important to go in with a willingness simply to listen, no matter what it is that I need to listen to. It may be family anecdotes or a lengthy tirade against a particular teacher, but is often a stream of consciousness about the inadequacies of the world, particularly the education system. Whilst I may well disagree with a great deal of the opinion which is expressed, this is neither the time to enter the debate, nor to reject the opinions, it is simply the time to listen and to value the opinions expressed. I have seen other practitioners who, for understandable and probably well-intentioned reason will interject with either: 'I can see that you are angry, but I have not come to discuss these things', or 'I have no intention of being spoken to in this manner ... please listen to what I have to say, or I will leave': I have never seen either approach enable them to develop any form of trusting relationship with the parent(s). The key is simple: listen.

I have found that arranging a series of visits in which I am quite willing to make no discernible progress during the first ones is essential. Equally important is time-limiting each one. Although I am willing to listen, I have to be clear that I cannot stay all night, so I need to set a time when I will leave. Equally I need to be clear as to who I am, what my role is and what it is possible for me to achieve. It is a grave mistake for me to ever suggest that I can sort out issues over which I have no control. I may be able to offer addresses or names of people who it would be appropriate to contact, but I cannot sort out issues of housing, employment, unpaid debts, etc.

Clearly the nature of the work with the parents will depend upon the reason behind the initial contact. For schools, I more than understand that this is time-consuming, may not be seen as part of a teacher's duties, and may not be seen to be 'worthwhile', but if we do have any notion of inclusivity and responding positively to disaffection, we have to understand that building links with parents is essential. Thus schools must:

- Make such contact part of some appropriate member of staff's job description.

- Make every effort to contact parents of young people who display signs of disaffection early.

- Ensure that parents see this as a supportive not a punitive intervention.

- Maintain contact with parents – the commonest complaint I hear is, 'that ******* school only ever rings me when things go wrong'.

- Keep a dialogue and a relationship going – it is only when parents feel valued and listened to that difficult issues can be raised and dealt with effectively.'

▓▓ Negotiating behaviour and change with parents in school

Those members of staff who work with small groups and with individual pupils inevitably find themselves wondering about motivating factors in a pupil's behaviour and attitude. Discussions with parents can set individual behaviour in context and greatly help a teacher's pastoral relationship with the child. These can, however, be difficult meetings for both members of staff and parents.

Much of the understanding of child and adolescent development found in specialised work is not new to Special Educational Needs departments, where a small team of experienced adults cultivate skills with individual pupils and parents. SEN staff use their understanding of the problems facing each child to draw up plans that require others – non-specialist adults, including parents, or the child's peers – to get involved with the solution. It is useful to share this understanding with other colleagues, so that more teachers can take into account home and school factors.

▓▓ A late-stage problem

Perhaps the most common motivation for secondary teachers to ensure they meet with parents is a problem that has developed to a stage where the school feels they cannot deal with it any longer on their own. Pastoral staff are likely to invite parents to this sort of meeting when a behaviour issue needs resolving. If the pupil is at a late stage in the school's disciplinary procedures, this is one of the most difficult situations to handle. It can be avoided by sharing the school's concerns with adults in the family before it gets so bad that everyone is looking for someone else to blame.

Parents are unlikely to trust a teacher's bad report if no warning has previously been given of a deteriorating situation. There is firstly the possibility that the pupil behaves very differently at home and school, so some detail is necessary in order for a parent to trust your version of the story and to recognise their child in it. The pupils concerned often do not pass on letters reporting problems and their version of the story might be quite different. When describing a problem, it is important to give a short history.

The manner of the teacher reporting needs to be sympathetic to the feelings of the parent hearing the information rather than angry with the child for having committed the misdemeanour. Otherwise, the problem could be taken as a personal criticism of the child or their family. Sensitivity needs to be akin to that of a doctor informing relatives of a bad diagnosis in the medical consulting room – amongst teachers, like doctors, seniority is no predictor of skill in this area. Dr Stuttaford comments that how doctors present bad news makes a great difference to the patient's welfare, and *'Research shows that patients' satisfaction with their treatment is correlated with doctors' ability to empathise.'* (Stuttaford, 1999). Creating a working alliance with a family is the first step to solving an individual problem, so there is no advantage to be gained from an antagonistic or disciplinarian manner.

Parents will be offended if they feel you have judged their son or daughter unfairly. If you say: 'Tony is too macho to admit he is wrong', the parent will hear that you are criticising their beloved and you may get a defensive or sullen response. Once a parent is feeling defensive, it is very difficult to get the conversation back onto an equal footing. Suspicions are close to the surface when there is a problem, a point illustrated by the language used by parents to each other, 'I was *hauled up* to the school today.' Criticising their child often feels like a personal attack rather than a comment of relevance to their life at school. You may then find that the parent cannot engage in an adult conversation because they are feeling as if they are being told off at school. The same parent would be more agreeable if you said in a more affectionate tone: 'Tony is always trying to be right. I say one thing and he corrects me!' The mother might allow herself to say: 'It is irritating, isn't it?'

It can help to imagine being in a similar position oneself or to rehearse out of the meeting how certain phrases come across. The aim is for parents to think about the problem, rather than prompting them to defend their child. If disciplinary measures are imminent, separate the painful task of telling parents this from the more personal discussion about what can be done about it. Parents of pupils with behaviour problems will usually be grateful if teachers can help them to think about it without making them feel like bad parents. This might involve acknowledging that to start with the pupil's efforts may not be completely successful, and where they break certain school rules they will be subject to the same rules as the other pupils. However, the staff member they are working with can convey that they appreciate the small shifts in behaviour that others in the school will not notice. Within an ongoing relationship in which the progress of the child is appreciated, it will be possible to separate the drama of incidents at school from the slow but steady plan for improvement.

▰▰▰ Good practice in SEN

An ongoing relationship is created at a much earlier stage by calling parents at the first opportunity when there is a sign of a behavioural

difficulty. It is important to explain to the parents that there is no serious cause for concern at this point, but that it is worth keeping an eye
on the child's behaviour. Schools that have only brief or one-off communication with parents as a child embarks on stage one of the SEN
Code of Practice tip parents into sudden shock when formal procedures
have to come into play at a much later date because problems have persisted. In most of the literature on involving parents more extensively,
teachers are encouraged to build communication as a preventative
measure to conflict or the breakdown of a pupil's place at the school. A
problem that becomes entrenched instead of leading to working to
modify behaviour or improve learning is more likely to become a label
that cannot be changed.

Communication with the SEN department regarding contact with the
parents of particular children then needs to be incorporated into regular staff meetings. Dealing with minor problems that used to be thought
of as the sole responsibility of SEN staff, are, in schools with an effective
policy for dealing with emotional and behaviour difficulties, becoming
a wider responsibility, but with clear procedures for specialist staff to
manage co-ordinated responses to severe problems.

▰▰ SEN at Llanrumney High, Cardiff

At Llanrumney High School, all arrangements for identifying special educational needs are conducted within
the context of a whole staff agreement that they are an
inclusive school. Learning Support issues are a stand-
ing item on the agenda of departmental meetings.
Monthly meetings between the Learning Support
Co-ordinator (the SENCO) and departmental link staff
result in early communication about any factors that
persistently inhibit a child's learning and early discussion with parents about the pupil's particular need for
support. The school's Learning Support Co-ordinator
ensures that all parents of children on the register are
contacted termly. 70% respond, and about 50% come
into school to discuss the problem. At the other end of
the spectrum, he may have daily telephone contact with
parents of children at stage 5. A number of Year 11
pupils with special needs or at risk of exclusion aim at
achieving Duke of Edinburgh Awards and educational
certificates.

One of the whole school SEN strategies involving parents is the STAR Group. It is run by a dedicated

member of staff alongside a youth worker, who work with up to sixty pupils in Years 7, 8 and 9 and all their parents and have contact with pupils at Key Stage 2. The group's aims are positive school attendance and reduced crime. The majority of parents come into the school, sometimes at a breakfast club. The meeting includes a discussion of basic educational targets for key skills. The problem-solving approach draws on parents' expertise and also ensures a positive start to the day. If parents do not come in, one of the workers visits them at home.

If some staff in schools find problems in communicating with an individual child, a pastoral tutor should make a special effort to talk with the family at a very early stage. Even if there is no cause for concern at the time, the child's lack of personal skills will predictably entail support at some point. Parents will then feel more trusting because they know that teachers have been getting to know their 'special' child and have developed an understanding of their qualities as well as their idiosyncrasies. Tutors will then be more involved and informed about the family, rather than waiting for the SEN department to do this groundwork at a later stage.

Working with parents will improve support for children with a whole range of special needs, from minor learning and behaviour difficulties to more severe and enduring problems. A common theoretical backdrop to the examples of good practice featured is seeing a child's place in a system of helping relationships, both internal and external to the school. Systemic understanding can help to draw attention to gaps and strengths in their support network. A map of the child's access to help can make both teachers and parents aware of the significant figures in their life, whether parents, friends, close family members or relatives. According to systemic theory, as one commentator puts it, *'Context is foreground not background'* (Jim Wilson, Cardiff Institute, lecture at the Institute of Family Therapy).

Learning from family work: the Marlborough Family Service Education Unit

Parents can be highly motivated to improve their children's behaviour and progress. They may not have previously admitted there was a problem. Talking about their child's development and how they relate to adults is one way of seeking a new way forward. The Marlborough Family Service Education Unit gradually enables children to make enormous progress and remain at, or re-integrate into, a mainstream environment. In many cases, only a special school would have been thought possible prior to their work with parents, carers and pupils.

The staff encourage the kind of observation that helps parents and teachers to start to talk about the child's behaviour. They focus on the cues and detailed interactions that produce certain kinds of behaviour, seeing the patterns in the way a child behaves with different adults known well to them. Together with their parents, they seek what the connections might be between the habitual patterns of behaviour in their key relationships at home and the undesirable behaviours in the school setting. They aim at both parents and children attending special sessions on up to four mornings per week. The children return to their mainstream school lessons in the afternoons. The obvious objection that 'parents will not have the time' is often heard, but they do achieve attendance, partly because matters have become so serious. Despite the difficulty for the parent(s) of taking time off work or making a major investment of time in resolving the problem, the consequences of not doing so, such as ongoing serious behavioural problems or permanent exclusion, could be far more difficult and have an even worse impact on their lives. If a child's extreme behavioural needs reduce, their quality of life and that of the whole family will improve.

The teacher-therapists at the unit facilitate a weekly discussion between all the parents of children referred at the time. They encourage them to share the difficulties that they are having in helping their children to manage better. This reduces the social isolation the parents commonly face, given the antisocial nature of these children's behaviour. By swapping stories and admitting how hard it is to change established patterns of behaviour, they support each other, reassuring the individual parent who feels they are failing that one setback does not mean the whole venture is worthless (Dawson and McHugh, 1986).

Case study 1: 'Jason'

> Jason was referred to the unit in his second year of secondary school due to his lack of concentration and unmanageable behaviour in the classroom. His style of disruption was experienced as challenging by staff because he would attempt to control their manner with him, demanding to be treated as a 'mate' rather than a child, and wreaking havoc if they did not comply. In response to feeling perturbed by him, staff attempted to distance themselves from him. His reaction was to push past this interpersonal barrier, trying to engage them even more provocatively.

His history from primary school records included several references to case reviews in which Social Services were involved. His mother had called the primary school on many occasions in crisis, and his father was a known substance misuser. Jason was the subject of case conferences at which his family was mentioned, particularly the attendance and behaviour problems of his older brother whom his mother had requested be taken into care several times. Jason's behaviour was cause for concern at primary school, but not seriously.

At the time his behaviour came to a head in secondary school, his father had died six months before and his brother was in a juvenile offenders unit. When the staff talked to his mother, she was still inconsolable, and given the extent of her problems, meeting her confirmed the feelings that school staff had had about Jason, that here was a family in such distress and a mother who was so overwhelmed that it was hard to imagine making any constructive suggestion. The feeling of despair she communicated to them made them feel that the problems were beyond any educationalist's reach. It was tempting to say that she just needed time, or that another professional might be better qualified to support her and Jason's problems would not go away until his mother had more help.

By classifying his mother as incapable, the danger presented was that Jason would be taken into care himself. This road promised few solutions to his educational problems. The staff at the Marlborough asked her to attend the unit and observed Jason's pattern of behaviour with her. What they saw was a pattern of flick-flack behaviour, in which he oscillated between behaving like a younger child to get her attention and then moving into an 'older' role because he saw she seemed fragile, which made him anxious. The way ahead included a tolerance of his lack of ability to learn, because he had had a lot to deal with that demanded his emotional energy and distracted him from learning. The solutions had to focus on increasing his ability to learn, and explaining to his mother why his behaviour led teachers at school to 'pick on him'. Her motivation to participate in the plan for improvement was clear, because she felt she had lost her husband and her eldest son and did not want to lose Jason too. She was nevertheless feeling very deprived herself, and by no means strong.

The plan they developed included a highly structured programme that would progress from one small achievement to a series of small achievements. All the targets developed were classroom focused, but had an impact on the mother's ability to parent too. The first was to arrive at school on time, the second to stay in his seat in class. In the unit during the morning his behaviour could be talked about in a small group, observing if he arrived on time and noticing why he missed instructions given by the teacher. If he was touching other children, he was not in his seat. If he was daydreaming or fidgeting, the small environment allowed his mother to focus on the problem with meeting the target. Staff involved her in praising and rewarding him when he succeeded, and persuading him to say what he had achieved for himself so he could start to take some ownership of his reputation at school. In the afternoons, back at school his form tutor was asked to remind him to carry a review card to mark off how he was doing, from which other teachers could see his goals that week or month.

Lessons where he achieved his targets were the first in which he felt fully integrated with his classmates, and could be used by him as evidence that he was trying and succeeding in other classes where he had more difficulty. Channelling his capacity to be independent into the activity of gathering evidence paid off in the school environment, while the more intensive support in the unit could help when he lost control and failed. They could trace back what had triggered the outburst.

Separately to the learning activities, the staff and parents at the unit supported Jason and his mother in the emotional issue of how Jason would be allowed to grieve for his father. His mother was still crying a lot as if she could not talk about him. Jason's grief was noticed by others, and so she heard other adults talking about his sadness. Their sensitivity helped them both to think about the fact that the first anniversary of his death was approaching.

His mother gradually regained the role as a parent with him that she had lost when his father had died. The intimate bond created by their bereavement, and the loss of the elder brother at home, had reinforced his feeling that he was her equal. They had entered a period in which she was grieving with him as a peer, which had been reflected in his behaviour at school.

(Interview with Brenda McHugh, teacher in charge and family psychotherapist)

Inviting parents to help their child in the SEN department at school, instead of referring out to an external unit, will engage support staff and teachers in developing successful approaches to improve behaviour and achievement. Elements of the work done at the Marlborough could be reproduced in a mainstream setting, if the staff concerned have the skills to create a 'no blame' atmosphere in discussions with the parents. One can get away from simply blaming the home or school for the problem, and thus avoiding thinking about how to resolve it, by noticing that a child demonstrates antisocial behaviour and allowing a curiosity to discover why and how this behaviour repeats itself. As a non-judgemental approach has distinguished the specialised interventions by pastoral staff and support workers who already work with parents, these staff might also be involved in family work alongside SEN staff and parents. Alternatively, if the support mechanisms for staff include the teacher support teams described in Chapter 7, an experienced home–school worker and an SEN staff member might form part of the core support team, enabling them to share their experience and skills.

Fitting in is crucial to pupils in the mainstream school environment and parents can help a child to understand why they may find themselves singled out, even for minor incidents, when they see them in this ordinary environment. In the case study above, Jason's mother evidently needed support, so a teacher could add a normalising dimension to external support by thinking of her if another school family was bereaved. Peer support amongst parents can be extremely helpful.

One function of inviting the parent into school to help the child with schoolwork is to learn how the child's behaviour is triggered automatically within the interpersonal dynamics of relationships with adults in that specific context. The staff and other parent volunteers present will also create a support network for both parent and child, made up of individuals who do not get caught up in the troubled behaviour and so can help to prevent the knee-jerk reactions by either or both parties that dominate in a difficult and emotional situation. By noticing and naming what the behaviour is that causes the problem, the staff are modelling an ability to think about the problem instead of immediately responding to it as would be appropriate in their roles as teachers or parents. Thinking together about how to change the habit that has developed which is causing difficulties in school should form the core of the meetings.

- Name the behaviour that needs to change.

- Agree with the pupil which small steps she or he feels are achievable.

- Discuss with the parent(s) how they can encourage the pupil in these ways.

- Agree how a pastoral staff member or particular subject teachers can encourage the pupil at school in these areas.

- Decide if the form tutor can monitor and communicate with the parent about their targets.

- List these daily or weekly targets.

- Nominate a member of staff to attend regular meetings with the parent, pupil and SEN/support staff about the pupil's progress.

Inclusive schools are already familiar with the process of devising behavioural targets and working with pupils to achieve change. The strength of family support for behavioural change is in the reinforcement that appears to make the difference between superficial and long-lasting change. Even this approach cannot promise universal success, but it will stimulate a higher standard of work with emotional and behavioural problems, and can set into a relevant theoretical framework discussions about children and families that would otherwise be purely subjective and often speculative. The approach seems behavioural, but the work of the unit draws on systemic theory in the assessment of the problem and in choosing which parties are involved in the solution, and attachment theory within the field of child psychology which acknowledges what young people need in order to grow and learn.

Case study 2: 'Life sentences' – labelling a child instead of involving their parents or carers

Parents of children with emotional and behavioural difficulties have often experienced their child's failure over a number of years. They describe the dread of being singled out in the playground for a '... little chat'. The parents are not alone in their feelings of powerlessness to make their child behave differently. A long line of teachers is likely to have experienced failure similar to the parents. This combination can lead to less optimism on both sides and to fewer attempts at discussing the nature of the problem or trying anything new.

Lines can easily become drawn, with the parents blaming the teachers for the lack of discipline and teachers feeling increasingly frustrated as parents fail to respond to letters or phone calls. The child's behaviour escalates in this vacuum until one or the other party is forced to take action. Unfortunately this action does not always attend to the real problem but often confirms the child as having sole responsibility for the disturbance.

An example of school refusal

Thirteen year-old Darren Collins was referred by his year head because of chronic school refusal. Shortly after Darren started to attend the Marlborough Family Service Education Unit, he and his parents failed to attend an arranged meeting.

A common feature of school refusal cases is that professionals expend a lot of energy taking action, making plans and arranging meetings. At best a message arrives saying that the parents cannot come because they have to take their child shopping for a new pair of trainers; at worst there is no word at all and once again everyone feels let down.

On this occasion we used the time to compare notes from the education welfare file and the school records. The pattern of non-attendance was first noticed when Darren was five: 'Irregular attendance hampers Darren's progress.' This was a common feature throughout his primary records. The education authority had been contacting Mrs Collins since Darren was six years old.

The pattern of non-attendance had been set for seven years. There needed to be a different kind of contact with Darren's family. In this case the difference was to persuade Mrs Collins to meet us with her parents, Darren's grandparents, to discuss ways of helping Darren get to school and to remain there.

We learned about the importance of the grandparents firstly from Darren and then from Mrs Collins' description of the amount of time they spent together, how the grandmother cooked all the meals and how grandfather could discipline Darren.

For seven years representatives of the education service had been talking to Mrs Collins on the assumption that she had the power in the family. Even though Mrs Collins had her own child she still functioned more as a child of her parents. She and Darren were more like siblings. By including the grandparents the family as a whole was able to devise its own plans to help Darren attend school regularly.

(Dawson and McHugh, 1987, p.120)

A systemic view of the problem involving significant family members and teachers is helpful in emphasising the power of relationships to improve behaviour. There is no threat, as is often the case when statutory agencies are involved, that the blame will be purely attributed to one party or the other. In the last twenty years, the work of psychologists and teachers has greatly increased the possibility of finding home–school solutions to entrenched problems that are being expressed through children's behaviour. The body of theory and a professional framework to support pioneering teachers undertaking this work have become more visible and more constructive.

'We apply some of the principles of how family attachments influence security to how relationships between social systems such as the school, the family and the psychological services affect the child's security ... Children feel more secure if they sense that each group is supportive of the other. However, if children, especially those in difficulties, sense that there is mistrust between the various organizations, their capacity to feel secure in each may be reduced, and learning can suffer.'

(Byng-Hall, 1994, p. xiv)

An awareness of the importance of the child's support system must equally take into account the role school plays in that child's life. For one child, school may represent a safe place to test boundaries if parents at home are fragile or not coping. For another, they may be behaving in the same way at home and at school, with good outcomes in the home environment and poor ones at school:

'Children's unacceptable behaviour at school can often be seen as useful behaviour at home. A child's noisy behaviour at home may be the only bright event that *stops a mother sinking into deep depression. At school the child's outbursts are hampering his development. Children, sadly, are often willing participants in sacrificing their futures for the sake of adults' needs ... Teachers may be the only people in a position to persuade them of the need for change for the child's sake.'*

(Dawson and McHugh, 1987, p.121)

When the matter requires a joint response from home and school, whether regarding behaviour, rules, rewards, homework or academic progress, the child needs to hear a unified message rather than conflicting ones. Once communication and a consistent approach have been established, other teachers need to know that things might become even more difficult. The work can take many months, but the benefits can endure for years. In-school work reduces the distance between the parties whose collaboration will benefit the pupil concerned. It increases the possibility that both home and school will reinforce the messages being given to the child.

▓ Children with severe communication difficulties – Langdon School

The intake at Langdon includes a number of children who have arrived from special schools with a whole range of learning and emotional or behavioural difficulties. About 20% of those on the register have statements, and of these children about 40% would be at special schools in other authorities. The SEN department at Langdon School works with parents in meetings focused on what the child needs to learn in order to attend school, with co-ordinated help from home and support in school.

The department makes contact with all parents of children with special needs from the earliest stage possible, and they sustain communication with them through to Year 11 when their children are leaving the school and receive their Record of Achievement at a Presentation Evening. Anne Macaulay, SENCO, attends their annual review meetings in Years 5 and 6 while they are still in special or mainstream primary school. Teachers and SEN assistants work with parents to articulate the children's familiar methods of coping at home and talk with them, for example, about how to ensure that the children develop different skills for coping more independently.

The inclusion of those with the most severe communication difficulties in a large mainstream school causes understandable levels of anxiety for their parents. They complete a Goal Setting Checklist which establishes the areas for the work and the nature of the support that will be necessary. There is a flat on the school site where living skills and independence can be practised.

The SEN staff monitor the achievement of individual goals from the start of the work, to influence their recommendations for support. One child had had full-time (100%) support at their specially-resourced primary school but was allocated only ten hours of Learning Support Assistant time at secondary school. By observing his ability to cope, they could set an immediate target to express his level of need. In order to achieve 'not shouting out', the replacement behaviour chosen was 'to put hand up at the appropriate time'. This child's initial lack of ability to do this resulted in an immediate increase in his support, followed by a phased plan to reduce the support gradually that would parallel his gradual ability to cope better on his own.

Although the nature of support and the skills of the staff involved are different from those needed in cases of milder difficulties, the level of structure in the individual plans and the systems for feedback about individual achievements between teachers, non-teaching staff and parents are similar. A range of specialised work involving parents can therefore be managed in the mainstream school environment using systems devised for interventions with individual families. A senior manager usually maintains an overview of the work, ensuring good practice is shared between different staff. They will then be in a good position to report back on behalf of the school to the local authority and other funding agencies on the progress of home–school work with the most disadvantaged members of the school community.

One issue for schools that rely on sessional staff for expertise in specialised areas of work is how to respond to the changing needs of pupils from year to year. This is more difficult in schools where there are a very small number of children with behavioural or learning difficulties, or where children are progressing through the care system and cannot remain at the school for long. Staffing requirements for individual plans in these situations can vary quite considerably. In general, schools that manage to stabilise their intake through minimal exclusions will enhance provision for pupils because staff skills will not need to change

Goal-setting checklist

Notes regarding assessment

Some of the sheets in this goal setting check list ask for an assessment.
Please use the following key to assess the students in each task.

1=Needs constant support---N.C.S.

2=Needs guided support---N.G.S.

3=Needs occasional support---N.O.S

4=Needs no support---N.N.S.

You may enter in either the abbreviation or the number for the assessment.
Further comments may be added under the "remarks" section.
Please enter the date each task was attempted.

SELF-CARE/HOUSEHOLD
Toileting

TOILETING

Item	Materials/Procedures	Performance	Assessment	Remarks
1. Sits on toilet seat	Toilet. cover raised	Sits until finished without rising	☐	
2. Urinates in toilet	Client does not have to take self to toilet	Use toilet (not more than one daytime accident per week)	☐	
3. Defecates in toilet	Client does not have to take self to toilet	Use toilet (not more than one daytime accident per week)	☐	
4. Verbalizes or gestures toilet needs (daytime)	Observe client	Asks or gestures need to go to toilet (even if too late to avoid accident)	☐	
5. Takes self to toilet	Observe client	a) Only occasional accidents	☐	
		b) No accidents	☐	
6. Cares for self in toilet	Observe client	Uses toilet correctly wipes when necessary and flushes toilet	☐	

SELF-CARE/HOUSEHOLD
Grooming

GROOMING

Item	Materials/Procedures	Performance	Assessment	Remarks
1. Wipes nose	Tissue/handkerchief	Wipes nose dry	☐	
2. Blows nose	Tissue/handkerchief	Blows and wipes nose	☐	
3. Uses handkerchief without reminder	Observe client	Gets tissue to blow nose as necessary	☐	
4. Combs or brushes own hair	Brush/comb. mirror	Combs/brushes sides. top front and back of hair while looking in mirror	☐	
5. Cleans own fingernails	Nail file	Removes visible dirt from all nails on each hand	☐	
6. Cuts own toenails	Nail clipper or scissors	Cuts all nails on each foot, so no sharp corners	☐	
7. Cuts own fingernails	Nail clipper or scissors	Cuts all nails on each hand, so no sharp corners	☐	

over short periods of time. Where fluctuations in the needs of the pupil population are inevitable, cluster arrangements with other schools or working with a Local Education Authority officer can increase the ability of the school to respond to changing needs in the school population. For example, sessional staff and home–school workers can rotate between local schools over a number of years. They will get to know local families well and may even be in a position to recommend which school will suit pupils with particular needs. Control mechanisms can also be introduced at the stage of admissions through a banding policy, such as that described in the case study of Camden School in the next chapter.

A combination of the specialised interventions described in this chapter and the mainstream strategies described earlier in the book will ensure whole school provision for the range of needs and abilities commonly found in a comprehensive school. Contextual policies that reinforce parental support have been discussed in their relevance to particular issues, such as homework, assessment and marking. While many of the specific recommendations will require secondary schools to rethink their current practice, many are not new. The same applies to school activities for parents and cultural events at the school, which will depend on an ethos encouraging the representation of different communities within the school and involving their families and social networks. It is often the ability of staff and senior managers to see the connections between the lives of the pupils in school and their lives outside school that makes the difference in these peripheral but vital activities involving parents.

10 SUSTAINING AN ETHOS OF PARENTAL INVOLVEMENT

The schools that feature in this book report that the contribution of parents to their school is essential. This is supported by research identifying good home–school relations as a key characteristic of school effectiveness (Sammons, Hillman, Mortimore, 1997). Parents are the largest, most active outside interest group a school can have; they form what amounts to an army of potential friends or enemies, albeit an often invisible one. Their commitment can sometimes be seen in their direct involvement with the school but more often exerts a behind-the-scenes influence on pupils that is less tangible. A school's commitment to them in return shows in the way they are kept in mind during the planning of all school strategies that have a bearing on their role, whether they are directly involved or not. Relevant strategies will range from practical arrangements for discussions with parents to the school's review of behaviour, anti-bullying and curricular policies.

Previous chapters have concentrated on including, informing and talking with parents; we will now look at how schools can recognise the role parents play in pupil development and progress. The principles of mutual recognition and appreciation can be translated into listening to their views and involving them in relevant decisions. At times, it will be important to organise events of only tangential benefit to individual pupils, in recognition of the value of parental interest in the life of the school community. Pastoral staff and senior managers will sustain the ethos of parental involvement if they convey to staff and pupils that parents' views are respected and taken seriously. Parents need to be seen as an essential resource to the school.

Leadership

Leadership evidently plays a crucial role in creating and sustaining the ethos of a school. In all of the case studies, a senior manager promoted or supported the introduction of new methods of working with parents. They keep their experience of child and adolescent development in mind and empathise with parents in order to encourage a school ethos that includes parents. Small details can make a difference. At Langdon School, the female headteacher, Vanessa Wiseman, had invited parents of new pupils to watch their children go to their classes on their first day from an upstairs balcony. In my interview with her, she mentioned how important it might be for parents to see who their children were with – an acknowledgement of the separation they would be feeling and a desire to make sure their children had company as they took their first steps in the new environment. Schools that recognise the ordinary, quite predictable feelings of care and concern of a parent in this way make parents feel understood, the first step to building trust in a school.

Change management

A review of home–school relations is likely to reveal the need for changes at all levels in a school. Reynolds and Packer's descriptors of typical resistance amongst staff to change in ineffective schools are:

- *'projections of individual teachers' deficiencies on to the children or the surrounding community and its parents, as excuses for ineffectiveness;*

- *"cling-ons" of past practice (we've always done it this way!);*

- *defences, whereby teachers have built walls to keep out threatening messages from outsiders;*

- *fear of attempting change because it may fail, associated with a reluctance to risk;*

- *the fantasy that change is someone else's job;*

- *the "safety in numbers" ploy, whereby the staff retreat into a ring-fenced mentality.'*

(Reynolds and Packer, 1992, p.179)

In a school that needs to improve quickly, the staff turnover may militate against forging stable relations with parents and getting to know local families. Or if a school has undergone extensive change, staff might find the adjustment to ordinary day-to-day communication with parents somewhat mundane. Really tough situations have a film-like quality; working in difficult environments, sorting out fights and dealing with social problems that may even involve the police at the sharp end of deprivation can be addictive. They tend to reinforce stereotypical images of parents, and create an embattled feel which will not help teachers to see parents as ordinary people. A part of the task of supporting those who work in these environments is not to judge their responses or defences, but to articulate a less threatening perspective. So if staff perceive parents as the opposition, anticipating a fight or anger, it can help to keep in mind that this woman approaching is the mother of her son or daughter, who nursed them through illnesses and survived the isolation of parenthood.

Supporting staff

It cannot be denied that the art of child development, of which education is a part, is unpredictable – it is hard to take responsibility for such slippery material as a child's development. Parents are the first parties responsible in a child's life. They hand the baton to teachers, and it can be unwieldy and difficult. The science of the quality of teaching and learning has been emphasised in recent years, but the developmental value of pastoral relationships with children and work with their parents is much less talked about. As long ago as the early 1960s, Michael Marland wrote: 'A mother who moved house during term was anxious to find out after a couple of weeks how her son was getting on. The class teacher was eventually and hesitantly spoken to. He was polite but baffled. What was the need to ask? The new boy was getting on quite normally, or they would have sent for her. No-one had the imagination to realise that some immediate reassurance would be welcome, or that this was the time to step out and interest the parent.' (Marland, 1964, pp. 15–16). In addition, it may be ten years before a new secondary teacher has experience of parenting adolescent children themselves and the age at which professional women have children is rising. Working with the parents of adolescent children can easily be intimidating. Senior managers need to appreciate teachers' insecurities and support them compassionately while not being afraid to challenge low expectations.

A school leader's role is to:

- show their commitment to working with families – one head sends a postcard to every new pupil at home before their first day, and greets them by name when they arrive with their parents

- delegate responsibility for working with parents and clarify who should get to know them

- focus on these staff, who will not just be teachers, and make useful observations about their style and approach with parents

- create a debate within the staffroom based on collective wisdom rather than received wisdom – get to know local families so that false generalisations can be challenged

- increase channels for more communication between parents and teachers so they feel motivated through personal contact to make an effort with each other

- make sure parents do not see them as a remote figure.

In addition to showing an interest by reviewing what other staff have done, and offering praise and encouragement, school leaders may lead a complementary activity, as was Michael Marland's approach as head of North Westminster Community School. Alongside targeted projects with minority ethnic communities led by home–school workers (described in Chapter 9), he invited the Bangladeshi ambassador to judge the English writing competition and to give out prizes at assembly. The public statement this made to pupils and parents about the wide horizons of the English-speaking world acted as a counterweight to the frequent categorisation of minority pupils as pupils with problems. Senior managers can helpfully make connections between the experiences and cultures of pupils in and out of school; between the microcosm of the school community and the macrocosm of the external world.

Egalitarianism

An important principle in work designed to improve communication with parents is its egalitarian nature. As we have seen, work with parents demands a commitment to communication with parents by staff at all levels of the school hierarchy. The non-authoritarian interpersonal skills required are easily observable when teachers and parents meet in person, which sets the tone for how to respond to parents. Leaders appear to set an example by their manner with parents as much as by the profile they give to parental initiatives. Demonstrable thought and effort about one's own style of communication helps to share power with parents, and to redress the balance between parents in different social classes. On an organisational level, issues of access and inclusiveness tend to be given due priority when initiatives are updated to embrace more parents than traditional meetings, as academic reviews have improved upon parents' evenings. In the next two examples, too, of headteacher-led approaches used by Dame Tamsyn Imison at Hampstead School, the newer event appears more inclusive. They were described by her in an interview in August, 2000.

▰ The head's open door

From 1984 to 1990, the headteacher held a monthly meeting where parents could raise any issue directly with her. The skills used in this meeting reflected this headteacher's awareness of the fear of teachers in general, which she related to their own experiences of rejection via the eleven-plus examination within the state system.

'The Head's Open Door was something I could run on my own because I started as head just as the industrial action by teachers started to limit participation by most staff. It was part of a broad range of activities, which included for example a summer fair run by the children, a helpline (although very few used it), and tutor group teas. They were necessary because parents otherwise tended to participate if all they had to do was appreciate their kids. There was a general fear of teachers, and of parents amongst teachers, that resulted in a need for groups like the Advisory Centre for Education. I had been involved with Parents' Action Groups myself, and I had two girls and one boy who had gone through the state system. Anyone over a certain age would have been subject to a selective system. Only 18% passed the eleven plus, so the vast majority of parents had been told they were not academic.

The Open Door was held at a regular time, such as the first Monday in the month. 6.30pm seemed the best time in our school. I asked the parents who came to sit in a circle. Individual parents had queries that sometimes led to a whole new approach. I invited Gill Morris, a specialist in Personal, Health and Social Education from the Local Education Authority, to come and talk to parents at one session about smoking and drugs. She was much more up-to-date than we would have been. She ran a session on coping with adolescence too. Thirty to forty parents is quite enough for this sort of discussion. A few parents were interested in much more information about what was being taught in Years 10 and 11. This led to a 'Post Home' initiative in the summer, in which every department gives a summary of which books are useful to read, and what homeworks will cover in general. On occasions, other members of staff attended, one deputy head in particular. It wasn't just mothers who came, there was a gender mix. It was a sounding board for policies too. At one stage it grew to 150 parents – we had to move it to the library.'

Year forums for parents

'When it was time to take a new approach, I sent a personal letter to all Year 7 parents inviting them to an informal Year Forum for Parents, from 6.30pm to about 8.30pm. It was organised with the school's home–school association who provided the food and drink. The head of year and tutors came. The parents who came, about a quarter of the 200 in the year, were seated around eight tables (by tutor group) with a large piece of flipchart paper. Any children who came with their parents sat together at another table. I asked them to write down 'What a child is like' (and the children wrote 'what a parent is like') and to choose a spokesperson to feed back. It was an icebreaker, and met their expectations in terms of teachers taking the organising role while also getting parents to participate actively. The exercise got them to see the similarities between children. It also structured the raising of issues in a manageable way as each group then discussed the problems, which varied from tidying their rooms to mobile phones, and suggested solutions too. The problem of getting them up for school was of evident value to the school's goal of improving punctuality, and the parents talked about what was needed the night before, how to monitor what was needed on different days, and organising clothes for school. Refugee parents came and translated for each other.

The feed back was reported in the school newsletter, the Hampstead Buzz. Other topics raised were homework, bullying and new coursework guidelines. I felt as a headteacher that I learnt what parents were feeling about the school. Parents were working too – everyone was doing their bit and learning what partnerships involve. Parents realised that we all play a role, and I think they understood the value of togetherness with the school. The Year Forums for Parents of students in Years 8 and 9 were also fun, and well attended. Unlike other types of parents' groups, they do not rely on regular meetings that always end up being dominated by a small number of parents who are particularly committed.'

These examples illustrate how a space can be created for parental voices to be heard and for the start of a dialogue with parents about issues with their children that affect their education. A challenge for schools across the UK is how to create more of a sense that parents are genuinely involved in decisions that affect them and their children, rather than paying lip-service to the ideal of engaging parents. Much will depend on the interpersonal skills of staff in conversations with parents about their child. Schools also need to consider the wider involvement of parents, in consultation about whole school policies and procedures. Their starting point must be that all parents are entitled to engage in relevant debate with the providers of education and with their children, in keeping with emerging traditions in state-provided public services in Britain.

Citizenship

Vincent and Martin have studied discussion-based parents' forums in search of a deliberative space vital for 'deliberative democracy' as epitomised by the development of parental engagement with the school (1999, 2000). A sociological perspective can equally be applied to the dynamics of individual parental involvement. The notion of citizenship (which in the UK is *still* fairly notional) introduces a contrast with the silent subject, such as the parent expected to listen silently to their child's report.

> 'The old ethos stressed habitual obedience rather than the critical thought and democratic practices of a citizenship culture as in the United States, France and post-war western Germany. The idea of 'a good citizen' was simply 'a good subject'. The traditional English idea of public service was from the top down.'

(Bernard Crick, TES, 30 June 2000, p.15)

The implication that there is an intrinsic value in challenge and debate sets a school's endeavour to modernise its relations with parents into a social and moral context. A more challenging citizen is assumed to have ideas of their own, with a right to debate and challenge those setting the agenda. However, in order to challenge the establishment, a parent needs to feel they are not the only one. Expecting an isolated parent to express critical views of the school is unrealistic – they will be worried about the backlash on their own child, with reason as children do report inappropriate remarks being made to them by teachers after meetings with their parents. But the problem with creating a public space for parents to complain about the school is that the image of the all-powerful state provider can prompt parents to become overly demanding. By grouping parents together and inviting them to speak, the result may be purely to create a space for discontent and opposition. In an impersonal public meeting, it is difficult to help the participants to be realistic in their demands or constructive in their suggestions. Schools trying to reform relations with parents need to create space for individual issues and problems, in discussions where parents feel safe enough to express themselves honestly. In the little time available for meetings with parents during the school year very significant things are said. The problem at the moment is that many of the conversations are not particularly focused or productive.

Consultation

Parents can be asked their opinion about the expectations that the school has of them, if asked in a suitable way. Approaches to consultation on the involvement they would like to have as well as on policy can be very similar to those employed for the audit described in Chapter 2, and home–school workers are ideally placed to ask questions neutrally. Ideas for policy development will benefit from the views of parents because they are not as invested as staff in the history or tradition of current policies. They may have creative ideas for solutions to old problems.

The Instep home–school project in Scotland involved parents in an interesting way during a period of substantial school review. A survey was taken to local parents requesting their opinion of the local secondary school against a list of a range of features describing an effective secondary school. The clarity of the results and the value of involving parents in setting priorities for school improvement and development in this way led to the survey being repeated two years later. Non-teaching staff and those who work specifically with parents can also support policy development by contributing views during a consultation exercise based on their experience.

The commonly disparaged annual meetings for parents could be used to much better effect, as has been shown in schools that seek out vehicles for consulting parents and debating issues with them (Bastiani, 1995). But formal meetings are bound to exclude those who are not comfortable with written procedures or meeting conventions – such as the setting of an agenda and the function of the chair. It may be necessary to use existing associations and parents' groups, including cultural associations and fund-raising groups, for consultation. These traditional groupings of parents can be valuable because their stable membership can encourage honesty and ensure diverse interests will be represented:

> 'The constructive discussion – where parents could agree to disagree – to a large extent resulted from the close relationships built on strong social ties inside and outside the school. The 'open' forum was rather more impersonal, with fewer parents knowing each other or having links outside the school ... The ease of relationships because of social ties between parents can encourage the active expression of parental voice in the forums.'
>
> (Martin, Ranson and Vincent, 2000, p.6)

Pressures on parents

It is important not to let listening to parents become a channel for pressures that merely serve to distract them from educational issues. One deputy head interviewed described how a detail of uniform became disproportionately important to parents at his school, when pupils were allowed to wear their own trainers with the uniform school sweatshirt and black trousers. Before regulation by the school, parents endured excessive pressure from their children over the detail of which trainers were allowed and what style was acceptable. They passed this pressure directly on to school staff – minor disciplinary incidents were blown out of proportion whenever the school tried to limit the eccentricities of fashion, as parents came into school to complain about the infringement of their child's freedom. The school then introduced a policy on uniform that effectively banned fashionable trainers, and started to loan black plimsolls to any pupil who attended in the wrong shoes which successfully stopped arguments with parents over this matter.

Policy development

Following consultation, a common challenge for a school today is how to engage a range of parents and teachers in discussions about policy issues and stimulate constructive suggestions, without merely creating a platform for complaints. In the case of the year forum described above, parents of children of a particular age were asked to discuss among themselves their preoccupations and possible solutions involving both home and school. The relevance to parental support of education was immediately apparent, and where conversation seemed to expect school solutions, the facilitator could ensure these were balanced by asking other parents how they would deal with a problem raised. Equally important was acknowledging the basic minimum that had to be done by the school for all parents: only if they were given better information directly by the school could parents help their children to prepare for school the night before, to ration television viewing and to assess the progress of coursework. This sort of debate then has implications for curricular policies, such as assessment and marking, which teachers should correlate to the discussion held.

At the Year Forum in Hampstead School, the structure of the exercise set and seating parents in small groups allowed a space where the voices of parents were heard. Action taken after each forum gave a profile to the new dialogue. The head sent out details of Year 10 courses in response to the open discussions with parents. Parental opinions were channelled into other discussions by printing the results of each meeting in the school newsletter, where teachers and governors of the school could take parents' experiences and views into account when planning and policy-making. The wording was not changed by staff and the broad dissemination of the newsletter enabled parents' views on a wide range of policy and practice issues to be shared. The next stage, as research on school-based parents' groups has shown, would be to define how these views had been taken on board (Vincent and Martin, 2000). Being responsive to what schools find parents' concerns to be helps the creation of two-way communication.

The educational research on school-based forums (Martin et al., 2000; Vincent and Martin, 2000) has confirmed that space for a genuine dialogue with parents is being created in schools in several types of forums. These approaches have begun to take account of the fact that most parents (not just the middle classes) do wish to honour their responsibilities, but they feel silenced by the range of hurdles and obstacles in their path (MacLure and Walker, 1999, 2000). A commitment to democracy in discussing issues with parents balances the inevitable feeling that a school is privileged territory for professionals and insiders. Many schools need to recognise that almost all parents of school pupils have a contribution to make, and that parents are motivated by altruism as well as self-interest. An ethos of parental involvement will strengthen through deliberation with parents about policy issues that relate but are not restricted to parental interest in their individual child.

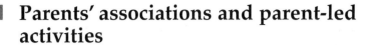

Parents' associations and parent-led activities

Recently it has become unfashionable to value Parents' Associations or old Parent–Teacher Associations within home–school strategies. These traditional groups are often discredited because of the desire to reduce inequalities in work with parents. However, the informal 'club' atmosphere of Parents' Associations enables parents to feel comfortable, as if they were with a group of friends – they are friendly with each other and they are united by being friends of the school. These social groups tend to create a clublike feel, which makes them appear exclusive to parents who would be in the minority. It is a mistake to think that they are all middle-class groupings – educational research with a sociological perspective has shown that this is not always the case. Those motivated to participate can be the ones who want to give something back to the school out of gratefulness, or out of 'not wanting something for nothing', which is not a class-specific value. This was a main reason reported by the parents interviewed:

> *'I like to think that I am putting something back. It improves the education system for the little bit of help I give, it benefits the children and the school, not just my own. I think that is a worthwhile job, I look at it as something I like doing.'*

(Clive, white father and Carson School Association Chair)

> *'Well we felt, because like the school had taken him on, we thought well, like it is only fair that we ought to try and do something toward the school. So we decided, well, me and the wife decided to join some sort of association, combined with the school.'*

(Peter, white father and Carson School Association Treasurer)
(Vincent and Martin, 2000, p.464)

Traditional Parent–Teacher Association meetings are not used as a space for negotiation and are not, in general, representative of all parents. But they provide a vital informal type of network that can support the aims of the school. Parent governors can provide an appropriate link between Parents' Associations and more concerted efforts made by school staff as part of the school development plan.

The Camden School Community Association (CASCA)

The emphasis on improving communication with parents and involving them in new forms of debate should not minimise the importance of channelling the more active contribution that small groups of parents can make into a range of parent-supported activities.

Camden School for Girls is a comprehensive school in North London with 950 pupils on roll. It has currently to raise £250,000 over a two-year period to meet its requirement as a Voluntary-Aided school to contribute 15%. The impecunious Frances Mary Buss foundation is behind it and a large-scale building project is now going ahead, for which 85% of the money comes from the state and the rest must be found by the governors through trusts and fund-raising. Parents usually help to raise more than £10,000 per year, and more during periods of intensive fund-raising.

The school introduced banding for the September 1999 intake. The banding is established by testing with the help of NFER, and the school draws up four separate catchment areas for each of the four ability bands, A to D, taking 25% of its intake from each band. The aim is to ensure a stable academic balance throughout the school with the accompanying benefits of planning staffing and the curriculum more consistently than if the roll was subject to an unpredictable academic mix from year to year.

Interview with Deborah Jackson, Secretary of CASCA

'Twenty to thirty parents or carers participate in the association in support of the school. The headteacher and one or two staff usually attend the meetings. No-one is excluded, even pupils – once a couple of sixth formers came to offer help in motivating the rest of the sixth form during a fund-raising exercise. Unlike many a PTA, this group seems to have the trust of the teaching staff, but maybe this is because it does not see its function as being a forum for decision-making about the school, or even low-level grumbling. The school supports different cultural communities and CASCA can play a helping role in some of these – for instance by organising a Bengali social group. It can also be a forum for anecdotal discussion of issues for parents, like the use of mobile telephones in school, difficulties with friendship groups, how to encourage teenagers to do their homework or GCSE coursework, and the amount of freedom allowed at different stages.'

Deborah described the fund-raising activities she had been involved in herself. One of these during 2000 was a Promises Auction, the first in the school for some years, which raised nearly £18,000.

Promises Auction

'Get your School Association to take the lead. If they want to do it, they should start planning at least nine months ahead. They need to tell parents when it will happen and start to gather ideas. It takes a long time to generate a good head of steam – first of all people do nothing about it, the idea has to sit around for a while and appear in the school newsletter, with some suggestions of what people can give. The basic principle is that everyone has something to give, whether it is an evening of babysitting, or something a bit more unusual. Those who buy at the auction are at least partly looking to give something to the school, so they will not be as demanding as if it was a commercial enterprise. Most of the lots will be fun, a few will be very eye-catching.'

Deborah quoted a school in America which had auctioned a parking space in front of the school gates for a year for thousands of dollars! The lots should be affordable and roughly in line with the sort of expenditure considered reasonable by the range of parents and employers in your school and local community. But do not fall prey to low expectations. You might be surprised what local people will come up with.

Getting people talking

A parent representative for each form will help to talk to people to see if they have any ideas. They might see each other at events organised at the school, so make sure they are sent details of these well in advance by post so they can make arrangements to attend. The telephone is used a lot to pursue ideas, so the school office may be able to help by making sure all phone numbers are up to date, with the proviso that confidentiality is respected too.

Once the idea of the Promises Auction is in circulation, inform staff and parents regularly about lots that have been offered. The bulk of the work until the day itself will now be compiling a catalogue, and making sure that each item is described as fully and accurately as possible – if a holiday cottage is on offer, what period exactly, and how many will it sleep? Are pets/smokers allowed? You want to be almost as careful about this as a commercial company might be, to avoid awkward misunderstandings.

The evening itself

'An auctioneer is needed, preferably with some professional experience of rattling through the bidding but also with a light touch and an understanding of how to

coax the optimum amount of money from bidders for a lot which might be decid-
edly quirky and have no well-defined commercial value. With your auctioneer,
work out how many lots you will be able to auction 'live' without the evening
dragging on until long after midnight.'

Deborah and Peter's group decided that no more than 120 could be sold
live during a single evening; the rest were 'silent' lots. These were to be
viewed before the live auction started, with either the object itself on
display, if tangible, or a good description of it, and a sheet of card on
which to enter bids, each one higher than the last. People walked round
placing their bids, and at the appointed hour the lots were sold to the
highest bidder, from £1 to £200, depending on the item. Their American
friends, whose auction was a more high-powered fund-raising event,
introduced an extra twist to this silent section by allowing a 'close-
out' – a notional value was placed on each lot, and if bidders wanted to
ensure success at the final outcome, they had merely to bid four times
that value. After that, no further bids were allowed.

'Meanwhile the auctioneer assembles everyone for the 'live' part of the evening.
The bidding is fast and furious, fuelled (with any luck) by alcohol and adrenaline,
and lots would tend to be sold for more than in the Silent Auction. Runners (stu-
dents from the school) would find the successful bidder and take their name and
telephone number in readiness for payment and collection of lots at the end of the
evening. Care needs to be taken over the paperwork, so that there is the minimum
of confusion later on about exactly who has bought what!'

Seeing Deborah at home before the auction with the phone ringing, and
her husband and eldest daughter talking about the latest offers made –
a dinner cooked by a famous food writer and singing lessons from a
world-class singer – I was reminded of the way in which this sort of
activity becomes a pleasurable part of family life. Schools that decide
not to encourage their Parents' Associations are really missing out on an
opportunity to create emotional and moral support for pupils by whole
families in the school, who express their valuing of education in the
time and commitment they give. The activities are fun, so parents will
become associated with a positive, lively and energetic form of support,
which will help teachers to appreciate them and will provide a balance
to the mutual surveillance which is an inevitable dynamic in the
home–school relationship.

CAMDEN SCHOOL FOR GIRLS
Sandall Road, London NW5

AUCTION OF PROMISES

ORGANISED BY CASCA
IN SUPPORT OF THE BUILDING APPEAL

FRIDAY 7th APRIL 2000
From 6 pm to 10.30 pm

Auctioneer: Roger Keverne

Timetable

6.00   Silent Auction and Education/Health Zone open

6.30   Bar and Snackbar open

7.00   Voucher Bazaar opens

7.30   Live Auction begins

9.30   Silent Auction and Education/Health Zone close

9.30   Grand Draw

10.30   Bar closes and evening ends

UNDER 16s WELCOME WITH RESPONSIBLE ADULT

Examples of lots

How to claim your Live Auction lot

If you are the successful bidder, a runner will come immediately to collect your details, and give you a card with the number and price of the lot. Please write a cheque payable to CASCA or have cash ready (no credit/debit cards) and bring it to the Cashier's Desk where you will be given details of how to claim your lot. You can make payment any time after buying the lot, but please allow time if the Cashier is busy. Portable lots should be collected on the night if possible.

PLEASE DO NOT REMOVE YOUR LOT UNTIL YOU HAVE HAD CLEARANCE FROM AN ORGANISER.

13 Pas de Deux
Watch a Royal Ballet class in the new Opera House. 2 tickets for the class 10.30-12 am, 24th April (Easter Monday). Lower age limit 12.
Sue Davis

14 Handy-Andy
A day's labour in the London area by a versatile builder: carpentry, bricklaying, painting, plastering (you supply materials). No plumbing or electrics.
Bill Drew

15 A Roaring Success
Two good tickets for a Saturday performance of The Lion King musical.
Angela Weir

16 Dine with a Stranger?
A meal for 2 and a bottle of house wine at the famous Magdala Tavern, South End Green.
Lindsay & Tish Campbell

17 An Absolute Snip
Haircut in top hairdressing salon, Cello (W1).
Petra Fried

ARTS & CRAFTS MOVEMENT

ART FURNITURE
Est. 1989
158 Camden Street London NW1 9PA
Tel 0207 267 4324   Fax. 0207 267 5199
E-mail arts-and-crafts@artfurniture.co.uk
Website www.artfurniture.co.uk
OPEN 7 DAYS 12-6

217 ABC of DTP
School Secretary, Barbara Goldsmith, offers a three hour tutorial for one or two beginners in the ins and outs of Desk Top Publishing using Microsoft Publisher, at school or at your home.
Barbara Goldsmith

218 Twang!
5 Guitar lessons for a complete beginner, guitar provided. Either in NW5 or at your home within 3 mile radius.
David Gaskell

219 Economical!
Six hours tutoring in A Level Economics from University of Westminster lecturer, within 4 miles of school.
Alec Gordon

220 English Patient
MA in Education offers 6 hours tutoring at A Level in English. Round the corner from CSG.
Roger Elliott

221 Raise Your Voice
Have you ever wanted to sing but never taken the plunge? Or do you want to take your voice a stage further? A great opportunity to take three lessons with Linda Hirst, distinguished international singer and Head of Vocal Studies at Trinity College of Music. She has a wide repertoire from jazz (as an ex Swingle singer) through mainstream to seriously difficult contemporary music.
Linda Hirst

HEALTH

250 Deeply Relaxing
A reflexology/aromatherapy session at donor's home in Hendon or locally (45-60 minutes): 'Treatment which helps the body to balance and heal itself'. Could be within wider North London area if parking available.
Janine Clinton-Smith

251 Back to Back
An hour's lesson with a trained instructor in the Alexander Technique in donor's home in Highbury.
Refia Sacks

252 Stretch Yourself
Private 1 hour yoga lesson (Iyengar) in Crouch End with Ros Bell, teacher for over 20 years and author of 'Simple Yoga Techniques'.
Ros Bell

253 Good Health
Address those aches and pains in a holistic way. A 90 minute session in your home with a professional homeopath.
Fran Sinclair-Taylor

254 Healthy by Nature
One consultation and two follow-up sessions in Camden area with a medical herbalist. Small charge for herbs at cost.
Sue Goddard

Specialist speakers on issues concerning parents

Some initiatives that clearly support a parent-friendly ethos have been part of school life for many years. Home–school work in many secondary schools has included occasional talks for parents, often by advisers in Local Education Authorities. These activities may acquire a new relevance when planned to reflect whole school development in particular policy areas, such as bullying, homework or behaviour. They enable parents to meet each other informally, encouraging a sense of a parental community within the school. They can be organised to reach out to particular parents if a need has been identified.

Community talks

Uniting parents by their community of interest outside school can be particularly important if they are in a minority. At North Westminster Community School, for example, Islamic parents were invited to discuss with the Imam of a nearby mosque whether swimming was acceptable during Ramadan.

Short courses on parenting

Outside speakers may also be willing to offer a series of talks or a short course for parents. Commonly, talks are popular on drugs, behaviour, sexual relationships, discipline and support for pupils as examinations approach. The humanity of the speaker is important, rather than their expert status, especially given the sensitive nature of personal and social topics. A proper discussion of emotional issues will contribute to better understanding of a teacher's position if problems arise at school. The speaker needs to convey that it is an inevitable part of parenthood that all parents will struggle some of the time.

Bob Sproson, Head of Cambridgeshire Secondary Support Service

In working with groups of parents, I have found on a fairly consistent basis that the vast majority are keen to learn more about the task of parenting. Rather like any group of 'practitioners' this majority tends to fall into the following groups:

■ Very capable, having few problems in relating to their offspring, but keen to add to their knowledge and/or to discuss and share 'practice' with others;

■ Very capable, but with a specific problem area or child which they wish to address;

■ Struggling with the task, keen to learn whatever is on offer, both by listening to 'experts' and sharing experiences with others;

■ Struggling with the task to the point where they are on the point of giving up and desperate for support of any kind.

Practical issues

I have run a variety of 'parenting support' and 'help' groups under a whole range of titles. Most have been centred upon a secondary school which has then offered its resources (venue, overhead projector, television, video, etc.), but some have been 'community based', most usually utilising a village hall or similar building. Clearly it helps if the venue can be warm, comfortable and accessible and if light refreshments (at the least tea and coffee) can be made available.

Initial sessions have always been well attended, provided that they have been appropriately advertised. Subsequent numbers depend upon the quality of the experience for the parents. A mixture of didactic delivery and the opportunity to talk in large or small groups (the latter are usually better ... at least more people get to actively participate) has worked well. The didactic section may come from a single speaker covering a range of topics or through a range of speakers. I have preferred the former because of the rapport which it is then possible to build with the group, but both, if well planned and delivered, will engage an audience.

Content

Three areas have consistently been rated highly in official and unofficial feedback from groups:

1. Theories of behaviour: I would never suggest that I can or should offer an in-depth course on the range of possible explanations for human behaviour, but sessions spread over two to three weeks (one hour of 'lecture' followed by small group discussions/tasks) have enabled me to give participants a good overview of the major bodies of thought (cognitive, behaviourist, psychoanalytic, perceptual-phenomenological, existential, eclectic) and to add to these areas the 'nature nurture' debate along with some information concerning labelling of behaviour. Inevitably there have been parents of children who have been diagnosed as ADHD, conduct-disordered, etc., or parents who want their child so diagnosed in order that they might access resources and much interesting subject matter arises for discussion. Equally inevitably many participants become more interested in examining and explaining their own behaviour than that of their offspring, but that is helpful both in terms of personal insight and of understanding how their own behaviour impinges upon all those people with whom they interact. I like to conclude with the notion that individuals rarely, if ever, act in a manner which takes no account of their environment. Behaviour is not a 'constant' which people carry around with them: thus everything in the home, from the way it looks to the values which the parents espouse, will influence the behaviour of the young people growing up in it.

2. Proactive parenting: It is this understanding, twinned with the idea that although there are many other factors which influence children's behaviour, the way that they are parented is arguably the single most influential factor, which leads parents to look at the way they structure their household, the way that they choose to relate to the other members of it. Again I like to use a three-week period to cover a range of topics and to provide plenty of opportunity for discussion in large and very small groups. Areas which I cover are:

- the creation of rules in the home,
- the notion of non-negotiable and negotiable rules and guidelines for behaviour,

- private space for young people – rules which govern the use of that, i.e. what does private mean?

- meal times,

- use of televisions, computers and whatever new technological wizardry is around,

- pocket money,

- friends – particularly when they are deemed to be 'undesirable',

- bedtimes,

- tidiness (or otherwise!).

When working with parents in secondary schools (it may well be argued that this is pertinent for lower age ranges also), I have utilised external speakers ('experts') to cover the areas of drug use and adolescent sexuality and, presuming that the speakers have been knowledgeable and able to present their information well, these sessions have proved to be highly successful.

3. Dealing with conflict when it does occur: It is essential to add to the notion that although, to a very large degree, children are the products of their parenting, there are occasions (anonymous case studies are helpful here) when children stray despite 'best efforts' on the part of their parents and, even in the calmest and most caring of homes, conflict will occur on occasion. Thus it is important that parents are clear how they will respond when 'tempers flare'. Again the notion of pre-planning is key, but other areas I cover are:

- If a is initial outburst, b is parental response to it and c is next behaviour on part of child, then c may well be more closely linked to b than it is to a.

- The anger cycle – there is a clear graph which can be plotted for most outbursts – what most people fail to understand is the amount of time which is required to 'come down' from extreme anger. Reasoning, reflecting and planning are not likely to be possible until after that period of time.

- The notion of 'doing the opposite' to the angry person – not always possible, but can be a useful strategy, e.g. child shouts, adult voice lowers.

- The need for self-support or mutual support by/amongst parents after difficult-to-manage incidents.

Two weeks is usually enough to cover these areas, although it is important to be aware that there almost inevitably will be parents for whom the examination of such 'incidents' is very painful (for some the pain comes from the fact that their own children behave in such a way, for others it comes from reflecting back upon 'flash points' with their own parents or carers). Individuals may need a lot of time to talk, but they must not come to believe that this is a forum in which they can deal in any great depth with such issues.

Targeted talks

When a concentration of issues or needs in a particular tutor or year group of pupils creates a challenge to normally effective teaching strategies, dynamics in particular years can be addressed through special talks for parents. These talks should be made accessible to all parents but with the possibility of dividing into small groups to discuss the content with form tutors or year heads.

Involving pupils in home-school work

One of the challenges in home–school communication can be the participation of pupils in meetings that concern them. As they approach adulthood, discussions can appropriately involve them, provided other channels exist for communication between parents and teachers. While they might find these discussions difficult on an emotional level, given the independence to which they become accustomed in the school environment, they will appreciate being offered a role. Teachers can also encourage their understanding of the need for communication with their parents about their well-being and progress.

Once their appreciation has developed of the benefit to them individually of parents and teachers meeting, the benefit to the school of parental involvement could also be discussed with pupils. Identifying all those whose lives are affected by the education a pupil receives could illustrate democratic principles or the notion of a stakeholder society.

Implications for the quality of teaching and learning

'The best thing is for the parents to be brought within the educational experience of the schoolchild by doing what they can do, and this with confidence. There are many ways in which the parents can help the child in his learning, which are within the parents' spheres of competence. If this happens, then the parent can feel adequate and confident both in relation to the child and the school. This may mean that the contents of the learning in school should be drawn much more from the child's experience in his family and community.'

(Bernstein, 1970, p.345)

Teachers have tended to follow Bernstein's advice only so far, except in schools where channels of consultation exist and home–school contact is frequent (Bastiani, 1995). Objections to the centralised parameters of the National Curriculum have obscured the fact that a large amount of freedom exists which teachers can use.

Teachers can share this freedom and refine their methods of involving parents in the support of their children's learning by informing parents and community groups about the knowledge and the abilities that will be developed through schemes of work. Sending out a list of topics due to be taught during the term or year can encourage discussion at home. The teacher or school's interpretation of the National Curriculum can thus be shared honestly with parents, and parents can see where they will be able to help and, equally important, where they cannot help. Informing parents in this way might also help pupils to make connections in their mind between what is learnt at school and the world outside school.

Family members might offer culturally-specific knowledge or perspectives which will enrich the school-taught curriculum. Once teachers understand local family lives, curriculum content can be planned that relates to pupils' experiences outside school to provide the maximum scope for reinforcement of school learning.

A teacher who does not understand the context or culture of each pupil will miss valuable opportunities to help the pupil develop their thinking, or even worse, may offend a pupil through lack of insight into their home situation. Communication with parents can mediate this problem at the core of what is taught and how it is taught. Not every teacher can get to know a child's family, but from all the teachers that a child has, a few should be responsible for developing an understanding of their particular situation. A parent who never feels connected with a staff member at the school could fail to help the pupil to think through aspects of their life and make conscious choices about their behaviour and achievement at school. Lessons devised in mainstream schools will probably be less culturally specific than the cultural lessons learnt at home. Where there are not enough teachers to represent the different cultural and faith communities within the school, key staff need to be responsible for learning enough to ensure that the school does not unintentionally discriminate against pupils from minority cultures.

Culture

In a multi-cultural school, cultural activities and customs initiated by pupils will help their parents to feel welcome too. The great differences between schools here and in their country of origin may otherwise reduce the motivation of minority parents to visit the school or talk with staff. They might feel alienated, or simply respect the professional expertise of teachers and not wish to intrude. Minority ethnic pupils and parents can easily regard school as a completely separate world from family life, which discourages these parents from relating to the school even if the school wished they had more involvement. First and second generation children may themselves need to learn about customs and schools in their country of origin in order to have ideas for how their school in this country might reflect their culture. The split between home and school can be reduced by encouraging pupils to bring home cultural experiences into school, as in North Westminster Community School where pupils put up notices about Ramadan. Supplementary and mother tongue schools linked with the school might help to generate material for displays.

School development

Substantial understanding amongst school staff of families' lives can influence arrangements made for home–school work and for children's education in general. The planning of meetings at the school should consider the fact that in some areas parents do a considerable amount of shift work, or few have private transport. This is a form of 'organisational listening', which will help to forge trust with the school.

Responses to parents' queries will communicate a school's respect for their contribution, and new forums for debate will extend the capacity of the school to take on board their concerns and views, while agreeing on the role and responsibilities of parents too.

Creative ideas for parental involvement might be encouraged once a trusted space has been created for open-minded debate. Parents may wish to attend sex or drugs education lessons, which could be delivered out of school hours. It may even be possible to develop debate with parents about adjusting the organisation of a school to suit the majority of families. By listening to issues for parents, schools might start to originate ideas that could lead to radical changes in the way education is delivered and organised, for example, times of the school day could be adjusted to include a long after-lunch session for community work and extra-curricular activities before completing lessons in the late afternoon. A variety of solutions that were previously only found in the private education sector might solve daily transport and childcare problems and accommodate family life. The impact of sustaining a dialogue with parents would then be felt on local educational provision as a whole, and Local Education Authorities would need to be involved to realise new plans. Most secondary schools have few areas for pupil relaxation and leisure away from normal classrooms, and staff contracts would need to accommodate different responsibilities.

Schools that take steps to engage and sustain the almost universal interest amongst parents in their children's education will experience the rewards. A belief that parents have something to offer needs to be reflected in public events as well as private meetings. By maintaining open communication and debate with parents, schools are creating avenues for greater parental influence on the life of a school community as a whole as well as improved support for individual pupils.

The changes brought about by teachers and others, in widely varying schools, suggest we are at a turning point in secondary school work with parents. A growing body of experience implies that the potential of parental support for pupil achievement and for comprehensive education is beginning to be realised. Although initial training is lacking, further professional training is available for staff development in interpersonal work and leadership. Experience gained from introducing new work with parents, and from increased communication with parents, will help teachers to reflect and learn about effective approaches. In addition, research findings on home–school communication will enable schools to draw on psychological and sociological insights in the development of new strategies. Newer practices are starting to resolve age-old difficulties between parents and teachers in secondary schools.

TABLE OF INFORMATION ON CASE STUDY SCHOOLS

School	Area	No. of pupils	Eligible for free school meals %	Ethnic minority pupils %	Key socio-economic factors	Feeder primaries	Full-time staff/ equivalent	Strategies included
Llanedeyrn High School	Roundwood, Cardiff	920	27%	9%	Part suburban, part estate community school	5 main feeders	52	Home-School Agreement, NRAs reports, planner
Deptford Green School	Lewisham, South-East London	1100	60%	51%	Situated within two poorest wards in Lewisham	8 main, 44 in total	70	Deptford Truancy Challenge, and Office Mgr. interviews, job descriptions
The Philip Morant School	Colchester, Essex	1647	7%	2.8%	Foundation, CTC Average CAT scores, varied intake, SEN Unit on site	5	105	Year 9 Options Evenings
Llanrumney High School	Llanrumney, Cardiff	800	37%	5%	Edge of estates	8	46.5	Review Days, SEN
Castlebrae Community High School	Edinburgh, Scotland	350	58%	0.003%	Urban outskirts	4 main, 1 dual, 9 in total	42.14 (teaching staff)	Instep Project – consulting parents, home visits
New Heys Community Comprehensive School	Garston/ Allerton, Liverpool	1030	39%	7%	Inner-city school	5 main, intake from linear strip across city	61	Review Days, family literacy project

School statistics refer to the year 1999–2000

TABLE OF INFORMATION ON CASE STUDY SCHOOLS

School	Area	No. of pupils	Eligible for free school meals %	Ethnic minority pupils %	Key socio-economic factors	Feeder primaries	Full-time staff/ equivalent	Strategies included
Hampstead School	North London	1300	34%	53.5%	80 home languages	7	128	HT Forum for Parents, newsletter, Somali Community Project
Camden School for Girls	North London	926	33%	33% EAL	Voluntary-aided girls' comprehensive Policy of banding – 25% from ability groups A–D	6	60 (teaching)	PTA – CASCA, Promises Auction, Book Fair
Cantonian High School	Cardiff	1250	26%	12%	Families mainly housed by the local authority, in large area of social deprivation	3 main, about 12 others	75 (teaching)	Consulting parents about Parents' Evenings
North Westminster Community School	London	1950	47%	89%	Inner London school on 3 sites	47	c. 215 adults	Family liaison and Refugee workers
Langdon School, Newham	East London	1926	43%	76%	Inclusive school (487 on SEN register; low exclusion) and diverse – 49+ home languages	5 main	c. 200 adults on site	Primary–secondary transition, planner, SEN, whole school ethos

School statistics refer to the year 1999–2000

FURTHER READING AND REFERENCES

Further Reading

Home backgrounds

Marland, M., 1974, 'The pupils in their times', *Pastoral Care*, Heinemann Educational.

Quinton, D. and Rutter, M., 1985, 'Parenting behaviour of mothers raised in care', in A. R. Nicol (ed), *Longitudinal Studies in Child Psychology and Psychiatry*.

Rutter, M., 1989, 'Pathways from childhood to adult life', *Journal of Child Psychology and Psychiatry*, vol. 30, no. 1, pp.23–51.

Home–school audit, policy-making and practice

Alexander, T., Bastiani, J. and Beresford, E., 1995, *Home–School Policies: A Practical Guide*, Jet Publications.

Beresford, E., Botcherby, S. and McNamara, O., 2000, *Parents and Secondary Schools – Enabling Parents to Support their Children's Learning*, Manchester School Improvement Service, Tel. 0161 610 3333.

Brighouse, T., 1993, 'Parental involvement from policy to practice: An education officer's view', in Merttens, R. and Vass, J. (eds), *Partnerships in Maths*, The Falmer Press, pp.175–80.

Burgess, R. G., 1985, 'Documenting pastoral care: Strategies for teachers and researchers', in P. Lang and M. Marland (eds), *New Directions in Pastoral Care*, Blackwell, NAPCE, ESRC.

DfEE, 1999, *How is Your Child Doing at School*, HMSO.

DfEE, 2000, *Learning Journey*, HMSO. Three guides to the curriculum, copies available to parents on request only, Tel. 08000 96 66 26.

Hailstone, E., 1984, *Stay-away Parents and How to Draw Them In*, Home and School Council, 2nd edn.

Marland, M. and Rogers, R., 1991, *Marketing the School*, Heinemann Educational.

Pastoral care
Bettelheim, B., 1987, *A Good Enough Parent*, Thames and Hudson.
Marland, M. and Rogers, R., 1997, *The Art of the Tutor*, David Fulton Publishers.

Effectiveness
Rutter, M., Maughan, B., Mortimore, P., Ouston, J. and Smith, A., 1979, *Fifteen Thousand Hours: Secondary Schools and the Effects on Children*, Open Books.
Walker, B. M., 1998, 'Meetings without communication: A study of parents' evenings in secondary schools', *British Educational Research Journal*, vol. 24, no. 2, pp.163–78.

Teacher support
Creese, A., Daniels, H. and Norwich, B., 1997, *Teacher Support Teams in Primary and Secondary Schools*, David Fulton Publishers.
IMPACT Games and Activities Pack. Available from the Impact Project, School of Education, UNL, Tel. 020 7753 7052.
PATCH English and Science packs. Available from the Partnership with Parents team, M-SIS, Acorn Centre, Tel. 0161 610 3311.

References

Alexander, T., Bastiani, J. and Beresford, E., 1995, *Home–School Policies: A Practical Guide*, JET Publications.
ATL, 2000a, *Teachers and Parents: Survey of Teachers' Views*, Opinion Research Corporation International.
ATL, 2000b, *What the Teachers Said*, (unpublished), IPPR Conference Workshop Paper, Association of Teachers and Lecturers.
Barber, M., 1994, *Parents and their Attitudes to Secondary Schools – Interim Report*, (unpublished), Centre for Successful Schools, University of Keele.
Bastiani, J., 1995, *Taking a Few Risks*, RSA.
Beresford, E., Botcherby, S. and McNamara, O., 2000, *Parents and Secondary Schools – Enabling Parents to Support their Children's Learning*, Manchester School Improvement Service, Tel. 0161 610 3333.
Berne, E., 1966, *Games People Play*, Penguin.
Bernstein, B., 1970, 'Education cannot compensate for society', *New Society*, 387, (26 February), pp.344–7.
Bettelheim, B., 1987, *A Good Enough Parent*, Thames and Hudson.
Brighouse, T., 1993, 'Parental involvement from policy to practice: An education officer's view', in R. Merttens and J. Vass (eds), *Partnerships in Maths*, The Falmer Press, pp.175–80.
Brown, D. and Pedder, J., 1989, *Introduction to Psychotherapy*, Routledge.

Byng-Hall, J., 1994, Foreword to second edition, in E. Dowling and E. Osborne (eds), *The Family and the School*, Routledge, pp. xiii–xiv.

Cowling, K. and Cowling, H., 1993, *Toe by Toe*, Baildon, W. Yorkshire, Tel. 01274 598807.

Daniels, H., Creese, A. and Norwich, B., 1998, 'Teacher support teams', in J. Dunham and V. Varma (eds)., *Stress in Teachers*, Whurr Publishers.

Dawson, N. and McHugh, B., 1986, 'Application of a family systems approach in an education unit', *Maladjustment and Therapeutic Education*, vol. 4, no. 2, pp.48–54.

Dawson, N. and McHugh, B., 1987, 'Learning to talk to parents', *British Journal of Special Education*, vol. 14, no. 3, pp.119–21.

DfEE, 1998a, *School Standards and Framework Act*, The Stationery Office Limited.

DfEE, 1998b, *Performance Assessment Survey: Careers Service Work with Parents and Guardians*, PA5, HMSO.

DfEE, 1998c, *Home–School Agreements Guidance for Schools*, PPY984, HMSO.

DfEE, 1998d, *Home–School Agreements What Every Parent Should Know*, PPY986, HMSO.

DfEE, 1999a, *How is Your Child Doing at School*, NB, HMSO.

DfEE, 1999b, *Pupil Mobility in Schools*, Research Brief No. 168, UCL, HMSO.

DfEE, 2000, *Learning Journey*, HMSO. Three guides to the curriculum, copies available to parents on request only, Tel. 08000 96 66 26.

DfEE, 2000b, *The Education (Pupil Information) (England) Regulations*, HMSO.

DfEE, 2001, *Schools achieving success*, The Stationery Office Limited.

EPLI–280, 2000, *Education, Public Law and the Individual*, vol. 5, 2 and 3.

Fletcher, B., 1993, *Not Just a Name – The Views of Young People in Foster and Residential Care*, National Consumer Council.

Grainger, J., Parkhouse, A. and Potter, E., 1999, *Schools' Liabilities to Pupils and Parents*, Croner Publications.

Hancock, R. and Cable, C., 2000, *Teaching Assistants' Skills and Experience*, (unpublished), Open University, Paper presented at BERA Conference.

Harding, J. and Pike, G., 1988, *Parental Involvement in Secondary Schools: A Guide for Reviewing Practice and Developing Policy*, ILEA.

Hopkins, J., 1990, 'The observed infant of attachment theory', *British Journal of Psychotherapy*, 6, pp.460–71.

Human Rights Act, 1998.

Johnson, D. and Ransom, E., 1983, *Family and School*, Croom Helm.

Jordan, D., 1998, *Report to Governors*, (unpublished), Llanedeyrn High School, Cardiff.

Jowett and Baginsky, 1991, *Building Bridges – Parental Involvement in Schools*, NFER.

Katz, Y., December 1997, 'Effective collaboration between teachers and parents in Israel: A strategy for improvement of the educational process', *Pastoral Care*, NAPCE, Blackwell.

Llewellyn, A., 2000, 'Perceptions of mainstreaming: A systems approach', *Developmental Medicine and Child Neurology*, 42, pp.106–15.

Macbeth, A., 1989, *Involving Parents*, Heinemann Educational.

Macbeth, A., Corner, T., Nesbit, N. et al., 1984, *The Child Between – A Report on School–Family Relations in the Countries of the European Community*, European Communities Commission, Belgium.

MacLure, M. and Walker, B., 1999, *Secondary School Parents' Evenings: A Qualitative Study, Final Report to the Economic and Social Research Council, Award no. R000222287*, University of East Anglia. Download from website: www.uea.ac.uk/care/research/parents.html.

MacLure, M. and Walker, B., 2000, 'Disenchanted evenings: The social organisation of talk in parent–teacher consultations in UK secondary schools', *British Journal of Sociology of Education*, vol. 21, no. 1, pp.5–25.

Marland, M., 1984, 'Could do better: How schools liaise with parents', *Westminster Studies in Education*, vol. 7, pp.45–55.

Marland, M., 1993, *The Craft of the Classroom*, Heinemann Educational.

Marland, M., 1997, *The Art of the Tutor*, David Fulton Publishers.

Marland, M., 1998, 'Moving from teaching to middle management', *Professional Development Today*, vol. 2, no. 1, pp.7–16.

Marland, M. and Rogers, R., 1991, *Marketing the School*, Heinemann Educational.

Marland, M., 1964, 'At Arm's Length', *Forum*, Vol. 7, No. 1.

Marriott, G., 2001, *Observing Teachers at Work*, Heinemann Educational.

Martin, J. and Vincent, C., 1999, 'Parental voice: An exploration', *International Studies in Sociology of Education*, vol. 9, no. 2, pp.133–54.

Martin, J., Ranson, S. and Vincent, C., 2000, *Little Polities: Schooling, Governance and Parental Participation*, The University of Birmingham.

Merttens, R. and Vass, J., 1993, *Partnerships in Maths*, The Falmer Press.

Miller, A., 1987, *The Drama of Being a Child*, Virago Press.

Morelli, G. A., Rogoff, B., Oppenheim, D. and Goldsmith, D., 1992, 'Cultural variation in infants' sleeping arrangements: Questions of independence', *Developmental Psychology*, 28, pp.604–13.

Morrow, V. and Richards, M., 1996, *Transitions into Adulthood*, Joseph Rowntree Foundation.

Nias, J., 1981, 'Highstones: Mirror-images and reflections', in *Case Studies in School Accountability*, vol. 2, SSRC, Cambridge Accountability Project.

OfSTED, 1995, *Framework for Inspection*, HMSO.

OfSTED, 1999, *Secondary Initial Teacher Training: Secondary Subject Inspections 1996–1998 Overview Report*.

Phillips, A., 1995, *Terrors and Experts*, Faber and Faber.

Plain English Campaign, 1991, 'How to write letters in plain English', www.plainenglish.co.uk.

Plowden Report, 1967, *Children and their Primary Schools*, HMSO.

Reilly, D. H., 1995, *How to Have Successful Schools*, University Press of America.

Reynolds, D. and Packer, A., 1992, 'School effectiveness and school improvement in the 1990s', in D. Reynolds and P. Cuttance (eds), *School Effectiveness Research, Policy and Practice*, Cassell.

Rogers, C. R., 1967, *On Becoming a Person*, Constable.

Rutter, M., 1989, 'Pathways from childhood to adult life.' *Journal of Child Psychology and Psychiatry*, vol. 30, no. 1, p.23–51.

Sammons, P., Hillman, J. and Mortimore, P., 1997, 'Key characteristics of effective schools: A review of school effectiveness research', in White and Barber (eds), *Perspectives on School Effectiveness and School Improvement*, Institute of Education, University of London, pp.77–124.

Singh, P. and Taylor, L., 1998, 'Parents add value to secondary mathematics', *ACE Bulletin*.

Stuttaford, T., 1999, 'The art of breaking bad news', *The Times*, 8 June 1999, p.18.

Sutton, R., 1995, *Assessment for Learning*, RS Publications.

Teacher–Parent Interviews: Some Materials for Teachers, 1983, Community Education Working Party, Nottingham University School of Education.

The Taylor Report: A New Partnership for our Schools, HMSO.

Vincent, C. and Martin, J., 2000, 'School-based parents' groups – A politics of voice and representation?', *Journal of Education Policy*, vol. 15, no. 5, pp.459–80.

Walker, B. M., 1998, 'Meetings without communication: A study of parents' evenings in secondary schools', *British Educational Research Journal*, vol. 24, no. 2, pp.163–78.

Weston, P., 1999, *Learning from Practice*, OfSTED.

Winnicott, D. W., 1960, 'The theory of the parent–infant relationship', in *The Maturational Processes and the Facilitating Environment: Studies in the Theory of Emotional Development*, 1965, The Hogarth Press and the Institute of Psychoanalysis.

Winnicott, D. W., 1962, 'Further thoughts on babies as persons', in *The Child and the Outside World*, Part 3, no. 2,

Winnicott, D. W., 1965, *The Maturational Processes and the Facilitating*

Environment: Studies in the Theory of Emotional Development, The Hogarth Press, London and the Institute of Psychoanalysis.

Winnicott, D. W., 1986, 'Children learning' in *Home is Where We Start From*, Penguin, pp.142–9.

Wolfendale, S. and Bastiani, J. (eds), 2000, *The Contribution of Parents to School Effectiveness*, David Fulton Publishers, London.

Woods, P., 1984, *Parents and School – A Report for Discussion on Liaison between Parents and Secondary Schools in Wales*, Welsh Consumer Council/former Schools Council Publication.

INDEX